Deleuze *on Cinema*

Deleuze *on Cinema*

RONALD BOGUE

Routledge
New York and London

Published in 2003 by
Routledge
29 West 35th Street
New York, NY 10001
routledge-ny.com

Published in Great Britain by
Routledge
11 New Fetter Lane
London EC4P 4EE
routledge.co.uk

10 9 8 7 6 5 4 3 2 1
Cataloging-in-Publication Data is available from the Library of Congress

ISBN-0-415-96603-5 (hb)
ISBN-0-415-96604-3 (pb)

For my son
Cameron

Contents

Abbreviations

All translations from Deleuze, Guattari, and Deleuze-Guattari are my own. For works that have appeared in English translation, citations include page numbers of the original French edition followed by the page numbers of the corresponding passages in the English translation.

B   Deleuze. *Le Bergsonisme.* Paris: Presses Universitaires de France, 1966. *Bergsonism.* Trans. Hugh Tomlinson and Barbara Habberjam. New York: Zone Books, 1991.

BR   Deleuze. "The Brain Is the Screen." Trans. Marie Therese Guirgis. In *The Brain Is the Screen: Deleuze and the Philosophy of Cinema.* Ed. Gregory Flaxman. Minneapolis: University of Minnesota Press, 2000, pp. 365–73.

DR   Deleuze. *Différence et répétition.* Paris: Presses Universitaires de France, 1968. *Difference and Repetition.* Trans. Paul Patton. New York: Columbia University Press, 1994.

IM   Deleuze. *Cinéma 1: L'image-mouvement.* Paris: Minuit, 1983. *Cinema 1: The Movement-Image.* Trans. Hugh Tomlinson and Barbara Habberjam. Minneapolis: University of Minnesota Press, 1986.

IT   Deleuze. *Cinéma 2: L'image-temps*. Paris, Minuit, 1985. *Cinema 2: The Time-Image*. Trans. Hugh Tomlinson and Robert Galeta. Minneapolis: University of Minnesota Press, 1989.

LS   Deleuze. *Logique du sens*. Paris: Minuit, 1969. *The Logic of Sense*. Trans. Mark Lester, w0ith Charles Stivale. Ed. Constantin V. Boundas. New York: Columbia University Press, 1990.

NP   Deleuze. *Nietzsche et la philosophie*. Paris: Presses Universitaires de France, 1962. *Nietzsche and Philosophy*. Trans. Hugh Tomlinson. Minneapolis: University of Minnesota Press, 1983.

PP   Deleuze. *Pourparlers*. Paris: Minuit, 1990. *Negotiations*. Trans. Martin Joughin. New York: Columbia University Press, 1995.

PS   Deleuze. *Proust et les signes*. 3rd edition. Paris: Presses Universitaires de France, 1976. *Proust and Signs*. Trans. Richard Howard. New York: G. Braziller, 1972.

QP   Deleuze and Guattari. *Qu'est-ce que la philosophie?* Paris: Minuit, 1991. *What Is Philosophy?* Trans. Hugh Tomlinson and Graham Burchell. New York: Columbia University Press, 1994.

DELEUZE ON CINEMA

Shortly after Gilles Deleuze's death on November 4, 1995, Serge Toubiana remarked that "of the great French thinkers who have counted these last thirty years, Deleuze was the only one who *truly* loved cinema" (Toubiana 1995, 20). That love of the cinema was certainly evident in Deleuze's *Cinema 1: The Movement-Image* (1983) and *Cinema 2: The Time-Image* (1985), with their wide-ranging references to films from all eras and most of the major movements and tendencies in world cinema. Yet these volumes surely came as a revelation to many of Deleuze's readers, for in the years preceding *Cinema 1* and *Cinema 2*, Deleuze had given little indication of his deep attachment to this particular art form. Besides publishing monographs on such philosophical figures as Hume (1953), Nietzsche (1962), Kant (1963), Bergson (1966), and Spinoza (1968, 1981), as well as extended expositions of his own thought in *The Logic of Sense* (1969), *Difference and Repetition* (1969) and the two volumes of *Capitalism and Schizophrenia* coauthored with Félix Guattari, *Anti-Oedipus* (1972) and *A Thousand Plateaus* (1980), Deleuze had frequently discussed literary works in many of his writings, devoting entire volumes to the study of Proust (1964; augmented 1970 and 1976), Sacher-Masoch (1967), and Kafka (1975, with Guattari). He had also articulated a theory of the theater in *Superpositions* (1979), and he had examined

1

music in *A Thousand Plateaus* and painting in his *Francis Bacon: The Logic of Sensation* (1981). Yet before *Cinema 1* and *Cinema 2,* the art that seems to have fascinated him most was scarcely manifest at all in his work. What those volumes revealed, however, was a long-standing and profound engagement with film, one that eventuated in books that clearly remain among Deleuze's greatest achievements, both as commentaries on the cinematic art and as works of philosophy.

Deleuze's object in *Cinema 1* and *Cinema 2* is to develop philosophical concepts that "relate only to cinema, to a given genre of film, to a given film or some other. Concepts proper to cinema, but which can only be formed philosophically" (PP 83; 58). Deleuze pursues this task through a close attention to individual films and particular images, but with constant reference to a general conception of cinema as a mode of thought. That mode of thought is inseparable from the films that embody it, but it requires a complex philosophical treatment of time, space, and movement to account for its diverse manifestations. Given the nature of this project, the books Deleuze produced make significant demands of the reader, who must follow Deleuze through thickets of dense reasoning and sweeping synthetic exegesis across the domains of both cinema and philosophy. Deleuze is not deliberately obscure, but his cinema texts are often difficult, primarily because they are so allusive and so highly condensed in their references. They presume an intimate familiarity with the films, directors, and cinematic movements he treats, a firm grasp of the extensive literature of film criticism and theory that has taken shape over the last century, and a detailed knowledge of the individual philosophers whose analyses he weaves into his own thought. Fortunately, Deleuze is scrupulous in documenting his sources, and a careful examination of his references and examples often clarifies the most dense and seemingly opaque passages. My effort in this book, therefore, has been to provide a reading of *Cinema 1* and *Cinema 2* by way of a reading *along with* Deleuze, an exposition of his thought through an exposition of his sources and examples. In my remarks on specific films and directors, I have generally sought not to extend Deleuze's observations to works he does not treat, but instead to draw out the implications of his often highly condensed comments on individual films. Frequently, the elucidation of his examples has required as well a detailed examination of other critics' and theorists' comments on the films to which Deleuze alludes. In my explication of

Deleuze's philosophical arguments, I have endeavored to flesh out his

often highly condensed comments on individual philosophers and debates, while providing explanations that are accessible to philosophers and non-philosophers alike. Finally, I have tried to extract from the myriad details of Deleuze's analyses the broad outlines of his argument, with the ultimate aim of demonstrating the coherence and originality of his thought on cinema as well as the significance of that thought for an understanding of his philosophy as a whole.

Deleuze's approach to cinema is predominantly Bergsonian in inspiration, and without a firm grasp of Bergson's conception of time much of *Cinema 1* and *Cinema 2* is obscure. In *Bergsonism* (1966), Deleuze offers a reading of Bergson that hinges on one of the most puzzling of Bergsonian propositions—that the things we commonly call space and time are merely extremes of the contraction and dilation of a single *durée,* or duration. The universe for Bergson is an open vibrational whole, a flow of matter-movement that contracts to form the fixed and discrete entities of the spatial world and dilates to form the temporal dimension of a universal past surging through the present and into the future. This notion of *durée* as the time-space flux of a vibrational whole informs Deleuze's entire conception of cinema, and in chapter 1 I show how Deleuze applies this notion to the general problem of movement and its relation to time, as well as to the specific problem of the cinematic image and its relation to time and movement in film.

In chapter 2, I consider the complex relation Deleuze establishes between the open whole of *durée* and the fundamental cinematic elements of the frame, the shot, and montage. The cinematic image is a framed image-in-movement. If the universe is a single flow of matter-movement, each framed image may be seen as a slice or chunk carved out of the matter-movement of the open whole. The frame delineates a slice or "mobile cut" of *durée,* and hence it demarcates a limited set of elements, but the open whole remains indirectly present in each mobile cut. The open whole is even more evident in the montage of images, though in the traditional cinema montage remains an indirect rather than a direct presentation of the open whole. The shot Deleuze sees as the intermediary between the frame and montage, each shot framing a limited set of entities and at the same time suggesting the relations beyond itself that may guide its assembly in a montage sequence. Frame, shot, and montage, then, are three different manifestations of time, three different ways in which the open whole of *durée* unfolds itself in movement-images. Of the three, however, it is montage that most clearly reveals a particular understanding of *durée,* and Deleuze finds in early filmmakers four approaches to montage that correspond to four different conceptions of the open whole. For Griffith, the whole is an organic unity of minimal intervals within a dilating totality. For Eisenstein and the Soviet school, the whole is a dialectical totality, a spiraling expansion of time that unfolds in leaps and starts through the shock of contrasting images. For many pre-war French directors, such as Gance, Clair, and L'Herbier, the whole is a mathematical infinite comprised of quantities of movement, whereas for German expressionists such as Murnau, Lang, and Wiene, the whole is a dynamic infinite made up of clashing intensities engaged in a perpetual war of moving light and shadow. In each case, Deleuze shows how specific techniques of framing, composition, lighting, camera movement, and montage emerge from a dominant conception of the open whole.

In chapter 3 I turn to Deleuze's taxonomy of the images and signs of the classic cinema. In *Matter and Memory,* Bergson argues that the epistemological conundrums posed by the opposition of subject and object may be overcome if we simply assume that the world is made up entirely of images. In this world of images, non-living entities are images that interact with surrounding images like so many billiard balls, whereas living entities are images that function as centers of indeterminacy, pausing before reacting to a collision with another image, say, or moving in an unexpected direction, or accelerating in an unpredictable fashion. Living images gain autonomy from surrounding images by mastering space and time—by perceiving impending encounters with other images, predicting their movements, planning counter-movements, and so forth. A "sensorimotor schema" organizes and coordinates the perceptions, feelings, and actions of each living image, and from that schema issues a particular configuration of the world centered on that given image. Deleuze finds implicit in Bergson's account three specialized images that come into existence with every living image: the perception-image, whereby the living image senses the outside world; the action-image, which structures the space surrounding the living image; and the affection-image, which connects the living image's outer perceptions, inner feelings, and motor responses to other images. It is on the basis of this tripartite Bergsonian division that Deleuze builds his classification of images.

This tripartite division soon gives way to a more complex taxonomy of images, however, for Deleuze sees in Charles Sanders Peirce's categories of Firstness, Secondness, and Thirdness certain parallels to Bergson's classification of images that suggest the existence of an additional three types of images—the "impulse-image," the "reflection-image," and the "relation-image." These six categories of images Deleuze then uses to construct a taxonomy of signs. Deleuze claims Peirce as his guide in articulating a non-linguistic theory of the sign, but he departs from Peirce in defining the sign as a particular image when viewed from the perspective of its genesis or its bipolar composition (the two poles of its composition being the minimal interval of movement and the maximal movement of the whole). Signs, then, are simply images subdivided into three categories—one genetic, the other two compositional. Since there are six kinds of images, and each kind may be divided into three categories of signs, it is possible to distinguish eighteen types of signs, each of which is a specific kind of image. Much of *Cinema 1* is devoted to an analysis of cinematic images in terms of this system of signs, and throughout chapter 3 my effort is to differentiate the various signs from one another and determine precisely how they are revealed in cinematic images.

The signs Deleuze identifies in *Cinema 1* are signs of the movement-image, which is the category under which Deleuze groups all images that are regulated by the sensori-motor schema. The sensori-motor schema provides the commonsense temporal and spatial coordinates of our everyday world, and the signs of the movement-image, which are the signs of the classic cinema, ultimately conform to the coordinates of that commonsense world. In the modern cinema, however, the sensori-motor schema breaks down, and with the collapse of that schema new images appear—time-images—as well as new kinds of signs. Chapter 4 traces the emergence of time-images in cinema, first in "opsigns" and "sonsigns," pure visual or sonic images that defy commonsense understanding; then in the "mnemosigns" of flashback memories and the "onirosigns" of dream landscapes; and finally in the "hyalosigns" of time crystals. Opsigns and sonsigns are shards of time, moments that resist assimilation within a measurable, chronometric time, and Deleuze finds in Italian neorealism the first sustained evidence of the emergence of this shattered temporality. Mnemosigns and onirosigns, though often recuperated within a commonsense time scheme in the classic cinema, point toward unorthodox forms of time—a bifurcating time in the flashback, a floating time in dream sequences and the oniric dance world of Hollywood musicals. But only with the hyalosign does a full time-image arise. Bergson argues that in order for memories to be formed, every actual present moment must be doubled by a coexisting virtual past moment, and that the virtual past extends as a single domain from the present point in time into the vast reaches of the past. Normally, we do not perceive the coexisting actual present and virtual past, but in certain experiences of déjà vu and automatism we receive faint intimations of time's double nature. Deleuze argues that in the modern cinema certain images and signs function as time crystals, as refracting, filtering, and reflecting surfaces in which the virtual and the actual are made visible and rendered indiscernible as they pass into one another in circuits of exchange. The interplay of the virtual and the actual may take on various configurations, and its effects may be traced in individual sequences of images, whole films, or the entire oeuvre of a director. Thus, Deleuze shows, the funhouse mirror scene at the end of Welles's *The Lady from Shanghai* may be seen as a time crystal, but likewise the entirety of Fellini's *And the Ship Sails On* may be viewed as one giant time crystal. And in the films of Ophuls, Renoir, Fellini, and Visconti we may identify four prevailing "states of the crystal": in Ophuls, the perfect crystal; in Renoir, the split crystal; in Fellini, the crystal in formation; and in Visconti, the crystal in dissolution.

In hyalosigns we see an unsettling double time of an interpenetrating virtual past and actual present, but in what Deleuze calls "chronosigns" we see even more disturbing and paradoxical images of time. Chapter 5 is devoted to such chronosigns, which Deleuze divides into two categories—those that concern the *order of time,* and those that concern *time as series.* The chronosigns of the order of time make visible either coexisting "sheets of the past" or mutually exclusive simultaneous "points of the present." In Resnais's films, characters inhabit realms that are like planes of coexisting past events, each plane metamorphosing into another, the film establishing transverse, puzzling passages between various planes of past time. In Robbe-Grillet's films, incommensurable present moments coexist simultaneously, and the commonsense temporal order of past-present-future gives way to a paradoxical time of presents-of-the-past, presents-of-the-present, and presents-of-the-future. The chronosigns that concern time as series are signs in which the becoming of time is rendered visible in the image. The onward thrust of a past through a present and into a future is manifest in images that incorporate a "before" and an "after" within a "now." Such images reveal the "power of the false," the power of the time of becoming, which undermines fixed identities and makes undecidable the distinction between the true and the false. Welles's Nietzschean tales of deception and fakery display the power of the false, as do Rouch's ethnofictions, in which Rouch and the subjects of his African documentaries together invent stories that construct the collective identity of a people-to-come. Clarke and Cassavetes invent a cinema of the body, in which images, characters, and plots issue from corporeal movements that fuse past, present, and future in gestural trajectories. And Godard creates a cinema of categories, in which categories of every type—aesthetic genres, colors, psychological faculties, logical and metaphysical categories, and so on—are treated as series engaged in a perpetual metamorphosis, each series disclosing a specific power of the false.

Deleuze argues that all chronosigns must also be regarded as both signs of thought, or "noosigns," and as signs that must be read, or "lectosigns." In chapter 6 I examine first noosigns, which are informed by specific relationships between the image and thought, and then lectosigns, which manifest particular dispositions of sight and sound. In the classic cinema, the image and thought are in mutual accord, the sensori-motor schema common to film and viewer allowing a ready passage between the screen world and the world of the spectator. In modern cinema, however, an alien thought is instigated by the image. A "spiritual automaton" arises from within the viewer, and at the same time the screen itself becomes the brain surface of a non-human thought. The gap *between* images functions as the principle of their interconnection, and in each gap the fissure of a pure outside is made present. The outside is a split in chronometric time and Newtonian space that escapes commonsense rationality, and in the noosigns of the modern cinema we see and enter into a world of thought-images beyond ordinary thought. In the modern cinema as well the gap between images is doubled by a gap between images and sounds, and that gap requires that visual and sonic signs be "read" in ways that cannot be anticipated in advance of their appearance. The lectosigns of the modern cinema are genuinely audio-visual signs, sounds constituting an autonomous sonic continuum, images a separate visual continuum, and the two put in relation to one another through their mutual differences. The films of Straub/Huillet, for example, reveal a stratigraphic space and an aerial free indirect discourse, the visual images and sound images communicating through a staggered back-and-forth passage between the two domains. In the cinema of Marguerite Duras, an oceanic flow of visual images coexists with a flow of words tending toward inarticulate cries, the two flows interacting without ever dissolving into one another. In each case, a particular image of time manifests a new form of thought and establishes a new relation between sight and sound.

This book is one of three I have written on Deleuze and the arts, the other two being *Deleuze on Literature* and *Deleuze on Music, Painting, and the Arts*. Each is designed as an autonomous entity, but all three form part of a single project. Deleuze's writings on cinema may be approached as a self-contained unit, yet much that he says about film illuminates his analyses of the other arts, and when considered in conjunction with his studies of literature, music, and painting, the cinema books contribute to a profound and original conception of the arts in general. I have therefore tried to address as wide an audience as possible in this book, in the hope that those with interests in any one of the arts might be encouraged not only to read and reread *Cinema 1* and *Cinema 2*, but also to explore the full range of Deleuze's writings on all the arts. I thus ask the indulgence of specialists who might find the occasional definition of terms too rudimentary, or the summary of long-standing debates unnecessary.

Over the last several years, a number of excellent works on Deleuze have appeared both in French and in English. I have profited greatly from many of them, but I have not engaged in extended discussion of any of these works, citing only those texts that help illuminate a particular point in Deleuze's arguments. I have found especially useful the studies of Deleuze's cinema theory by Rodowick, Kennedy, and Marks, as well as the collective volumes edited by Flaxman, Serrano, and Fahle and Engell. Anyone interested in grappling with the difficulties of *Cinema 1* and *Cinema 2* will find these works well worth reading.

I have been engaged in this project for more than a decade, and many have provided invaluable assistance throughout those years. I am grateful to the University of Georgia Research Foundation and the University of Georgia Center for Humanities and Arts for grants that allowed time for research and writing. Charles Stivale, Costas Boundas,

Ian Buchanan, and Paul Patton offered encouragement at key moments of this endeavor. I am especially indebted to Jerry Herron for his friendship and support, and to Florin Berindeanu for his enthusiastic comments on the entire manuscript. I have learned much as well from students in my seminars, including Michael Baltasi, Ravinder Kaur Banerjee, Andrew Brown, Balance Chow, Hyung-chul Chung, Letitia Guran, Paulo Oneto, Aaron Parrett, Wei Qin, Astra Taylor, and Maria Chung-min Tu. My greatest debt, however, is to the members of my family, who have remained faithful and cheerful companions throughout the long journey.

Chapter One

BERGSON AND CINEMA

Of all the arts, cinema is the one Deleuze examines most thoroughly. In *Cinema 1: The Movement-Image* and *Cinema 2: The Time-Image,* he makes reference to hundreds of films by directors from around the world, cites the major film theorists, and comments on the development of cinema from the silent era to the modern age. Yet his two-volume study, he says, is not a history of cinema, but "a taxonomy, an essay in the classification of images and signs" (IM 7; xiv). The "great *auteurs* of cinema" Deleuze sees as comparable "not only to painters, architects, and musicians, but also to thinkers. They think with movement-images and time-images instead of concepts" (IM 7–8; xiv). His object is to articulate the logic of that thought in movement-images and time-images and to situate it within a general account of the relationship of matter to images, movement and time. In this chapter, we will consider some of the broad philosophical concerns that guide the formation of this taxonomy of images and signs.

DELEUZE'S BERGSON

In *Cinema 2: The Time-Image,* Deleuze cites with approval Tarkovsky's statement that in modern film "time becomes the basis of bases in cinema, like sound in music, like color in painting" (IT 60; 288). If indeed time can be the fundamental element of cinema, it is not surprising that the thought of Henri Bergson should inspire Deleuze in his explorations of cinema. As Kolakowski observes, according to Bergson each great philosopher has only one thing to say, and "if we attempt to apply Bergson's remark to himself, we may sum up his philosophy in a single idea: time is real" (Kolakowski 1985, 2). Bergson's influence on Deleuze is early and profound, first evident in Deleuze's lengthy 1956 article "La conception de la différence chez Bergson," and then in his 1957 edition of Bergsonian excerpts, *Mémoire et vie: textes choisis,* and his 1966 book, *Bergsonism.*[1] Throughout the cinema volumes, Deleuze relies heavily on Bergson's philosophy of time to construct the basic framework of his analysis, and a measure of familiarity with Deleuze's Bergson helps clarify some of the more difficult facets of his argument.

In *Bergsonism,* Deleuze notes that "the Bergsonian dualisms are famous: duration-space, quality-quantity, heterogeneous-homogeneous, continuous-discontinuous, the two multiplicities, memory-matter, recollection-perception, contraction-relaxation [*détente*], instinct-intelligence, the two sources, etc." (B 11; 21). Many assert that Bergson's philosophy is essentially dualistic, and some that its dualisms mask fundamental inconsistencies in his thought.[2] Kolakowski, for example, argues that "in Bergson's writings there are two philosophies incompatible with each other" (Kolakowski 103), one based on a theory of consciousness that opposes time and space, the other on a cosmology that opposes life and matter.[3] Deleuze's object in *Bergsonism* is to demonstrate the coherence of Bergson's work by interrelating the central Bergsonian concepts of *durée,* memory, and élan vital, and to show that if Bergson is dualistic, it is in the most complex of senses, the course of Bergson's analysis taking him from an illusory dualism to a clarifying dualism, then to a higher monism, and finally to a generative dualism and pluralism.

Durée, or duration, the dynamic movement of passing yet continuing time, remains a constant preoccupation of Bergson's throughout his work. In his first book, *Essay on the Immediate Data of Consciousness* (1889; published in English as *Time and Free Will* in 1910), Bergson articulates the basic elements of his theory of *durée,* and though in *Matter and Memory* (1896; English Translation, 1911) and *Creative Evolution* (1907; English, 1913) he significantly modifies his initially clear-cut distinctions, it is useful to consider the way in which he first approaches the topic. His opening concern in *Essay* is to argue against the possibility of quantifying internal, psychological states. He shows first that supposedly quantitative increases and decreases in such emotions as joy and sadness (more joy, more sorrow, etc.) actually represent qualitative shifts from one subtle complex of emotions to another (say, from a vague sense of well-being, to an enthusiastic participation in one's activities, to an ecstatic embrace of the world). He then argues that even changes in the most basic of physical sensations are also qualitative rather than quantitative. Each degree of contraction of a given muscle is accompanied by a qualitatively shifting involvement of various parts of the body. The passage from a gentle pinprick to a piercing stab involves not quantities of tickling or pain but a succession of qualitatively differentiable sense experiences. Bergson concludes that all internal psychological states may be ranged between the extremes of abstract emotions like joy and sorrow and such physical sensations as muscle contractions and pinpricks, and that in all of them the illusion of the possibility of quantification arises from a spatialization of internal states. The very concept of number itself, he claims, is grounded in a spatial model. To think of a quantity is to treat qualitatively different elements as homogeneous and simultaneously co-present entities (twenty individually distinct and moving sheep being converted during quantification into so many interchangeable points on a plane). The number *line* is not simply a convenient means of representing numbers but a basic element of quantification. To quantify psychological states is to change a sequence of heterogeneous complexes unfolding in time into homogeneous units in a timeless space, within which one may measure various degrees of joy or sorrow, exertion or relaxation, pleasure or pain, by comparing psychological events to one another as static and completed objects simultaneously present in a fixed space.[4]

What underlies this illusory quantification of qualitative psychological states is a fundamental opposition of space and time, one that is masked by our habitual and unreflective treatment of time as a form of space. We tend to think of time as an abstract, homogeneous element, which we measure by the ticks of the clock. But the sixty marks on the clock face are merely interchangeable, static points, and the *passage* of time is more than a mere succession of states marked into discrete and even intervals. Our basic psychological experience of time is that of *durée,* of a dynamic continuation of a past into a present and toward a future. _Durée,_ suggests Bergson, should be thought of as a musical melody. Although we tend to spatialize and hence distort melody through the graphic representations of musical scores or the visualization of keys on a piano, melody is actually an indivisible multiplicity changing qualitatively in an ongoing movement. The melody does not so much consist of discrete notes as it passes through the notes, the entire succession of notes forming a single process—a process which, however, is not a simple unity, but an indivisible heterogeneity. Each note interpenetrates the next note, the first and second note continuing into the third note, the first, second and third into the fourth, and so on, each phase of the passage of the melody (second note, third note, fourth note) functioning as a qualitatively different moment, each pushing into the next in a single movement which eventuates in the completed melody. (We should of course undo all the spatial terms in this description, erasing the distinction between individual notes, between first, second, third and fourth moments, etc.) With each note also something new comes into existence. Against the background of subsequent notes, which together form a qualitatively distinct ensemble, an unpredictable new note emerges, which then forms with the subsequent notes a new qualitatively distinct ensemble. _Durée_ is in this regard fundamentally _indeterminate,_ the future truly open and unforeseeable. The Laplacean cosmos of universal cause-and-effect relations, in which the future may be predicted given a total knowledge of all bodies and their present relations, is essentially timeless, for in the succession of necessary causes-and-effects time makes no real difference. The deterministic universe is basically spatial, the fixed past and the inevitable future easily plotted on a single and complete graph. _Durée,_ by contrast, is time that makes a difference, each moment bringing forth something qualitatively new.

The apparently opposing notions of duration and succession are combined in _durée,_ for the passage from moment to moment also entails a cumulative continuation of interpenetrating moments in an indivisible process. Indeed, without this combination of duration and succession there would be no _movement_ of time, no passage from one moment into the next—in short, no _real_ time, in any meaningful sense. In his first book, Bergson approaches _durée_ as a psychological phenomenon, identifying _durée_ and consciousness, and that continuation of a past moment into its succeeding moment with _memory._ He neatly divides the external world of space from the internal world of *durée,* the one comprising a homogeneous quantitative multiplicity of infinitely divisible terms external to one another, the other a heterogeneous qualitative multiplicity of indivisible, inseparable terms. Within the self, "there is succession without reciprocal exteriority; outside the self, reciprocal exteriority without succession" (1959, 72–73; 1910, 108).⁵ In the absence of a consciousness to perceive it, there is no movement from one moment to the next, no *durée,* for there is no memory to retain and prolong a past-present into a succeeding present. Our sense of a spatialized internal world and a temporal external world comes about simply through "a kind of exchange" between internal *durée* and external space "analogous to what physicists call a phenomenon of endosmosis" (1959, 73; 1910, 109). In *Matter and Memory* and *Creative Evolution* Bergson abandons this simple opposition of external space and internal human *durée,* but in all his subsequent works he continues to associate *durée* with consciousness and memory, albeit in a widely extended sense of those terms. In *Matter and Memory,* he speaks of *durée* in general and develops especially the notions of memory and the virtual past. He asserts that the past "conserves itself by itself, automatically" [1959, 498; 1913, 5]. The past is conserved not in the material brain but in itself, and all past moments coexist in a virtual dimension. This virtual past is a giant memory, which extends from the infinitesimal point of the present into an expanding, unbounded past. Unconscious until actualized in specific memory-images, virtual memory forms part of the onward thrust of *durée* from an ever accumulating past into an open future. In *Creative Evolution* Bergson links *durée* and élan vital, the vital impulse or impetus that characterizes all living entities. *Durée,* he remarks, "signifies invention, creation of forms, continuous elaboration of the absolutely new" (1959, 503; 1913, 11), and the attributes of consciousness, "continuity of change, the conservation of the past in the present, true *durée*" (1959, 513; 1913, 23), he finds in the evolution of living beings. He thus concludes that "life is invention, like conscious activity, incessant creation" (1959, 513; 1913, 23), and that life is "the continuation of a single and same impulse [*élan*] which is divided out into divergent lines of evolution" (1959, 540; 1913, 53).

At times in *Creative Evolution* Bergson speaks as if he adheres to a dualistic opposition of the inanimate and the animate, of inorganic matter and élan vital (e.g., "life is, above all, a tendency to act on brute matter" [1959, 577; 1913, 96]), but Deleuze argues that this is not the case. Élan vital must be systematically related to the concepts of *durée* and memory, claims Deleuze. *Durée* is "essentially a virtual multiplicity (*that which differs in nature*)" (B 119; 112–13), or "more precisely, the virtual insofar as it is actualized, in the process of being actualized, inseparable from the movement of its actualization" (B 36; 42–43). Memory is "the coexistence of all degrees of difference in this multiplicity, in this virtuality" (B 119; 113). And élan vital "designates the actualization of this virtual following lines of differentiation that correspond to the degrees" (B 119; 113). Put simply, memory is the coexisting virtual past, *durée* the flow of time whereby that virtual past presses forward into the actual present toward an open future, and élan vital is *durée* as it unfolds itself into the future in the various forms of the created and ever-creating universe. The opposition of matter and life is not primary, for inert material entities and living beings are simply different degrees of contraction and relaxation of *durée*-memory, which in the dynamic unfolding of the universe divides into the forms of the inanimate and the animate.

This notion of *durée*-memory's contraction and relaxation (*détente* is Bergson's term, translated often by the neologism "detension," in the sense of a loosening of tension) Deleuze takes from some of the most difficult sections of *Matter and Memory* and *Creative Evolution* (see especially 1959, 337–56; 1911, 267–98, 1959, 376; 1911, 330, 1959, 696–720; 1913, 236–66).[6] Frequently Bergson insists on the illusory nature of the corpuscular view of matter, according to which the world is made up of various combinations of solid, impenetrable bodies. (The atomistic theory is one such corpuscular view of matter.) Our most basic experience of the world, however, is one of constant change, movement, and flux, and this experience Bergson finds increasingly confirmed in the developments of physics (the tendencies of which he discerns in 1896 and 1907 with remarkable prescience, as Capek demonstrates at length). Physicists recognize the existence of a universal interaction of forces, such that the separation of entities into discrete and autonomous units is called into question, and explorations of the microscopic constituents of matter suggest that there are no irreducible bodies in the world, simply "*modifications, perturbations,* changes in *tension* or *energy,* and nothing else" (1959, 337; 1911, 266), no things but only actions (1959, 705; 1913, 248) or movements (1959, 707; 1913, 249–50). In

Creative Evolution, Bergson asserts that "in reality, life is a movement, materiality is the inverse movement, and each of the two movements is simple—matter, which forms a world, being an undivided flux; life, which cuts matter up into living creatures, also being undivided" (1959, 707; 1913, 249). Bergson here suggests that the movement of matter is that of entropy, a dissipative tendency toward homogeneity, stasis, and undifferentiation, and that of life is an inverse tendency toward hetero-geneity, metamorphosis, and creative differentiation. In this regard, entropic matter is simply a decrease in tension in a field of energy, and creative life an increase in tension in that same field. But Bergson indicates as well that matter is relaxed *durée,* and that the apparent dif-ferences between quantities and qualities, the extended and the un-extended, bodies and minds, are ultimately only differences in the relative contraction or relaxation of *durée.* When I look at a red spot, I perceive a simple quality, but I know that 400 trillion vibrations of light per second make up that quality, and if I were to grasp each vibration in terms of the minimal temporal units of human consciousness (which Exner establishes at 0.002 seconds per event), it would take me 250 cen-turies to experience each vibration separately (1959, 340–41; 1911, 272). This suggests that there are different temporal rhythms in the universe and that qualities and quantities form a continuum, my most fleeting perception of the quality of red being a temporal contraction of trillions of nearly identical oscillations into a single moment. Bergson finds intimations of the extremes of contraction and relaxation in two psy-chological experiences—those of concerted actions and dreams. When I exert my will to the utmost in a given action, I contract the totality of my personhood, my entire past, into a present moment. At that instant I sense most fully the identity of consciousness and *durée* as well as the freedom and openness of *durée.* Conversely, in dreams I experience a minimal contraction of the past into the present, a relaxation of will and memory in which my connection to the present grows increasingly attenuated and past recollections separate from one another as discon-nected, mutually external entities. Here I have a glimpse of the tempo-rality of inert matter, and my personality "descends in the direction of space" (1959, 666; 1913, 201).

Bergson's example of dream consciousness may seem more confus-ing than helpful, but his basic point is that inert matter represents a minimal contraction of one moment into the next (although every

moment contains a latent connection with the entire virtual past, however tenuous that tie may be) and that the properties common sense
attributes to space arise naturally from the temporality of minimal contractions. Let us consider as an instance of minimal contraction two
discrete moments, A and B, separated by an infinitely small interval. (A
spatial model of this sort, of course, is merely a convenient fiction
adopted temporarily for explanatory purposes.) The distance between
moment A and moment B is so narrow that only the slightest amount
of change from one state to the next can take place. Also, given that
moment B emerges against the background of moment A, that background is so thin, including within it so little of the past, that the degree
of newness of moment B is infinitesimally small. For all practical purposes, moments A and B are identical. Their qualitative differences may
be ignored, and the newness of moment B may be treated as a virtually
predictable repetition of moment A. In other words, moments A and B
tend to become homogeneous and the relation of moment A to
moment B tends to become deterministic. Finally, as the connection
between past and present grows increasingly reduced, as the interval
between moments A and B becomes smaller and smaller, the moments
tend to take on the property of mutual externality. At a limit point,
when all connection between successive moments is suppressed, the
universe consists of a sequence of present moments instantaneously
arising and disappearing, each moment external to the other. As Deleuze
comments, "An infinitely relaxed, loosened [décontractée] durée places its
moments outside one another; one moment must have disappeared
when the other appears. What these moments lose in reciprocal penetration, they gain in respective spreading. What they lose in tension,
they gain in extension. So that, at each moment, everything tends to
spread out into an instantaneous, infinitely divisible continuum, which
will not prolong itself into the other instant, but will die to be reborn
at each succeeding instant, in an ever-recommenced blinking or shiver"
(B 89; 86–87).

　　Yet this movement toward total relaxation never reaches an
absolute end point, for there is no space completely devoid of durée.
Inert matter is durée's tendency toward that end point, and the space of
common sense, geometry, and Newtonian physics is simply an ideal, the
never realized limit of a timeless, instantaneously co-present expanse. At
that ideal limit, matter takes on the appearance of interchangeable,

mutually external corpuscles deterministically related within a homogeneous space-container, a "pure space" of infinitely divisible quantities unaffected in any meaningful way by the flow of time. Such a "pure space," says Bergson, "is only the *schema* of the terminal stage at which this movement would come to an end" (1959, 667; 1913, 202). Conversely, the extreme of an extensionless, totally contracted "pure" *durée*, a consciousness separated from matter, is also an ideal limit. However vast may be the virtual past that memory contracts, that past pushes into an actualized, physical present. However immaterial our inner states may seem, they participate in the material. All our sensations are extensive, "voluminous" to some degree,[7] and all our thoughts and emotions are embodied and connected to the physical world.

What is essential, says Deleuze, "is to see how relaxation [*détente*] and contraction are relative, and relative to one another. What relaxes [*se détend*] if not the contracted—and what contracts, if not the extended [*étendu*], the relaxed [*détendu*]? *This is why there is always extensivity [de l'étendu] in our durée, and always durée in matter*" (B 90; 87). To frame this insight in another form, we might say that *durée* and matter, time and space, are inseparable functions of one another, and that the various forms of the universe, ranging from the most elemental entities to the most complex organisms, are simply different rhythms in a vibrational whole. This "vibrational whole" we might call "time-space" or "movement-matter," but only with great caution. The vibrations of this whole are not vibrations *of* something—they are not the movement *of* matter, temporal elements *of* space. Our inherent tendency is to use visual, spatial imagery to speak about time, and hence to think of bodies as entities distinct from their movements. But movement is inseparable from that which moves, and as soon as we speak of a thing as distinct from its action we reinstate a division between movement and the moving entity. And as Bergson observes, physics increasingly shows us that the corpuscular theory of matter is untenable, that there are no irreducible, impenetrable bodies in nature, no "things" in motion. Hence Bergson's frequent reference to a universe of "flows," "modifications," "perturbations," and "vibrations"—all efforts to avoid the visual image of bodies and the concomitant and inevitable abstraction of movement (i.e., time) from that which moves. But with the phrases "time-space" and "movement-matter" we also risk reinstating an opposition of the mental and the physical, of mind and brute matter, and in the process once again denying the reality of time. When grasped as dynamic movement, time always entails at least a minimal retention of the past into the present (a memory of some sort) as well as a minimal impulse toward a future (an élan or will), and that "retention-impulsion," or "memory-will," makes up the essence of consciousness. The implication is that even the most microscopic of subatomic events exhibits some form of consciousness, some degree of dynamic contraction of a past into a present toward a future. Conversely, the most complex forms of consciousness are part of a single continuum of rhythmic flows. What differentiates subatomic events from human consciousness is their relative speeds and degrees of contraction, the size of the intervals they encompass between events and the amounts of the past they contract into an active present.

The vibrational whole of the universe, then, is at once mind and matter—if both terms are taken in a very special sense—and in this regard Bergson is a monist. But as Deleuze points out, Bergson's monism must also be seen as a generative dualism or even pluralism, for the vibrational whole that constantly unfolds does so in forms that naturally invite the distinction between the organic and the inorganic, between mind and matter, and in an irreducible multiplicity of rhythms (i.e., in the rhythms of the various qualitatively distinct contractions of durée common sense identifies as the bodies that make up the universe). Though a timeless, deterministic space of homogeneous, infinitely divisible quantities exists only as an ideal limit, those most relaxed contractions of durée actualized in the vibrational whole of the universe approach that ideal limit and thereby generate what we call inert matter. Conversely, the most intense contractions of durée generate phenomena that approach an ideal limit we identify as extensionless mind. And though there is only a single durée, that durée is a qualitative multiplicity, an indivisible plurality that constantly divides itself and qualitatively changes at each moment of its division, the multiple forms of the self-creating universe being so many differentiations of durée as it perpetually unfolds itself.[8] Hence Deleuze's identification of four moments in Bergson's thought: a first moment, in which Bergson critiques the conventional false dualisms of mind and body, quality and quantity, space and time; a second, in which he distinguishes between qualitative and quantitative multiplicities, separating an internal durée from an external space, and thereby clarifying what conventional dualisms confuse through their spatialization of time; a third, in which he shows that the dualism of *durée* and matter is actually a monism of rhythmic contractions and relaxations of a vibrational whole; and a fourth, in which he explains how *durée* actualizes itself through the creative activity of the qualitative multiplicity of élan vital, unfolding itself in the dual forms of the inorganic and the organic and in the plural forms of the various entities of the universe.

THREE BERGSONIAN THESES ON MOVEMENT

Deleuze opens *Cinema 1: The Movement-Image* with a commentary on three sections from Bergson's *Creative Evolution,* each of which articulates a thesis on movement that Deleuze finds apposite for a theory of cinema. In the first, Bergson reiterates his well-known critique of traditional treatments of movement, which confuse the act of moving with the space through which the motion takes place. What Deleuze finds striking, however, is that Bergson here identifies the error common to all spatializations of time as a "cinematographic" illusion. Suppose, says Bergson, that we want to reproduce the movement of a military regiment on a screen. The easiest procedure would be to take "a series of snapshots [*instantanés*] and project those snapshots on the screen, in such a manner that they replace one another very quickly. This is what the cinema projector does." Perception, intellection, and language operate in the same fashion, and "whether it is a matter of thinking becoming, or expressing it, or even perceiving it, we scarcely do anything other than activate a sort of internal cinema projector" (1959, 753; 1913, 306). In sum, we try to comprehend movement by slicing time into a sequence of static moments, or immobile cuts, and then somehow melding them back together again. Rather than grasping each particular movement as an indivisible whole with its own concrete *durée*, in which there is no distinction between motion and that which moves, we imagine a single, homogeneous space-container, within which we situate the moments of an object's movement as so many static, co-present points, and from this spatial image we develop the concept of an abstract, mechanical time as a regular repetition of homogeneous, interchangeable moments. Real movement and concrete *durée* give way to immobile cuts (*coupes immobiles,* immobile slices or cross sections) and abstract time. The mechanism of cinema aptly illustrates consciousness' inherent distortions of movement, but Bergson's apparent misgivings about the cinema itself are misplaced, Deleuze points out, for the cinematic image projected on the screen is perceived not as a set of still photographs to which motion is somehow added from the outside, but as an image directly and immediately in motion, a moving picture, or movement-image. In fact, Deleuze argues, it is Bergson himself who best understands such movement-images, and this differentiation of immobile cuts/abstract time and real movement/concrete *durée* provides an important first step toward the development of a general theory of cinema.

The second section of *Creative Evolution* that Deleuze examines contains a thesis on movement that commentators often ignore. In the fourth chapter of *Creative Evolution,* Bergson points out that there are actually two ways in which movement has been theorized in the West. The ancients conceived of movement in terms of privileged moments and ideal poses. The growth of an adult man, for example, was thought of as a passage from one fixed and quintessential statuelike pose to another, "the infant," "the boy," "the adolescent," "the adult," each statue summing up a phase of a process, the transition from one phase to another being part of the essential tendency of the body in question—in this case, the generative tendency of a male human being. With the advent of modern science, essential tendencies and privileged moments are abandoned. Galileo studies the fall of an object without respect to any specific moment of its descent. Time consists not of a string of indivisible, quintessential moments, but of a sequence of equidistant, indifferent, and interchangeable instants—*instants quelconques,* as Bergson and Deleuze call them, "any-instants-whatever." It is the latter, scientific view of time that the cinematic mechanism makes patent, though both ancients and moderns distort movement by spatializing time. "It is the same cinematographic mechanism in both cases," says Bergson, "but in the second it attains a precision that it does not have in the first" (1959, 776; 1913, 332). Deleuze points out, however, that in the scientific view there is the potential for an adequate conception of movement that is in keeping with the thrust of Bergson's thought. To illustrate the precision attained in modern science's application of the cinematographic mechanism, Bergson observes that "in the gallop of a horse our eye perceives above all a characteristic attitude, essential or rather schematic, a form that appears to spread out over an entire period and thus fill up a 'unit of gallop-time' [*un temps de galop*]: this is the attitude that sculpture has fixed on the friezes of the Parthenon. But still photography [*la photographie instantanée*] isolates any moment whatever [*n'importe quel moment*]; it puts all moments on the same level, and thus a horse's gallop spreads itself out in whatever number of successive attitudes one likes, instead of gathering itself together in a unique attitude, which would shine in a privileged instant and light up an entire period" (1959, 776; 1913, 332). What Bergson does not say, and perhaps does not fully realize, Deleuze observes, is that photography and cinema make possible a new means of understanding privileged moments, one that relies not on idealizing poses but on the very discovery of the *instant quelconque*. Muybridge's proto-cinematic stills of a galloping horse divide movement into a series of any-moments-whatever, yet within that galloping we find singular moments when now one, now three, now two feet touch the ground. Instead of the ancient series of ideal poses, we have a sequence of instants, no one of which is privileged over any other, each selected through an indifferent, impartial and uniform mechanism, yet any one of which may prove to be singular or regular. "The remarkable or singular instant remains an any instant whatever among the others" (IM 15; 6) The privileged instants of cinema, such as the images of crisis, paroxysm, and intensity that Eisenstein creates in his films, are such singular instants extracted from *instants quelconques*. Such remarkable instants are immanent within movement, and their extraction represents the emergence of something new. One of Bergson's central questions is, "How is something new possible?" and the cinema points toward an answer. "When one relates movement to any-moments-whatever, one must become capable of thinking the production of the new, i.e., the remarkable and the singular, at any of its moments whatever: it is a total conversion of philosophy and that is what Bergson proposed to do finally, to give modern science the metaphysics that corresponds to it, that it lacks" (IM 17; 7). Deleuze's proposal in his turn is to complete what Bergson started and give cinema the corresponding metaphysics that it lacks.

The third thesis on movement that Deleuze finds in *Creative Evolution* is the most important of the three. If one were to phrase it in "a crude formula, one would say: not only is the instant an immobile cut of *durée*, but movement is a mobile cut of *durée*, that is, of the Whole or of a whole [*du Tout ou d'un tout*]" (IM 18; 8). Movement is commonly looked on as "a translation in space" (IM 18; 8), that is, as a shifting of positions of objects in space. The tortoise and the hare begin their race at the starting line, and at the conclusion of the race, their bodies have assumed new positions within space. But true movement, insists Bergson, is transformation rather than translation (1959, 521; 1913, 32). The movement of the tortoise must be taken as an indivisible, qualitatively changing whole, and the same is true of the movement of the hare. Equally important, however, is that through this shift in positions a qualitative change takes place that affects the tortoise, the hare, and the space they have traveled—a change in a whole.

Bergson makes this point in *Creative Evolution* when he reflects on the time it takes for sugar to dissolve in a glass of water. If he wants a drink of sugar water, he must wait for the sugar to dissolve. In his impatience he experiences *durée*, but this sense of time's onward thrust is not simply psychological; the time of the sugar's dissolution coincides with his waiting, which indicates that the sugar and the water also partake of *durée*. "What does this say," he asks, "except that the glass of water, the sugar, and the process of the dissolution in the water are without doubt abstractions, and that the Whole [*le Tout*] within which they have been cut out by my senses and my understanding progresses perhaps in the manner of a consciousness?" (1959, 502; 1913, 10). As we have noted, for Bergson there are ultimately no things in the universe but simply vibrations of a whole. The water, sugar, glass, and observer are all merely perturbations, movements, flows, each a different rhythm of an unfolding *durée*. The quality of the water obviously changes as the sugar dissolves, but the observer also changes, as does the glass (albeit at a very slow pace). And there is no reason to restrict the number of changing elements to the water, sugar, glass, and observer. In this regard, Bergson comments that "the operation through which science isolates and closes a system is not an entirely artificial operation," since "matter has a tendency to constitute isolable systems" (1959, 502; 1913, 10). But this is only a tendency, and even science recognizes that systems can be isolated from one another only provisionally. For all practical purposes, our solar system is a closed unit, but the sun sends rays to the most distant planets, and "it moves, carrying with it the planets and their satellites in a specific direction. The thread which attaches it to the rest of the universe is doubtlessly very thin. Yet throughout the length of this thread, the *durée* immanent to the entire universe is transmitted, even to the smallest particle of the world where we live" (1959, 503; 1913, 10–11).

Every individual movement, then, is part of the movement of the Whole [*le Tout*], but that whole, Deleuze points out, is an open whole. In *Creative Evolution,* Bergson critiques determinism and finalism by observing that in both "*tout est donné*" (1959, 526; 1913, 37), everything is given. The cause-and-effect relation fundamental to determinism presumes an action already completed, a sequence of already past moments that make up a whole whose necessity is retroactively constructed. By extension, the entire universe is already "given" in determinism, since it assumes that a total knowledge of the present positions and relations of all bodies would make predictable all future states of the universe. In finalism the whole is also given, for in its most extreme form finalism presumes a teleological order in which all things and beings develop according to pre-constructed programs, whose end results are built into them from the beginning. *Durée,* however, is never given, nor can it be given, for the future is genuinely new and undetermined. The universe is a vibrational whole—a virtual past, coextensive with all that has ever happened, continually contracted into a present always pushing forward into an open and unpredictable future. As Deleuze phrases it, the whole is not giveable "because it is the Open, and because its nature is to change ceaselessly and to make something new surge forth, in short, to endure [*durer,* i.e., to "durate" or manifest *durée*]" (IM 20; 9).

Yet "matter has a tendency to constitute isolable systems" (1959, 502; 1913, 10), observes Bergson, and the commonsense regularities of stable objects in a uniform space are reasonable approximations of genuine movements of *durée* when it is minimally contracted. Hence, Deleuze argues, we must distinguish between the whole and *ensembles,*[9] isolable systems or closed *sets* (in the mathematical sense), the open *whole* manifesting *durée* as universal vibration and flow, and provisionally isolated sets within that Whole exhibiting the characteristics of commonsense space and time. Within sets, the "cinematographic illusion" prevails. Individual entities within sets are "immobile cuts," like still photographs, arranged in a mechanical, abstract time. One may say as well that each set is itself an immobile cut, and its temporal prolongation a succession of immobile cuts in an abstract time. Thus, we may make a preliminary distinction between the whole as *durée* and sets as immobile cuts exhibiting abstract time.

What is the relationship between the whole and sets? Sets are merely subdivisions of the whole, but subdivisions whose organization creates the cinematographic illusion of solid bodies in a homogeneous space and an abstract time. These sets, however, are insistent illusions that we automatically perceive and cannot eradicate—and for good reason, since they are approximations of realities that are useful for our survival in the world. So, if we consider movement within a closed set, we tend to see unchanging bodies shifting positions within a space-container. Yet we know that such a "translation" of bodies is also a transformation of a whole, that the movement of the bodies is actually a specific, local manifestation of the vibrational flux of the universe, a portion of *durée*. How, then, may we think of the manner in which *durée* manifests itself in our commonsense world? How do we *see durée?* To answer this question, Deleuze extends Bergson's thought by introducing two concepts that are not strictly Bergsonian—*durée* as the whole of relations, and movement as the expression of *durée*. Deleuze admits that the problem of relations is not explicitly developed by Bergson, but he argues that the whole may be defined as "the whole of relations" (IM 21; 10).[10] As Deleuze frequently asserts, relations are external to their terms. They "do not belong to bodies, but to the whole, as long as one does not confuse the whole with a closed set of objects" (IM 20; 10). In a closed set, objects change respective positions, but "through the relations, the whole transforms itself or changes in quality" (IM 21; 10). When we see objects move through space, we also see changes in the relations between objects, and those changes extend into a whole beyond the specific objects under consideration. The *movement* of the bodies, in a sense, serves as the intermediary between closed sets and the open whole, in that the movement may be seen simultaneously as bodies changing positions and as an ongoing transformation of relations between bodies. The movement of bodies, in this regard, may be said to *express durée,* or manifest the whole through a specific set of qualitatively changing relations between bodies. "Movement thus has two faces, in a way," says Deleuze. "On one hand, it is what happens between objects or parts; on the other, it is what expresses *durée* or the whole" (IM 22; 11).

The concept of expression Deleuze develops at length in *Spinoza or the Problem of Expression* (1969), and it plays an important role in much of his work. The notion of expression has its origin in medieval Neoplatonism, and Deleuze argues that it is the controlling model in Spinoza's conception of the relationship between the One and the

Multiple. The One, or God, expresses itself in the form of the created world. Expression is a process of *explication,* or unfolding (Latin *ex-plicare,* to un-fold), whereby the One unfolds itself in the Multiple. But the One also is enfolded, or *implicated,* in each entity of the Multiple. Explication and implication finally imply a synthetic *complication,* or simultaneous presence of the Multiple in the One and the One in the Multiple, and this triad of explication, implication, and complication forms the core of the concept of expression. Explication is a process of development, through which the One expresses itself in the Multiple. What is expressed remains enveloped in each entity of the Multiple, but only in a hidden, partially evident manner. The enveloped One is a sign, a hieroglyph that points beyond itself (as the shining lunar surface may be said to be a sign of the dark side of the moon). That which is enveloped may be explicated, or unfolded, however, at which point the hidden dimensions of the enveloped One may be revealed.

In Deleuze's explication of Bergsonian *durée, durée* may be said to explicate or unfold itself in closed sets, and closed sets implicate or enfold *durée.* Each closed set is an actualization of *durée,* a specific locus in which the vibrational whole, through its minimal contraction of time, forms a provisionally isolable system, and immanent within each closed set is *durée,* a maximum contraction of the entire past into an open future, a virtual, "ungiveable" whole of constantly changing qual-itative relations. *Durée,* "in changing its nature, divides itself in objects, and objects, in becoming deeper, in losing their contours, are reunited in *durée.* One can thus say that movement relates the objects of a closed system to open *durée,* and *durée* to the objects of the system that it forces to open up. Movement relates the objects between which it is estab-lished to the changing whole that it expresses, and vice versa. Through movement, the whole divides itself in the objects, and the objects are reunited in the whole: and between the two, indeed, 'everything' changes [*'tout' change*]" (IM 22; 11). As I look out my window now, I see a dog dozing beneath a tree and a girl bringing food to the dog. The dog eats, the girl pets the dog, and the leaves of the tree rustle in the breeze. I see a translation of bodies in space, a shift in the positions of the girl and the dog, a slight undulation of the leaves of the tree. But I also see in the movements of these bodies an ongoing transformation of relations between them, metamorphosing configurations of girl-dog-tree, and that change in relations is a qualitative change in a constant temporal flow, the dog passing from sleeping, to eating, to having been fed, the girl from bringing food to petting the dog. The movement-relations I observe extend beyond the frame of my window into an open vibrational whole, some of whose effects are invisible, and others visible, such as the rustling of the leaves touched by the wind, or the variegated patterns of light created by the play of the sun overhead through the clouds. The girl, dog, and tree are actualizations of *durée*, bodies whose temporal contractions induce the cinematographic illusion of stable entities shifting positions within a homogeneous space-container, yet their movements also express *durée* in the qualitatively changing configuration of relations between the objects, a configuration that extends beyond the confines of this particular group of elements and opens the closed set to the outside.

Movement can be seen in two ways, then, as a translation of bodies and as a transformation of relations among bodies, and hence a closed set may also be taken in two ways. When I look out my window and see the girl and dog shifting positions around the tree, the cinematographic illusion prevails. In this sense, the closed set delineated by my window demarcates a collection of immobile cuts in an abstract time. But when I see transforming girl-dog-tree relations, my window carves out a portion of the vibrational whole of *durée*. In this sense, the closed set is no longer an immobile cut but a mobile cut, a slice or chunk of *durée*. Hence, we may distinguish between *immobile cuts,* closed sets in which movement is a translation of objects in space; *mobile cuts,* slices of *durée* in which movement is a transformation of relations; and *durée* itself. And on the basis of this distinction, says Deleuze, the profound thesis of the first chapter of *Matter and Memory* becomes evident: "1) not only are there instantaneous, snapshot images [*images instantanées*], that is, immobile cuts of movement; 2) there are also movement-images, which are mobile cuts of *durée*; 3) and finally there are time-images, that is, *durée*-images, change-images, relation-images, volume-images, beyond movement itself" (IM 22; 11). Here, of course, we find the broad categories with which Deleuze organizes his analysis of cinema—the movement-image and the time-image—and as we shall see in the next chapter, the notions of immobile cut, mobile cut and *durée* structure Deleuze's treatment of the frame, the cut, the shot, and montage. But before turning to that analysis, we must consider Deleuze's second commentary on Bergson (*Cinema 1,* chapter 4), in which Deleuze extracts from Bergson's *Matter and Memory* the three varieties of the movement-image: the perception-image, the action-image, and the affection-image.

IMAGE, MOVEMENT, MATTER, LIGHT

In his preface to the seventh edition of *Matter and Memory*, Bergson explains that the object of his first chapter is to show that idealism and realism are "two equally excessive theses," and he proposes to do so by treating matter simply as "a collection of 'images' " (1959, 161; 1911, xi).[11] Common sense so regards matter, he claims, and with good reason. The philosophically uninitiated would be startled to be told that the tangible and visible objects before them exist only in their minds, or that the objects are completely different from the way they appear, their qualities (color, resistance, etc.) being simple mental additions to the object. For common sense, "the object exists in itself and, on the other hand, the object is, in itself, pictorial [*pittoresque*], as we perceive it: it is an image, but an image which exists in itself" (1959, 162; 1911, xii). The image is something more than what the idealist calls a "representation" and something less than what the realist calls a "thing." "In a word," says Bergson, with the concept of the image he will be able to consider "matter before the dissociation that idealism and realism have brought about between matter's existence and its appearance" (1959, 162; 1911, xii–xiii). As Deleuze points out, Bergson's effort to bridge the divide between subject and object, between perceiver and perceived, is similar to that of phenomenologists like Husserl, who insist that consciousness is always consciousness *of* something, that the object and the perceiving subject form an indivisible unit. Phenomenologists, however, begin their analysis by presuming the existence of consciousness, whereas Bergson makes the startling claim that he commences simply with a universal flow of matter-images and then "deduces" consciousness as a particular kind of image within that flow.

Let us presume a world made up of nothing but images, says Bergson, of things-as-they-appear. "All these images act on and react against one another in all their elementary parts according to constant laws, which I call the laws of nature" (1959, 169; 1911, 1). These images generally interact in a predictable fashion, each action directly inducing a reaction, all the images jostling one another like so many agitated billiard balls. But there are certain images for which an action does not lead directly to an opposite and predictable reaction, certain billiard balls which, when struck, hesitate before moving, and then possibly move in an unpredictable direction. Such images are living beings, which may be defined as "centers of indetermination" (1959, 186; 1911, 28). They introduce a gap in the universal interplay of mechanical causes and effects, a delay in reaction and frequently a shift in direction that exhibit what we may call choice. From the amoeba to the neurologically most sophisticated of animals, the living image may be viewed as a system for relaying movements—for receiving movements from outside and generating its own movements from within. A dog, for example, is bitten by a flea. A neural impulse is transferred centripetally from the skin to the brain, after which centrifugal neural impulses are communicated to various muscles and the dog scratches (or twitches, or rolls over). The dog's neural system introduces a delay between an external movement (the flea bite) and an internally generated movement, as well as a rudimentary choice (scratch, twitch, or roll, etc.).

Perception is a means whereby living images receive movements, and perception is always linked to action, for which reason all perception is sensori-motor, an instrument for translating an external movement via the senses into an ensuing motor action. The function of our neural system is not to form representations but to receive excitations and provide choices for future action, and perception is simply an instrument for furthering such action. Perception helps a living being control and negotiate its surrounding space; the more space it can control, the greater its options will be and the more time it will have to exercise those options. Yet perception helps the living being control its environment not by adding something to things, but by *subtracting* from them, selecting those features of surrounding objects that interest and concern the living being and ignoring those that are irrelevant to its existence. In order to increase the scope of its action, the living being decreases the number of elements with which it must deal. In this regard, elementary particles of matter are more responsive to their environment than living beings, for they react equally to all surrounding forces and bodies, whereas living beings react only to those entities and circumstances that concern their future action.

Bergson explains this notion of perception as subtraction via a meditation on the conversion of images as simple presences into images as what we commonly call representations, and in the process he makes

use of a complex set of models involving light and vision. Let us assume
the existence of a material object, a present image, of which we have a
representation. What differentiates the present image from its representation? The present image, or material object, acts on and is acted
upon by all surrounding images, such that finally it is "only the path-
way through which pass in all directions the modifications that are
propagated throughout the immensity of the universe" (1959, 186;
1911, 28). The present image becomes a representation when it is isolated from other images, not by more light being cast on it, but by a
diminution of light, a darkening of its contours. Hence, if present
images are light, representations are subtractions of quantities of light,
or selective filterings of light. When we perceive objects, it is "as if we
reflected on their surfaces the light that emanates from them, light
which would never be revealed if it passed on unopposed" (1959, 186;
1911, 29). To speak somewhat simplistically, we may say that an object
(a merely present image) emits light and that some rays of light pass
through us unnoticed, while others are reflected back onto the object.
Our representation of that object consists of the light rays we reflect,
that is, the object's total number of rays minus the rays we ignore or do
not reflect. An organ of perception functions as the mirror that reflects
the rays that interest us and that serve our future actions.

Bergson's model of light and mirrors is none too easy to follow, for
it would seem that light rays issue from objects, some of them meet the
reflective surface of our perceptual apparatus, return to the object, and
then bounce back to some receptive surface of our body on which a representational image is formed. And indeed, Bergson compounds the
confusion when he likens perception to a black screen on which a photograph is captured. If one considers "any place whatever in the universe," he says, "one can say that the action of matter in its entirety
passes through that place without resistance and without loss, and that
the photograph of the whole is translucent there: what is lacking,
behind the plate, is a black screen on which the image could become
clearly outlined. Our 'zones of indetermination' in some sort play the
role of the screen" (1959, 188; 1911, 32). But Bergson makes this observation only after having objected to the common assumption that perception is "like a photographic view of things, which is taken from a
fixed point with a special apparatus, such as the organ of perception,
and which is then developed in the cerebral substance by who knows

what chemical and psychic process of elaboration." If there is a photograph, he remarks, "it is already taken, already developed, in the very interior of things and for all points in space" (1959, 188; 31). Perception, he claims, is not within the perceiver, as the photographic model might suggest. When I observe a luminous point P, its rays strike my retina at cells a, b, and c, and neural impulses are then conveyed to the brain. I may speak as if perception takes place in the eye or the brain, but "the truth is that the point P, the rays it emits, the retina and the nervous elements affected, form a single whole; that the luminous point P is a part of this whole; and that it is really in P, and not elsewhere, that the image of P is formed and perceived" (1959, 192; 1911, 37–38).

Bergson's point is that perception is not representation at all, but a constituent part of action. There is no divide between an external, extended material world and an internal, unextended mental reality, no split between *being* and *being perceived*. A living image acts on and reacts to a second image, and as part of its action it responds to some aspects of the second image while not registering others. One image perceives another, and the relationship of the perception to the object is that of a part to the whole from which it is extracted. The object remains what it is—an image—and the perceived object is likewise that same image, only minus those qualities that are irrelevant to the perceiver. The qualities perceived in the object genuinely belong to that object, and perception's subtractive selection of qualities is part of the interaction of perceiver and perceived, and thus something that takes place in the extended world. Hence, if perception is said to take place in any specific location at all, it is not within the perceiver, but at the object perceived where the genuine qualities reside. Perception is in things, then, not inside the perceiver.[12]

In *Matter and Memory*, Bergson's purpose is not to elaborate a full theory of visual perception. He uses visual examples (such as luminous point P) and the models of mirrors and photographs primarily as tools to undo a representational model of perception and to integrate perception within the overall activities of living entities. As we have seen, for Bergson the universe is a vibrational whole, various entities being diverse contractions and dilations of *durée*, and that vibrational whole may be thought of (with due caution) as time-space or matter-flow— that is, as universal movement, in which there is no division between motion and things moving. In the first chapter of *Matter and Memory*, Bergson cautions that for clarity of exposition he is temporarily ignoring the role of memory in his description of perception, and that the "pure perception" he is detailing, a perception without the memory basic to *durée,* is a fiction. Nevertheless, his account of perception is not static—indeed, its fundamental terms are those of movement. His "deduction" of consciousness and perception presumes an initial cosmic matter-flow of mutually interacting images, within which the living image emerges as a center of indetermination, a temporal interruption and possibly a directional modification of the flow. Perception, too, is accounted for in terms of movement and action, the living image's perception being simply a selection, and hence a reduction, of the number of interactions it shares with surrounding images. "In a sense, one could say that the perception of any unconscious material point whatever, in its instantaneousness, is infinitely greater and more complete than our own, since this point gathers and transmits the actions of all the points of the material world, whereas our consciousness reaches only certain parts along certain sides of those parts" (1959, 188; 1911, 30-31). Earlier, we noted that Bergson's notion of contractions and dilations of *durée* establishes a continuum between inert matter and living beings, and that the smallest temporal contraction of a subatomic particle implies the existence of some sort of proto-consciousness. Here, Bergson temporarily ignores *durée,* but a continuum between the inert and the vital remains, given that perception, or the gathering and transmission of action, is immanent within all things, at every "unconscious material point whatever," and the perception of living beings is simply a subtractive, reduced version of the perception of non-living entities (a perception which, as Deleuze implies, resembles Whitehead's "prehension" [IM 94; 64]).

Deleuze aptly characterizes Bergson's primal cosmos of images as "a gaseous state," a "world of universal variation, universal undulation, universal rippling: there are neither axes nor center, neither right nor left, high nor low . . ." (IM 86; 58). In this world, the image exists in itself, "the in-itself of the image is matter," and there is an "absolute identity of the image and movement" such that "*image-movement* and *matter-flow* are strictly the same thing" (IM 86-87; 59). This Bergsonian universe of image/matter/movement constitutes "a sort of plane of immanence" (IM 86; 58-59). Since it is a universe temporarily considered without *durée,* it is not the open whole, but it is "a mobile cut, a temporal cut or perspective. It is a block of space-time, since the time of the movement that functions within it belongs to it each time [*chaque fois*]. There will even be an infinite series of such mobile blocks or cuts, which will be like so many presentations of the plane, corresponding to the succession of movements of the universe" (IM 87; 59).

Deleuze's equation of image, matter, and movement follows Bergson fairly closely, as does his description of the *durée*-free universe of image-movement/matter-flow as a mobile cut or block of space-time. But Deleuze adds to the equation something that transforms Bergson's account. The plane of immanence, says Deleuze, is "in its entirety Light. . . . The identity of the image and movement has as its reason the identity of matter and light. The image is movement as matter is light" (IM 88; 60). In *Matter and Memory,* Bergson nowhere explicitly equates matter and light, and throughout his discussion of perception he blurs the distinction between image as general thing-as-it-appears and image as visual appearance, moving indifferently in the examples of images he treats from visual images to sonic images or tactile images. His figures of perception as a mirror and as a photographic screen carry with them the figure of a universe of light, but it seems doubtful that Bergson is embracing an ontological identification of matter with light, since such a position would render problematic the status of non-visual modes of perception. By equating matter and light, however, Deleuze brings to the fore the implications of Bergson's theory of perception for an analysis of visual images and reveals the potential of that theory for a conceptualization of the relationship between the cinematic visual image and the material world.[13] If things are light, then what we commonly call visual images, whether directly perceptual or cinematic, are made of the same "matter." Our visual perception of a thing filters its light, selectively reducing its range of wavelengths (e.g., ignoring ultraviolet and infrared rays), framing its emissions, orienting them according to possible actions. The thing by itself, the image in itself, is a virtual image, a given "block" of light, its perception an actualization of a portion of that block. Its actualization takes place within the flow of light when a living image—itself a specific configuration of matter-light—selectively reflects light and brings into existence a given indivisible circuit of light (e.g., luminous point P, retina sites a, b, c, brain). Visual perception, then, is truly *in* things, both in the sense that perception takes place at the perceived object and that the perceiver is itself an emergent configuration of light. "In other words," concludes Deleuze, "the eye is in things, in the luminous images themselves" (IM 89; 60). Consciousness, as a mirroring configuration of light, is no longer to be conceived of in its traditional role as a kind of flashlight illuminating a dark world, but as itself a constituent component of light. "In short, it is not consciousness that is light, it is the set of images, or light, that is consciousness, immanent within matter" (IM 90; 61). And since the cosmic flow of matter-light consists of virtual images in themselves—and not simply static snapshot images, but movement-images—we may ultimately look on "the universe as cinema in itself, a metacinema" (IM 88; 59).

THE THREE MOVEMENT-IMAGES

The eye is in things, consciousness immanent within the metacinema of matter, and what actualizes virtual movement-images is the "center of indetermination" of a living image, an *interval* or gap in the universal interaction of matter-flows. Deleuze extracts from Bergson's account of perception in *Matter and Memory* three types of movement-image, each related in a specific way to the interval of a living center of indetermination. A living image, we recall, is a kind of relay system, receiving the external movements of other entities and converting them into the movements of its own actions. Perception is part of a sensori-motor system, for which reason the living image is an "instrument of analysis in regard to the received movement and an instrument of selection in regard to the executed movement" (1959, 181; 1911, 20). The interval that is a living image, then, has two "sides," one incoming and one outgoing, the first related to perception *per se,* the second to an ensuing action. What Deleuze calls a "perception-image" is a movement-image related to the first side of the interval, a selective registering of incoming movements, a *framing* whereby some elements are ignored and others rendered visible. The perception-image, in short, is the "thing" *minus* those features filtered out by perception. But Deleuze notes that Bergson suggests the possibility of a second kind of movement-image when he argues for the inseparability of perception and action. Bergson observes that our perception of the external world is subtly affected by our expectations and anticipations of future events, and by the possibilities open to us for future action. As a "center of indetermination," each of us is the center of a world oriented toward our action. Our horizon curves around us, and objects are situated in relation to our anticipations of their movements and our own choices of actions. Deleuze, then, identifies the *action-image* as a second kind of movement-image, one related to the "outgoing" side of the interval. Unlike the perception-image, which is characterized by "elimination, selection or framing," the action-image puts into effect an "incurvation of the universe, from which arise simultaneously the virtual action of things on us and our possible action on things" (IM 95; 65).

The third movement-image, the *affection-image*, is a bit more difficult to grasp. In his description of the affection-image, Deleuze makes use of two of Bergson's analyses, one regarding qualities in *Creative Evolution*, the other concerning affections in *Matter and Memory*. In *Creative Evolution* (1959, 748–51; 1913, 300–304), Bergson shows how the basic categories of language—adjective, verb, and noun—arise naturally as we negotiate the cosmic flows of the vibrational whole. Initially, we sense mere transient *qualities*, to each of which we gradually attribute a common identity—hence adjectives. Then we use the emergent continuities in sensible qualities to delineate discrete *bodies*—whence nouns—and finally extract from those bodies a separate, repeatable *action*—thus verbs. To these proto-linguistic categories Deleuze draws parallels among the three movement-images, perception-images corresponding to nouns (in that the selective framing of the perception-image delineates objects), action-images to verbs, and affection-images to adjectives.

Deleuze sees an essential relationship between the primary qualities of these proto-adjectives and what Bergson refers to as "affections" in *Matter and Memory*. Often, notes Bergson, it is argued that perception must be a form of internal sensation since a perceptual stimulus, such as a beam of light or wave of sound, can cause pain to the receptive organ if made sufficiently intense. Bergson counters that sensations, and bodily feelings in general, or "affections," are qualitatively distinct from perceptions, though sensation/affection bears a necessary relationship to perception and in fact always accompanies it.[14] When an external movement impinges on the surface of an amoeba, the entire organism responds to that movement. The amoeba's surface as a whole is a perceptual organ, a sensory organ and a motor organ. In more complex organisms, there is a specialization of tissues, whereby some register external movements while remaining immobile, and others execute motor activities. In humans, the eyes and ears are relatively immobile receptors of external movement, whereas the legs are organs of locomotion. When a beam of light hurts the eye or a blast of sound hurts the ear, the eye or ear experiences pain because it is encountering an external movement to which it cannot respond with motor flight. Its pain expresses its vain effort to escape, and in this regard its pain is "a sort of motor tendency on a sensible nerve" (1959, 204; 1911, 56).

Perception always takes place at the object, but when a light is so intense that it is blinding, the object of perception is no longer the light but the surface of the eye. At this point, and this point only, perception and sensation/affection come together. What we commonly call perception is actually a mixture of external perception and internal affection, and this mixture is necessitated by our corporeal existence. We are "centers of indetermination," which selectively reflect images and thereby bring into existence perceptions, but we are also extended bodies in an interactive field of forces and movements. Our perceptions allow us to assess at a distance the potential actions of things on us and our possible actions on them. As the distance between things and our bodies decreases, our possibilities for action diminish, until at a certain point, our bodies directly encounter external movements to which they must respond. Since our calculation of impending external movements and possible responses depends on an awareness of our bodily situation in the world, our perception is necessarily tied to our corporeal sensations/affections. But perception and affection remain qualitatively distinct. Perception takes place in the object, affection in the body. Since we are embodied perceivers, however, "there is no perception without affection. Affection is thus that which, from the interior of our body, we mix with the image of exterior bodies" (1959, 206; 1911, 60). Perception "measures the reflective power of the body, affection its absorbent power" (1959, 205; 1911, 57). We can see, then, that the eye has a dual function, in that it is an organ of perception that reflects and filters external movements at a distance as well as a tactile surface of the body that undergoes the affections of direct contact with external movements.[15]

What Deleuze draws from these discussions is that the affection-image "marks the coincidence of the subject and the object in a pure quality" (IM 96; 65). Affection occupies the interval between incoming perception and outgoing action; it is, one might say, in the interval itself. On the incoming side which links perception and affection, subject and object coincide, in that the object of perception is felt in conjunction with a bodily sensation. Perception reflects external movements, but in every perception some movement is also absorbed by the body, and that movement is related to "a 'quality' as lived state [état vécu]" (IM 96; 65).

Through this quality, the living image perceives itself along its corporeal surface, and thereby experiences its interiority. (Bergson says that among the images I know "from the outside through perceptions," there is one I know "from the inside through affections: my body" [1959, 169; 1911, 1].) In affection, movement is absorbed and registered as "a sort of motor tendency on a sensible nerve," in Bergson's phrase, or as Deleuze puts it, as "a motor effort on an immobilized receptive plate [*plaque*, photographic plate, such as Bergson refers to in his characterization of perception as "a black screen" behind "the plate" (1959, 188; 1911, 32)]" (IM 96; 66). But besides marking a coincidence of object and subject, affection also connects the interval's incoming side of perception to its outgoing side of action. The living image is an interruption in the direct interactions of matter-movement, and hence it introduces a discontinuity between received movements (perceptions) and executed movements (actions), such that the two kinds of movements are rendered "in some sense incommensurable" (IM 97; 66). Affection "reestablishes the relation" between the two movements, not through a third "movement of translation," or actual movement in space, but through a "movement of expression, that is, quality, simple tendency agitating an immobile element" (IM 97; 66).[16] It is not surprising, says Deleuze, that for the living images called human beings the paradigmatic site of the affection-image is the face, a relatively immobile surface on which are registered motor tendencies, expressions of pure qualities that suggest the connections between incoming perceptions and outgoing actions.

The three kinds of movement-images, then, arise automatically when a center of indetermination comes into existence in the midst of the matter-flow of universally interacting movement-images. These three movement-images are directly tied to the sensori-motor activities of the living image. The perception-image is a portion of the world that the living image selectively frames according to its interests and purposes. The action-image is an environment curved around the living image as center of potential encounters and possible responses. The affection-image is a motor tendency registered on a receptive surface, an image of a portion of the living image itself as it absorbs external movement and expresses a pure quality. Like the other two movement-images, the affection-image reveals the corporeal involvement of the living image in its environment; the affective quality expresses the coincidence of the subject as site of sensation and the object as locus of perception (since perception is always in the object, not the subject), while indicating as well through movements of expression (simple motor tendencies) the connection between the movements of incoming perceptions and outgoing actions.

In *Cinema 2: The Time-Image* Deleuze neatly summarizes the material we have considered in this chapter. He identifies a "vertical axis" and a "horizontal axis" in the "system of the movement image" (IT 43; 28), the vertical axis relating to the immobile cut, the mobile cut, and the open whole, the horizontal axis to the three kinds of movement-images. The vertical axis is one of *differentiation,* in that the virtual multiplicity of the open whole of *durée* continually divides or differentiates itself into the closed sets of actual objects in a homogeneous space and an abstract time, while that open whole remains everywhere indirectly expressed through the movements of the objects within the closed sets.[17] The horizontal axis is one of *specification,* in that the movement-image forms three *species* of movement-images when related to the interval of the living image or center of indetermination. (Although Deleuze does not say as much, we might also identify the vertical axis as the axis of *durée* and the horizontal as the axis of pure perception, or movement without *durée.*) Together, the components of the vertical and horizontal axes comprise "a plastic mass, an a-signifying and a-syntactic matter, a non-linguistically formed matter, though a matter that is not amorphous but semiotically, aesthetically and pragmatically formed" (IT 44; 29). This plastic mass, when treated in terms of its virtual rather than its actual divisions, is a plane of consistency of image/movement/matter/*durée.* And though Deleuze identifies that image/movement/matter with light in *Cinema 1,* he here broadens its conception to include all forms of matter/flow, the plastic mass being "a *signaletic matter* that bears the characteristics of modulations of all sorts, sensorial (visual and sonic), kinetic, intensive, affective, rhythmic, tonal, and even verbal (oral and written)" (IT 43–44; 29). This plastic mass is the "stuff" of which films are made—and of which we, too, are made, for "each of us, the special image or contingent center, is nothing but an assemblage [*agencement*] of three images, a consolidation of perception-images, action-images and affection-images" (IM 97; 66). In the following chapters we will consider the ways in which great directors shape this signaletic matter through the vertical processes of framings, cuts, shots, and montage, and through the horizontal processes of long-shot perception-images, medium-shot action-images, and close-up affection-images.

Chapter Two

FRAME, SHOT, AND MONTAGE

In his commentary on Bergson's *Creative Evolution,* as we have seen, Deleuze distinguishes between closed sets and the open whole, noting that matter naturally tends to form isolable systems yet without completely severing connections to the whole of *durée.* Movement functions as the intermediary between closed sets and the open whole, in that movement can be seen both as the change of position of discrete objects in a space container (the closed-set view of movement) and as the qualitative transformation of an open totality of relations (the open-whole perspective). The closed set may be treated as an immobile cut when movement is regarded as a mere change in the position of objects. In such a set we approach the ideal limit of a space free of *durée,* within which motion is conceived of as a succession of instantaneous slices of space regulated through an abstract time. But in the closed set, or isolated system of entities, the movement of objects may be seen as expressing *durée,* in which case the closed set functions as a mobile cut, a chunk or slice of the space-time of the vibrational whole.

Two triads of terms are thus operative in this analysis: closed sets/movement (as intermediary between sets and the whole)/open whole of *durée;* and immobile cuts/mobile cuts/open whole of *durée.* These triads, however, may be reduced to a single dyad of closed sets/open whole, the closed set functioning either as immobile cut or mobile cut depending on how movement is regarded within the set. On the basis of these distinctions Deleuze approaches the fundamental cinematic elements of the frame, the shot, and montage, which are present in films of all kinds— silent, sound, classic, modern, commercial, documentary, experimental, and all others. The frame of the camera delimits a closed set of elements. The shot is a discrete set of elements enduring in time, and hence a unit of movement in which objects change positions and by doing so express the transformation of a whole. And montage, as that process of cutting and splicing whereby shots are literally put in relation to one another, is the means whereby the open whole of *durée* plays through and informs the entire film.

FRAME AND SHOT

The camera always frames a portion of the world, carves out a block of space-time. The framed image is eventually projected onto a screen of fixed dimensions, the screen functioning as the "frame of frames" (IM 27; 14). Whether a close-up of a glaring eye or a panoramic view of the Grand Canyon or the Milky Way, the framed image fills the same screen space, and in this sense the screen provides "a common measure for that which has none" (IM 27; 14). Such a common measure tends not to unify so much as to disorient, for it forces a juxtaposition of qualitatively different views of things within an arbitrarily delineated surface area. Thus, the frame of the camera detaches a block of the world from its surrounding context, and the frame of the screen temporally juxtaposes heterogeneous blocks. No matter how hard one may try to normalize the cinematic image, then, there is inherent in it a destabilizing force. The frame, whether camera frame or screen frame, at the most rudimentary level "assures a deterritorialization of the image" (IM 27; 15).

The frame of the camera demarcates a closed set of elements, and "framing is the art of choosing parts of all sorts that enter into a set" (IM 31; 18). Deleuze identifies five features of the framed image.

(1) In terms of its content, the closed set of elements isolated by the frame provides information. The more information that fills the framed image, the more it may be said to be "saturated"; the less information, the more "rarefied" the image becomes, until it reaches the limit of the empty black or white screen.

(2) The frame itself as limiting border of the image functions either geometrically or dynamically. In the first case (the more common of the two), the frame establishes a fixed compositional grid of horizontal, vertical, and diagonal coordinates within which elements are organized in various patterns. In the second, the frame varies dynamically with that which is framed, the most striking instances of this practice being Griffith's iris shots and Gance's variable screen that opens and closes like a "visual accordion" (IM 25; 13).

(3) The elements enclosed by the frame are distinct parts, but also components of a single composition. In this sense, the frame both separates and unites the included elements, and the disposition of elements may again be either geometric or dynamic. Dreyer's arrangements of elements in horizontals and verticals, German expressionist configurations of diagonals and triangles, Western landscapes divided along a vast sky-desert horizon, all relate parts geometrically. Images of fogs, fluids, shifting shadows, undulating shapes and metamorphosing forms, by contrast, relate parts dynamically, the changing configuration of elements interacting as a Bergsonian qualitative multiplicity, not divisible or indivisible, but "dividual" (IM 26;14), the closed set of elements dividing itself at each moment into a qualitatively different set of elements.

(4) Every frame implies an "angle of framing," a position in space from which the framed image is shot. The frame's implicit point of view may be unexceptionable or unusual, and if unusual, eventually "justified" or not. A shot from the floor to the ceiling, for example, may prove to be the groggy detective's view upon awaking from a beating; alternatively, the shot may remain unexplained in narrative or pragmatic terms, in which case it may function as what Bonitzer calls a "deframing" [*décadrage*], an unsettling angle of framing that suggests a non-narrative motivation for the shot, one that must be "read" or interpreted.

(5) Finally, the frame both includes and excludes, necessarily determining the field of entities within a closed set as well as an "out-of-field" (*hors-champ*) beyond the framed image. In *Theory of Film Practice* Noël Burch distinguishes six spatial axes in the out-of-field—above or below the frame, to the right or the left, in depth away from the camera (e.g., the space beyond a closed door at the center of a shot) or toward the camera and beyond it in the audience's direction (17). But Deleuze proposes that in addition to this spatial conception of the out-of-field, which he calls a "relative out-of-field," we should distinguish an "absolute

out-of-field" of *durée*. Spatially, every framed set of elements may be included within a larger frame, the succession of frames extending in principle until an ultimate frame of frames includes the entire universe. Such an ultimate frame would not constitute a whole, however, for if conceived in strictly spatial terms, it would be without *durée*. Yet the open whole of *durée* is always present, though it can never be "given" as such. Within every framed image, *durée* "insists" or "subsists," manifesting in a disquieting way "a more radical Elsewhere, outside homogeneous space and time" (IM 30; 17). For every frame, then, there are two out-of-fields, one relative and one absolute, and Deleuze argues that the degree to which each is manifest within the framed image varies in an inverse proportion. The framed image and its relative out-of-field form part of the three-dimensional, six-vector space of common sense and ordinary experience—a space, as Bergson notes, that also reinforces the illusion of an abstract, homogeneous time. The greater the continuity between the framed image and the out-of-field—the more, say, a character's glance offscreen matches up with her interlocutor's spatial position in the succeeding shot—the more the image will be seen as belonging to a normal space and time, and the less it will be experienced as a slice of *durée*. Conversely, the more the image is separated from the relative out-of-field, and hence disconnected from the spatio-temporal coordinates of commonsense experience, the greater will be the disquieting "insistence" of the absolute out-of-field.

This distinction between the relative and absolute out-of-field leads Deleuze directly into a discussion of the shot, for the shot translates the relative movement of the immobile cut while expressing the absolute movement of the mobile cut of *durée*. In his remarks on the shot, Deleuze engages an extended debate in French film theory. As many French critics note, in English one may distinguish between the "shot" and the "take," the shot referring to the spatial distance of the subject from the camera (long shot, medium shot, close-up), the take to the temporal duration of a single recording of a scene. No such distinction is readily available in French. As Jean Mitry observes, the French term for the shot, *plan* (literally "plan" or "plane"), has its origin in the early silent cinema, when filmmakers spoke of establishing continuity between planes of action in succeeding scenes. Distances from the camera came to be described in terms of *plans—gros plan* (close-up), *plan moyen* (medium shot), *plan d'ensemble* (long shot)—and Mitry, for one, proposes that *plan* be restricted to characterizations of spatial distance and that such spatio-temporal "hybrids" as Bazin's *plan-séquence* (sequence shot), coined to describe tracking shots in which the camera moves about in a continuous take, be avoided (Mitry 64). Deleuze sides with those who oppose Mitry's strictly spatial definition of the *plan,* arguing that the unity of the *plan* is a "unity of movement" (IM 43; 27), every unity being determined by an act that brings together a multiplicity of elements. Hence, "*plans,* as immobile spatial determinations, in this sense can perfectly well be the multiplicity that corresponds to the unity of *the plan,* as mobile cut or temporal perspective" (IM 41; 25). The double sense of *plan* as spatial distance and temporal continuity, then, aptly captures the nature of movement as indivisible qualitative multiplicity, and the specific dimensions of any given *plan* will vary according to the number and extent of the multiple elements subsumed within a unifying movement. For Deleuze, then, the *plan* may consist of a single take from a fixed angle, a single tracking shot, or a succession of shots, whether fixed or tracking, edited to form a continuous movement. Yet it may be regarded as well in larger units, extending even to include the entire film as a single *plan-séquence,* a single movement that expresses the open whole of *durée* while distributing the multiple elements within various sets and subsets of the film.

What is crucial for Deleuze, however, is not the length of the *plan* but its relationship to movement. Movement "has two faces, as inseparable as inside and outside, verso and recto: *it is the relation between parts, and it is the affection of the whole*" (IM 32; 19). The *plan* "is movement, considered in its double aspect: translation of parts of a set which extends in space, change of a whole which transforms itself in *durée*" (IM 32; 20). Hence, the *plan* is the "intermediary between the framing of the set and the montage of the whole" (IM 33; 19), the frame isolating a closed set of spatial elements, montage assembling a temporal whole, and each *plan* manifesting the spatial repositioning of elements while simultaneously expressing the movement of *durée.* To illustrate the dual nature of movement, Deleuze describes a sequence from Hitchcock's *Frenzy* in which the camera follows a man and woman up a set of stairs to a door; the two enter the door while the camera pulls back, descends the stairway, travels along the sidewalk, and ascends the apartment building wall until it reaches the opaque window of the apartment. The figures of the man and woman move within the frame, the camera's own movement modifies the positions of various mobile and immobile elements, but at the same time these spatial repositionings express something that is happening, "a change in a whole that itself passes by way of these modifications: the woman is about to be murdered, she entered free, but can expect no help, the murder is inexorable" (IM 33; 19). The changing whole in this case is described in narrative terms, but it need not be, nor should narrative be seen as the unifying cause that subsumes the parts within a whole. The point is that in the *plan durée* divides itself into separate parts while continuing to unite them within a single indivisible multiplicity. In the *plan,* movement "decomposes" and "recomposes," splits into local configurations and combines in broad patterns, those configurations and patterns taking on identifiable formal shapes. Eric Rohmer, for example, shows that movements of contraction and expansion characterize the whole of Murnau's *Faust,* and François Regnault argues that various Hitchcock films have a global formal unity—the straight line of *Rope,* the broken line of *Psycho,* the spiral of *Vertigo.* Such movements also structure individual scenes and sequences, in some cases manifesting themselves as explicit motifs, as in *Vertigo,* where the spiral becomes "the vertigo of the hero, but also the circuit he traces with his car, or the curl in the heroine's hair" (IM 36; 21–22).

The *plan* "is the movement-image," and to the extent that it relates movement to a whole that changes, "it is the mobile cut of a *durée*" (IM 36; 22). We naturally tend to see movement as an attribute of solid and stable bodies, something that "belongs" to them, but in the cinematic image we are able to see movement disengaged from bodies. And the fundamental devices that help us see such disengaged motion are the movement of the camera and the movement between shots established in montage. Various mechanical means are used to move the camera—it may be mounted on a dolly, a crane, a shoulder harness, a truck, an airplane—but its function is "to extract from vehicles or moving entities the movement that is their common substance, or to extract from movements the mobility that is their essence" (IM 37; 23). Though diverse methods may be used to rationalize and normalize camera movements within commonsense spatio-temporal schemas, the mobile camera tends to extract a pure movement from bodies, one that takes on an existence independent of any specific character or point of view. Similarly, continuities between shots may be scrupulously maintained in editing, but the movement engendered through montage remains one that to some degree always escapes the bodies from which it issues. Montage and the mobile camera in a sense add something to the fixed shot, but in another they simply activate a potential inherent in the moving bodies within every shot. In this regard, the fixed shot of the earliest films "had a tendency to yield a pure movement-image, a tendency that imperceptibly came into action through the mobilization in space of the camera or through the montage in time of mobile or merely fixed *plans*" (IM 41; 25).

The *plan* as mobile cut not only expresses the whole of *durée* but also puts into variation "the bodies, parts, aspects, dimensions, distances, and the respective positions of the bodies that comprise a set [*ensemble*] in the image" (IM 38; 23). Every film in this regard is like a cubist painting of Léger, in which, according to Jean Epstein, "all the surfaces divide, truncate, decompose, break apart, as one would imagine them in the thousand-faceted eye of an insect" (cited in IM 38; 23). Each of these splintered surfaces provides its own perspective on the world, with no common denominator coordinating the relations between the various perspectives. Likewise, every film divides in time into multiple *plans,* each with its own incommensurable perspective. Each *plan* is a particular slice of movement, and hence each provides a specific view of time, or temporal perspective. And each perspective is itself dynamic, in constant variation. Bazin points out that the static image recorded in still photography is like a fixed mold of the world, whereas the cinematic image is a ceaselessly varying mold. Such ceaseless molding Deleuze calls *modulation,* and each *plan* is a kind of modulator, not simply registering passively the variable movements of the entities within the shot but actively putting them in variation through techniques of framing, camera movement, and montage.[1] In this regard, then, the *plan* as mobile cut may be defined as "a *temporal perspective or a modulation*" (IM 39; 24), the sum of such temporal perspectives or modulations being like the multiple facets of a cubist painting, each a particular division of the whole that expresses the whole in its individual way.

The *plan* is a temporal perspective, and as such it "acts like a consciousness" (IM 34; 20). The cinematic consciousness, however, "is not us, the spectator, nor the hero, but the camera, now human, now inhuman, or super-human" (IM 34; 20). In his commentary on Bergson, as we have seen, Deleuze argues that consciousness is in things, virtually present in the prehensions of brute matter and actualized in various organic forms as living "centers of indetermination." The universe is a "metacinema," and in the images of the cinema itself we see that consciousness-in-things—or rather, we see *as* that consciousness-in-things. Yet that consciousness is always a *camera* consciousness, one that may temporarily take on human or non-human functions or qualities, but that remains autonomous. It is this autonomy, in fact, that makes possible the extraction of movement from bodies and the presentation of movement-in-itself in the *plan*.[2]

MONTAGE: ORGANIC AND DIALECTIC

The *plan*, then, is the fundamental unit of movement in each film, varying in its extent according to the number of elements it combines as an indivisible qualitative multiplicity. In the *plan* we see movement's dual nature as translation of parts and expression of the whole. As expression of the whole, the *plan* is a mobile cut of *durée*, each mobile cut functioning as a temporal perspective, or continuous modulation of time, and a camera consciousness. The *plan* as movement-image is the intermediary between the frame and montage, between the closed set of elements demarcated by the frame and the open whole implicit in montage. Yet the three elements are only relatively distinct, since every *plan* is always framed, and montage is often already "in" the *plan* (as in the extended tracking shots of Welles's *Magnificent Ambersons*, where, for example, the continuous movement of the camera from two characters at the foot of the stairs to a second pair on the landing above serves the same purpose as a splicing of two separate scenes in montage.)

If the *plan* is "the determination of the movement that is established in the closed system" (IM 32; 18), montage is "the determination of the Whole" (IM 46; 29). Put another way, the *plan* is the movement-image, and montage "is the composition, the assemblage [*agencement*] of movement-images as constituting an indirect image of time" (IM 47; 30). It would be easy enough to translate Deleuze's definitions into more conventional terms, to see the whole as the unifying concept of the film (plot, theme, thesis, and so on), montage as the splicing of shots in accordance with that concept, and individual shots as the actual manifestations of the unifying concept, which itself can only be presented in an indirect fashion, not in any one shot but between the shots and in the organizing scheme of all the shots as a totality. For

Deleuze, however, a film's unifying concept, whether plot, theme, or thesis, is secondary to its form of time. Narrative, motivic, or discursive continuities issue forth from the matter-flows of the open whole of *durée*, which can take on a number of configurations. In the montage practices of certain early filmmakers Deleuze finds four tendencies— American organic, Soviet dialectic, French quantitative, and German intensive—that represent four basic ways of relating movement-images to the whole of *durée*.

The organic tendency is most fully met with in the films of D. W. Griffith, who conceives of the whole as "an organization, an organism, a great organic unity" (IM 47; 30). From this organic conception come Griffith's basic montage practices. An organism is made up of distinct parts, which may be presented in an alternation of binary pairs— rich/poor, male/female, North/South—hence Griffith's use of parallel, alternating montage. Parts must be related to the whole, however, and thus Griffith's development of the close-up as an inserted representation of an aspect of the whole. Parts finally must interact with one another, and in Griffith's films that interaction frequently takes the form of a convergence of parallel actions toward a single end—whence Griffith's celebrated use of concurrent or convergent montage, as when the Klan's rescue in *Birth of a Nation* is presented as an accelerated alternation between the approaching posse and the increasingly endangered innocents. Three forms of rhythmic alternation, then, inform Griffith's montage, "the alternation of differentiated parts, that of relative dimensions, that of convergent actions" (IM 49; 31), and these are the basic forms followed in mainstream American films from Griffith's day on.

Despite the clear narrative utility of these forms, however, Deleuze insists that "it is narrativity that derives from this conception of montage" (IM 49; 31). In Griffith's *Intolerance*, for instance, sweeping narratives from distant civilizations are the units of composition, and the montage of these units ultimately forms a figure of time as both the whole of the movement of the universe and the interval marking the smallest unit of movement. Time as a whole is like the circling flight of a bird, open at each end of its spiral; time as interval is like the moment between each beat of the bird's wings, an "accelerated variable present" (IM 50; 32). When infinitely contracted, the time of the bird's spiral is compressed into the interval of an individual beat; when infinitely dilated, the time of the interval expands across the extent of the bird's open-ended spiral.

In *Intolerance,* the bird's spiral is seen in the broad parallels between ancient and contemporary life, such as that of the Babylonian chariot chase and the modern American automobile-train pursuit, and the bird's beating wings in the recurring motif of the endlessly rocking cradle. In the converging montage of the Babylonian and American chase sequences, the time of the whole contracts within a narrowing interval, whereas in the rocking of the cradle the time of the variable present interval appears as the dilating, generative movement of the whole. It is from this fundamental movement of contracting and dilating time that the film takes on its narrative structure.

The dialectic tendency Deleuze finds best exemplified in the films of the great Soviet directors Sergei Eisenstein, Vsevolod Pudovkin, Alexander Dovzhenko, and Dziga Vertov, and its basic principles he distills from Eisenstein's extensive theoretical writings on montage. In *Film Form* Eisenstein praises Griffith's innovations in montage, but he points out that Griffith's formal alternations between parallel plots betray a bourgeois acceptance of social divisions as given and unalterable. Montage thinking "is inseparable from the general content of thinking as a whole" (234), and Griffith, "a master of *parallel montage*" (234), juxtaposes shots from parallel plots in the same uncritical manner as he thematically presents the struggles between rich and poor. Eisenstein calls instead for an "organic" treatment of film form, one that is not dualistic but "monistic and dialectic" (235). Actually, says Deleuze, both Griffith and Eisenstein adopt an organic approach to montage, but whereas Griffith thinks of the whole as an already constructed organism, Eisenstein conceives of it as a generative process of organic growth. For Eisenstein the shot is a "montage *cell,*" and "just as cells in their division form a phenomenon of another order, the organism or embryo, so, on the other side of the dialectical leap from the shot, there is montage" (Film Form 37). Each film should grow as a living being, each shot functioning as an animate cell. Yet the growth of the film proceeds not so much through division of the individual cell as through a juxtaposition of cells, for conflict or collision is what Eisenstein sees as fundamental to film. Montage "is conflict," he says, and conflict within the shot is "potential montage" (38). Through the collision of opposites a higher synthesis is produced, and the structure of each film is generated through a montage of conflicting parts that form larger synthetic units, the units increasing in size until they constitute the totality of the unified work.

The formal principle of such generative growth Eisenstein identifies as the Golden Section,[3] a ratio of parts to whole (roughly 8:13) that fascinated Renaissance painters and architects, and that Eisenstein regards as basic to the formation of natural entities and artworks alike. What is crucial about the Golden Section is that its parts are unequal (and hence unstable) yet harmoniously related to one another when subsumed within a larger unit, and each larger unit may itself be subsumed within another unit that is larger still. As Eisenstein demonstrates in *Nonindifferent Nature* (especially 10–16, 31–34), his own *Battleship Potemkin* may be seen as a collision of conflicting parts at every level, from the composition of individual shots to the editing of particular sequences (such as the famous "Odessa Steps" sequence), to the structuring of the plot as a whole (five sections, each of which is divided unequally in two parts, the five sections grouped in units of three and two), and within each of these levels the ratio of the Golden Section prevails.

The whole is a collection of colliding parts, and the collision itself Eisenstein describes as "a leap," a "transition from quantity to quality," a "transition into the opposite" (Nonindifferent Nature 35). This for Eisenstein is the essence of montage—a juxtaposition of conflicting shots that generates what he calls *pathos,* a "*moment* of culmination," "*a revolutionary explosion*" (35), a passage from one state to another, such as from water into steam. That passage, says Deleuze, ensures that "there is not simply an organic link between two instants, but a pathetic jump, in which the second instant acquires a new power, because the first has passed into it" (IM 53; 35). If the organic whole is a spiral (and in *Nonindifferent Nature* Eisenstein provides a diagram of a spiral as "the mathematical image" [17] of the Golden Section), the leaps of pathos "are like chords of an arc" (*cordes d'un arc,* which may also be translated as "strings of a bow") (IM 53; 35), straight lines that short-circuit an arc, each leap being at once "the chord/string [*corde*] and the arrow, the change of the quality and the sudden surging forth of the new quality, its elevation to the squared power, to the second power" (IM 54; 35). There is then in Eisenstein's dialectical form a continuity of organic growth yet also a discontinuity of generative force that produces something qualitatively new in each collision of opposites. And this discontinuity is manifest in montage practices that may be set in opposition to each of Griffith's three "forms of montage or rhythmic alternation" (IM 49; 31)—those of differentiated parts, relative dimensions, and convergent

actions. "For Griffith's parallel montage [the montage of "differentiated parts"] Eisenstein substitutes a montage of oppositions; for convergent or concurrent montage, he substitutes a montage of qualitative
leaps" (IM 56; 36). And for Griffith's use of the close-up as a simple vehicle for connecting a part to a larger whole (the montage of "relative
dimensions") Eisenstein substitutes a new treatment of the close-up as
qualitative break, the close-up being exploited for its qualitative difference in size from contrasting shots (the leap) and for its ability to distill
from an entity a specific affective quality (pathos).

In Griffith's organic montage, the movements of the whole of *durée*
and the variable present moment are related to one another as the open
spiral of a bird's flight and the individual intervals between beats of its
wings. In Eisenstein's dialectic montage, the whole remains an open spiral, but it is no longer simply an assemblage of parts that happen to function together. Instead, the spiral becomes a generative organic form that
grows through a synthesis of conflicting parts within larger and larger
units, each of which is structured by the ratio of the Golden Section. As
in Griffith's montage, the whole continues to be contracted within the
minimal interval of the variable present moment, but in Eisenstein the
interval becomes more than a site of alternation, functioning instead as
a qualitative leap. In Eisenstein, then, "time remains an indirect image
that is born of the organic composition of movement-images, *but the
interval as well as the whole take on a new sense*" (IM 56; 37), the interval
becoming a qualitative leap, the whole a generative spiral in which
"dialectical reality ceaselessly produces itself and grows" (IM 57; 37).

Deleuze regards Eisenstein as the chief theorist and practitioner of
the dialectic tendency in montage, and this tendency he finds as well in
a number of early Soviet films, especially those of Eisenstein's contemporaries Pudovkin and Dovzhenko. Despite clear differences in their
editing styles (Eisenstein's montage of abrupt "collision," for example,
is commonly contrasted with Pudovkin's montage of unobtrusive "linkage"), all three approach the whole as an organic form generated
through a synthesis of oppositions, Pudovkin concentrating in his films
on the progression of sudden shifts in consciousness through which
characters come to awareness of their class situation, Dovzhenko emphasizing the "triadic relation of parts, the ensemble and the whole" (IM 58;
38), diverse shots of individual characters, for example, being subsumed
within the imagery of a collective millennial past (*Zvenigora*) or grand

planetary future (*Aerograd*). It is only in Vertov that Deleuze sees a gen- uine break in the dialectic tendency, one made possible by "the radical affirmation of a dialectic of matter in itself" (IM 59; 39). For Eisenstein, Pudovkin, and Dovzhenko, materialism is above all historical, and Nature is dialectical only when "integrated into a human totality" (IM 59; 39). For Vertov, by contrast, there is a life in matter—in machines, landscapes, buildings, people—that sets them in interaction, and the interval of the qualitative leap is not that of an exclusively human con- sciousness but a camera consciousness, a superhuman perception in matter. In *The Man with a Movie Camera,* Vertov extends the dialectic beyond the human such that "the whole merges with the infinite set [*ensemble*] of matter, and the interval merges with an eye in matter, the Camera" (IM 61; 40). And in the process, Vertov suggests an alternative to the conception of montage as organic composition, one based on the principle of rhythm as a ceaseless adaptation of "transformations of movements in the material universe to the interval of movement in the eye of the camera" (IM 60; 40).

MONTAGE: QUANTITATIVE AND INTENSIVE

Vertov's dialectic of matter is one way of breaking with the principle of organic composition, but Deleuze finds additional means to this end in the montage tendencies of two groups of filmmakers from the 1920s and early 1930s, the French directors Abel Gance, Jean Epstein, Marcel L'Herbier, Jean Grémillon, René Clair, Jean Renoir, Jean Vigo, Germaine Dulac, and Louis Delluc, and the German expressionist directors Robert Wiene, Paul Wegener, Fritz Lang, F. W. Murnau, G. W. Pabst, Lupu Pick, and E. A. Dupont. Though the two groups are often con- trasted as French impressionists to German expressionists, Deleuze prefers to frame their differences in terms of a quantitative as opposed to an intensive approach to movement. In the French approach, the variable present is treated as a numeric unity, in the German, as an intensive degree, and at the level of the open whole, the French and German tendencies are opposed as Kant's mathematical and dynamic sublime, the one infinite in number, the other infinite in power.

Deleuze describes the French tendency in montage as "a kind of Cartesianism,"[4] characterized by a controlling interest in "the *quantity of movement,* and in the metrical relations that allow one to define it" (IM

61; 41), which gives rise not to organic or dialectic structures, but to "a vast mechanical composition of movement-images" (IM 62; 41). Such scenes as Epstein's traveling fair in *Coeur fidèle,* L'Herbier's ball in *El Dorado,* and Grémillon's farandole in *Maldone* are frequently cited as defining images of early French cinematic style, and in each Deleuze sees an effort to extract from the moving objects "a maximum quantity of movement in a given space" (IM 62; 41). Jean Epstein best describes this process of extraction in his account of a Spanish cabaret dance scene in L'Herbier's *El Dorado:*

> By means of a soft focus that becomes progressively intensified, the dancers gradually lose their personal differentiations, cease to be recognizable as distinct individuals, become merged in a common visual term: *the* dancer, an element henceforth anonymous, impossible to distinguish from twenty or fifty equivalent elements, which together come to constitute another generality, another abstraction: not this fandango, or that fandango, but *the* fandango, that is, the structure, rendered visible, of the musical rhythm of all fandangos. (Epstein, v. 2: 67–68)

The dance becomes a machine, the dancers its moving parts, and *the* dancer is extracted from the dance as the metrical unit of its functioning, a maximum quantity of movement for a given space—*the* dancer for *the* fandango. This mechanical approach to movement Deleuze finds explicitly demonstrated in the French school's images of machines, which he says are of two types—automata, which produce "an automatic ballet whose motor itself circulates across the movement" (IM 63; 42), and steam or combustion engines, "the powerful energetic machine that produces movement from something else, and ceaselessly affirms a heterogeneity whose terms it links—the mechanical and the living, the inside and the outside, the mechanic and the force" (IM 63–64; 42). Unlike the automata of German expressionist films, with their eerie and threatening inorganic life, French automata tend to be presented as mere geometric configurations in mechanical interaction with other regularly moving entities. In Vigo's *L'Atalante,* for example, when Juliette stops to look at the puppets in the storefront window, we see in one especially complex shot the extension of the puppets' mechanical movements to patterns of action beyond. The camera looks out from inside the store to Juliette on the sidewalk, the backs of the puppets in the foreground, Juliette's image in the middle space, the window reflection of the moving puppets floating in the background, a rhythmic flow of pedestrians passing behind her on a plane seemingly between her and the puppets' reflection. The superimposed movements of automata and people blend in a single movement composition, the motor of the puppet-human machine circulating throughout the parts.[5] In their handling of the second kind of machine—steam or combustion engines—the French directors differ especially from the Soviet school, in which various industrial machines are typically shown in dialectical unity with their human operators. Among the French, the engine and the engineer remain separate components of a single kinetic system, the engine determining a quantity of movement, the engineer a direction of movement in an annexed "soul" of the machine. Here, Deleuze has in mind especially the images of the train wreck in Gance's *The Wheel* [*La roue*], in which the accelerating movements of the locomotive combine with the complex passions of the engineer Sisif to form a tragic machine-with-human-soul, a "Bête humaine" (IM 64; 43) akin to the locomotive-engineer machine Renoir creates in his 1938 rendition of Zola's novel.

Such an approach to machines is indicative of a pervasive treatment of movement among French directors, one that manifests itself in such abstract avant-garde compositions as Léger's *Ballet mécanique,* and even in the French school's fascination with water, which represents no departure from mechanism but simply "a passage from a mechanics of solids to a mechanics of fluids" (IM 65; 43). French directors are intrigued by what Delluc, Dulac, and Epstein call "photogeny," that aspect of objects that makes them particularly suitable for filming. As Epstein explains, French directors early came upon "a mystery"—that certain objects were enhanced when filmed, others not—and they soon concluded that photogeny was "above all a function of mobility" and that movement was "the first aesthetic quality of images on the screen" (1974, v. 2: 65). That mystery, says Deleuze, led them to a new conception of the interval of the variable present as "a numerical unity that produces in the image a maximum quantity of movement *in relation to other determinable factors,* and that varies from one image to another according to the variation of the factors themselves" (IM 66; 44). Unlike Eisenstein's dialectical leap, the French interval functions as a unit of measure for constructing a movement-machine, each movement-machine having its own basic motion-units and standards of measure. In L'Herbier's fandango, the basic motion-unit is a rhythmic sequence of gestures and movements, repeated by various dancers, but finally extracted as a quantitatively specified temporal "unit of fandango," from which is constructed *the* fandango, the "maximum quantity of movement" for any and all fandango-machines. The numerical unit varies according to the ensemble of elements which it regulates, and hence the "maximum quantity" of movement does not necessarily mean the *fastest* movement, but simply "the 'best' quantity when considered in relation to all of its elements" (IM 67; 45). Hence, in Gance's *The Wheel* the maximum quantity of the train wreck sequence is a progressively accelerating unit of movement, whereas in the famous slow-motion sequence of Epstein's *Fall of the House of Usher,* the maximum quantity is an extremely elongated unit. In each movement-sequence, the motion-unit is determined by various factors—lighting, space, camera angle and distance, the objects/events filmed, the interrelated movements of objects and camera—and in each sequence, the montage of images is governed by the metrical unit of movement that generates the optimal rhythm for that particular configuration of factors.

The optimal numerical unit is a "maximum quantity of movement" that is relative to the ensemble of elements it organizes, but besides this *relative* maximum quantity there is in the French school of montage an *absolute* maximum quantity of movement at the level of the open whole of *durée*. The movement-image always has two sides, a recto and a verso, one facing the relative movement of the set, the other the open-ended and hence infinite movement of *durée*. In the *Critique of Judgment,* Kant observes that mathematical numbers allow us to conceive of something we cannot grasp with our senses—the infinite, an absolute magnitude without maximum, that which is "absolutely great in every point of view (great beyond all comparison)" (Kant, 88). Kant defines the sublime as "that, the mere ability to think which shows a faculty of the mind surpassing every standard of sense" (Kant 89), and the sublime generated via the estimation of magnitude through numbers he calls the "mathematical sublime." The mathematical sublime is something beyond the measure of the senses but graspable by reason, and Deleuze argues that the quantitative numerical units of the French school, the intervals of the variable present, express an infinite whole that is similar to the mathematical sublime, "something immeasurable, Too Much or Excess in relation to every measure, which can only be conceived by a thinking soul" (IM 70; 47). A dualism of matter and spirit prevails in the French school, the relative mechanical movements of material elements co-existing with an absolute movement of a conceptual, mental whole. That dualism is evident in Gance's locomotive-engineer machine, but also in L'Herbier's fandango. During the dance, the relative movements of the dancers come to form a single machine with mobile, circulating motor, but at the same time an absolute movement pervades the whole, "an independent Soul that 'envelops' and 'precedes' the bodies" (IM 70; 47), a spirit whose indirect image is the blur itself of the soft focus, the atmospheric envelope of the whole.

For the French school, the ideal toward which relative quantitative movement tends is that of a simultaneous co-presence of temporal movements, an infinite comprised of superimposed successive moments grasped simultaneously as a whole. "The ideal of simultaneism," says Deleuze, "never stopped haunting the French cinema, just as it inspired painting, music and even literature" (IM 69; 46), and indeed, Delaunay's simultaneism in painting did inspire Cendrars in literature, and Cendrars's close collaboration with Gance and other avant-garde figures generated considerable discussion of simultaneity among early filmmakers (evident in Epstein's essays from the 1920s, for example, and most prominently in Gance's writings on the concept of poly-vision).[6] In this regard, Deleuze sees in Gance's use of superimpressions and the triple screen in *Napoleon* the logical end point toward which the French school's quantitative tendency aspires. When Gance superimposes Napoleon's face over multiply layered images of the schoolboys' snowball fight, or when he juxtaposes three separate battle scenes in screens side by side, he knows that the viewer cannot take in everything at once, yet something is presented that goes beyond the senses, "an image as absolute movement of the whole that changes" (IM 71; 48). In the multiple superimposed or juxtaposed images one sees "the Simultaneous, the immeasurable, the immense, which reduces imagination to impotence and confronts it with its own limit, giving birth in the mind [*esprit*] to the pure thought of an absolute quantity of movement that expresses its whole history or its change, its universe" (IM 72; 48). The open whole is no longer conceived of as an organic spiral, as in Griffith and Eisenstein, but as a "great spiritual helix" (IM 71; 48), a geometric figure of multiple movements grasped as simultaneously co-present to one another in a single mental reality. Hence, Gance's technical innovations, though unique to his own practice, make explicitly visible the idea of time implicit throughout the French school, a dualism of material numerical units and spiritual simultaneities, from which arises a conception of montage that is "mathematical-spiritual, extensive-psychic, quantitative-poetic" (IM 72–73; 49).

The French school and German expressionism, says Deleuze, may be opposed "point by point" (IM 73; 49), but his primary concern is to differentiate the two through their respective understandings of the relationship of movement to light. Deleuze accepts as givens the features generally said to characterize German expressionist cinema—sharp contrasts of light and shadow, dramatic chiaroscuro effects, unstable compositions of diagonals, oblique angles, and contorted surfaces, as well as themes of madness, hallucination, violence, possession, the supernatural, and the diabolic. What he attempts to show is that the themes, the atmosphere, and the formal elements of these films all arise from a single conception of movement and light, one that brings together Worringer's notion of the Gothic line of non-organic life and Goethe's theory of color. In this sensibility, movement and light are forms of intensity, affective quantities that spread forth into space to varying degrees and that ultimately generate a dynamic sublime of apocalyptic power.

Like the directors of the French school, the German expressionists break with the organic conception of composition, though not through a Cartesian mechanism but through a Gothic non-organic vitalism, a "pre-organic germinality, common to the animate and the inanimate, to a matter that raises itself to the point of life and to a life that spreads itself throughout all matter" (IM 76; 51). In her classic study of German expressionist cinema, Lotte Eisner remarks that "the Germans have an eerie gift for animating objects," and she notes in expressionist films not only an obsession with bewitched objects and animate automata but also a general approach to settings—especially, buildings, streets, and rooms—as dynamic entities that "seem to have an insidious life of their own" (Eisner 23). This approach she links to Worringer's notion of a Gothic sensibility of " 'spiritual unrest' creating the 'animation of the inorganic' " (23). Deleuze concurs and sees throughout German expressionist cinema a conception of movement as vital non-organic force. Worringer finds the essence of Gothic art in the abrupt, zigzag line of its decorative designs, which passes *between* things and in the process imbues the figures of people, animals, plants, metals, and minerals with a common nervous energy.[7] This line is as much an expressionistic line as a Gothic line, in Deleuze's analysis, and its movement gives rise to a dynamic geometry of diagonals, extreme angles and jagged edges that actively constructs space rather than merely describing it. If the French school operates through a geometry of measure and metrical quantity, the German school shapes its images through a geometry of "prolongation and accumulation" (IM 77; 51), of kinetic lines, surfaces, and volumes that at once prolong movements beyond fixed limits and at the same time bring vectors together in intersecting junctures of accumulation. If both the French and German schools combine the human and non-human in interacting assemblages of motion, in the French a mechanical geometry of regular quantities determines the measure and rhythm of a given set of elements, whereas in the German a dynamic geometry of intensive forces connects elements in a network of changing and developing relations.

Nowhere is the movement of that vital non-organic force more evident than in the German expressionist handling of light. In Deleuze's reading of Bergson, we recall, image = movement = matter = light, and hence every movement-image is a light-image, but there are various ways in which light may be related to movement. In the French school, light is conceived of as a function of movement, something that "ceaselessly circulates in a homogeneous space and creates luminous forms through its own mobility rather than through its encounter with moving objects" (IM 67; 44). Light and shadow are merely rhythmic alternations of a luminous matter, the celebrated "luminous gray" of the French school being the midpoint in light's regular oscillation. As in Delaunay's simultaneism, light is a "pure mobility" that "creates its luminous forms" (IM 72; 224) as it spreads out in space.[8] In German expressionism, by contrast, light is treated as "a potent movement of intensity, intensive movement par excellence" (IM 73; 49). A Goethean conception of light prevails, according to which light and shadow are separate, infinite forces in perpetual conflict.[9] Goethe argues that light in itself is invisible, and that the visible comes into existence only through light's encounter with shadows. All the colors of the visible world are varying degrees of opacity, "degrees of shadow *in* light, according to a relation of *more* and *less*" (Escoubas 234). In light's contact with objects, the shadowy contours of objects "thicken" light and render the objects visible. In German expressionist film, light and shadow are like two separate entities in constant conflict. Each shade of light is a degree of intensity in relation to darkness, an intensive quantity that takes on its value in relation to the zero degree of black. The shadow surfaces of objects thicken light, block it, filter it, and render it visible. From this confrontation of the forces of shadow and light issue the typical compositional structures of expressionist shots—the stark diagonals, sharp striations, and acute contrasts of dark and light, as well as the shifting and unstable chiaroscuro interminglings of black and white. And throughout this struggle of light and shadow the intensity of a non-organic life moves in zigzag patterns, delineating trajectories that guide the montage links between shots.

In German expressionist cinema, light and shadow are forces in motion, intensive vectors that interconnect objects, buildings, landscapes, atmospheres, and people in configurations that move with an eerie life of their own, a life inherent in light and shadow as dynamic forces. These configurations of movement-images derive their temporal structure from the interplay of the forces of light and shadow, and each configuration has a temporal organization that is determined by the specific degrees of intensity of its given forces. One may say, then, that the smallest temporal unit of each configuration, the moment of the variable present, is the "intensive degree" (IM 82; 55). But each configuration also expresses the whole of *durée,* and in German expressionism the whole is the intensive degree raised to a higher power, a qualitatively distinct *durée* of infinite intensification. Intimations of this *durée* are to be found, as one might expect, in certain effects of light. Deleuze notes that in Goethe's color theory white and black represent the minimum and maximum of opacity through which invisible light becomes visible, and yellow and blue are *movements of intensification,* yellow resulting from a progressive addition of shadow to white, blue arising from a gradual subtraction of shadow from black. If white and black are the left and right end points of a continuum, yellow is created in a left-to-right movement toward black, blue in a right-to-left movement toward white; and if the two movements of intensification are continued, they meet in the center at a point of maximum intensity—which Goethe says is a reddish-purple. Goethe also observes that as yellow and blue become more intense, they are imbued with a reddish reflection or shimmer. He concludes that red-purple is not only the most intense color, but also a total color-of-colors that accompanies all other colors as what we might call a kind of "essence of brilliance." As Escoubas phrases it in his commentary on Goethe's color theory, red-purple is "the incandescent," "flash, brilliance, the turbulence of fire, which is the very excess of the visible" (241). Light in itself is invisible, and the world of color makes up the visible, but between invisible light and visible color is brilliance, dazzling and blinding light at the edge of the visible, an excess of visual sensation that can scintillate but also burn, and hence a possible source of both pleasure and pain for the eye. Goethean light ultimately "is *fire*," and in the scintillation of red-purple that fire flashes before and within the eye.

> There is thus a becoming-purple of the world. What does Goethe say? That red makes one see the world in a terrible light (*ein furcht-bares Licht*), as at the day of the last judgment. Thus, light is terrible. Terrible is the world of the visible, for the visible is burn, fire, lightning. . . . The eye, parent of the visible, is always burned, burning. The eye burns in the daylight of the world, the eye burns the world. (Escoubas 241)

Hence, effects of brilliance—scintillation, glistening, sparkling, fluorescence, phosphorescence, shimmers, auras, halos—are manifestations of the terrible, burning fire of red-purple light, and Deleuze finds such effects throughout German expressionist film. That burning light also appears directly in such images as the incantatory circle of flames in *The Golem* and in *Faust,* the phosphorescent demon's head in *The Golem,* the blazing head of Mabuse and of Mephisto, the silhouetted figure of Nosferatu as he emerges from a depthless luminous space and enters Hutter's room. What one sees in these images, says Deleuze, is "a pure incandescence or flaming of a terrible light that burn[s] the world and its creatures. It is as if finite intensity had now, at the summit of its own intensification, regained a flash of the infinite from which it had parted" (IM 78; 53). The effects of brilliance in expressionist film—those widespread shimmers, scintillations, glows and halos of intense light—intimate the presence of an infinite non-organic force animating the natural world. And the images of burning incandescence—the rings of flame, blazing heads, luminous silhouettes—directly present the light of infinite intensification as "the spirit of evil that burns Nature in its entirety" (IM 78–79; 53).

This terrible, burning light Deleuze regards as an instance of Kant's "dynamic sublime," a sublime generated not through mathematical number but through overwhelming force. Certain objects in nature— volcanoes, hurricanes, sea storms, waterfalls—fill us with terror, for they are forces that threaten to destroy us, yet if we contemplate them safely we feel great joy. In the dynamic sublime, says Kant, "we find a superiority to nature even in its immensity" (101), and by overcoming our fear, we "become conscious that we are superior to nature within, and therefore also to nature without us (so far as it influences us)" (104). Ultimately, we are able to transcend nature in the dynamic sublime and discover our spiritual "destination" (Kant 104) through the autonomy of our contemplation of overwhelming force. The brilliant, fiery light of expressionist cinema is an infinite, apocalyptic force in which "*the non-organic life of things* culminates in a fire that burns us and burns all of Nature, functioning as the spirit of evil or of darkness" (IM 80; 54), but Deleuze argues that at rare moments that terrible, burning light is shown to be something else, the light of the color-of-all-colors, the light of "a *non-psychological life of the spirit* which belongs neither to nature nor to our organic individuality, which is the divine part in us, the spiritual relation in which we are alone with God" (IM 80; 54). Hence, at the conclusion of Murnau's *Faust* we see first the flames of Gretchen and Faust at the stake, but through a slow dissolve we ascend through clouds to an incandescent blaze of radiating divine light. It is through the sacrifice of Gretchen that destructive fire is transformed into spiritual light, and in the screaming close-up face of Gretchen, superimposed over the mobile shot of the rushing earth, we see the essence of the expressionist dynamic sublime, "which marks both the horror of non-organic life and the perhaps illusory opening of a spiritual universe" (IM 81; 54).

The forces of shadow and light, raised to an infinite degree of intensity, become burning fire and supernatural light, and in this infinity of intensive fire/light force we find German expressionism's open whole of *durée*. In the open whole of the French school, all the mechanistic movements of individual configurations of elements are subsumed within a single, infinite dimension of simultaneous co-present movements. In the German open whole, however, the time of individual movements is not so much subsumed within an infinite totality as it is shattered entirely. Light and shadow are dynamic forces, and force, when raised to the infinite, becomes explosive power, a kind of Big Bang of destructive fire or creative light that ceases to have temporal coordinates. Thus, if the American and Soviet whole is a spiral of time, open at one end toward an infinite past and at the other toward an infinite future, and if the French whole is an infinite helix of simultaneous time, the German whole is "the ideal summit of a pyramid that pushes away its base as it ceaselessly rises" (IM 81; 54). The whole is an infinite intensification of force, a ceaselessly contracting locus of concentrated power that sucks time into a single shrinking point. But the whole consists not simply of the non-organic life of things but also of the non-psychological life of the spirit, and in its infinite intensification, the whole "is disengaged from all its degrees"; it "has passed through the fire, but only in order to break its sensible attachments with the material, the organic and the human" (IM 81; 54–55). The infinitely rising tip of the pyramid thus contracts all force into a single shrinking point, but it also is perpetually in the process of breaking away from its base as the non-psychological spirit severs its ties with the natural world, and if there is a time at all in this infinitely contracting and rising point, it is that which emerges when the whole is able "to detach itself from all states of the past and thus discover the abstract spiritual Form of the future" (IM 81; 54–55).[10]

In his remarks on montage in the French and German schools, Deleuze offers few examples of montage techniques per se. His arguments often seem to hinge on narrative or thematic considerations, and even when they engage distinctly formal elements, such as patterns of movement or arrangements of light, they seem to focus on the composition of shots more than the connections between shots. Amid Deleuze's dizzying melange of brief references to shots, sequences, entire films, oeuvres, schools, theories, and philosophies, it is easy to lose track of his main point, which is that montage is always guided by a conception of the open whole of *durée*. That conception no doubt varies in some ways from film to film and from director to director, but overall one may discern four broad tendencies in the understanding and treatment of the open whole. In each of its guises, the whole contracts into a minimum moment of the variable present and dilates into a corresponding form of the infinite. In the American tendency, the minimum is a simple interval, its corresponding maximum an organic infinite assembled through an equally simple process of open-ended accretion of parts. In the Soviet, the minimum is a qualitative leap, the maximum a dialectical infinite of ceaseless generative growth. In the French, a numerical unity is the minimum, and its corresponding maximum is an ideal infinity of all mechanical movements simultaneously co-present to one another. And in the German, an intensive degree is the minimum, and its maximum is an ideal infinity of all intensive forces contracted into a single ever-shrinking concentration of force. When Deleuze seems to be simply discussing plots or themes, he is instead attempting to disengage from these elements the implicit conception of the whole that informs them. Hence, when he speaks of the expressionist obsession with automata and animated objects, or of clashes between good and evil, sacrificial deaths, malevolent and beneficent spirits, his object is to extract from these motifs the implicit whole of an infinite contraction of intensive forces, which are manifest in the non-organic vital movements of light and shadow. When Deleuze elides questions of specific montage technique, it is because seemingly identical techniques take on a new sense when in the service of a different conception of the whole. Thus, though one may regard parallel montage as a technique common to all film, in the Soviet tendency it functions as a "montage of opposition," and in the German as a "montage of contrast" (IM 82; 55). What is important is less the individual techniques themselves than the whole that directs their use. For the same reason it is not crucial that Deleuze differentiate scrupulously between analyses of shots and analyses of montage, since the whole is as much evident in the shot as in montage. Indeed, the dual nature of the shot, as both immobile cut of commonsense time and mobile cut of *durée,* is that which ensures an interconnection between frames, shots, and montage. The shot is the movement-image, and the movement-image always expresses the whole of *durée.* If Deleuze's goal is to describe the characteristics of a given whole, then, it matters little whether shots or connections among shots are used to delineate its features.

The frame, the shot, and montage are the fundamental elements of cinema. Of the three, the shot has a special role, for it stands at the intersection of what Deleuze calls the vertical axis of differentiation (closed set/open whole) and the horizontal axis of specification (perception-image/action-image/affection-image). The shot is the movement-image, and the movement-image has three basic subdivisions—perception-image, action-image, affection-image. In the next chapter we will see how Deleuze develops this tripartite division into an elaborate taxonomy of cinematic signs.

Chapter Three
_____

EIGHTEEN SIGNS (MORE OR LESS)

Deleuze describes his study of film as "a taxonomy, an attempt at a clas-sification of images and signs" (IM 7; xiv), and much of *Cinema 1* is devoted to an explication of the signs related to the movement-image. Deleuze starts his classification of images with the tripartite division of the movement-image into the perception-image, the action-image and the affection-image, but he eventually identifies three more images, and each of these six gives rise to three signs, for a total of eighteen signs. That number, however, is hardly certain, as we will see while investigat-ing what Deleuze means by a sign and what functions he attributes to signs in the cinema.

PEIRCE AND SIGNS

In the preface to *Cinema 1*, Deleuze cites Bergson and Charles Sanders Peirce as the philosophical predecessors most important for his enter-prise. Peirce he recognizes as "the philosopher who went furthest in a systematic classification of images. The founder of semiology, he neces-sarily added to it a classification of signs, which is the richest and the most numerous ever established" (IM 101; 69). Peirce's inspiration, however, is more general than specific, and despite Deleuze's frequent

linear, broken into parts; Continuous, like cinema, not reality

human time → not his time not reality

references to Peirce's work, the semiotic framework of *Cinema 1* and *Cinema 2* is much more Bergsonian than Peircean. What Deleuze appreciates most in Peirce is his commitment to a non-linguistic theory of the sign. It has often been noted that Saussure and Peirce independently developed the concept of a general theory of signs, and that Saussure's semiology has its basis in the linguistic opposition of signifier and signified, whereas Peirce's semiotics is founded on a non-linguistic triad of representamen-object-interpretant. Many French cinema theorists adopt a Saussurean approach to the sign, and Deleuze's effort is to propose an alternative that maintains the autonomy of the visual sign from the linguistic sign. Such autonomy is necessary above all because the notion of film as a language tends to privilege narrative as the fundamental dimension of cinema.

schema = human's, not time

For Deleuze, however, narrative is a secondary product of a structure of time and space. The regularities and continuities of narrative have as their condition of possibility the regularities and continuities of a commonsense space-time organized to increase the effectiveness of human action. Our pragmatic world is structured by our needs, desires, purposes, and projects, and the practical application of our perceptions and actions to meet those ends depends on a coordinated interconnection of our sensory and motor faculties. Hence, a "sensori-motor schema" (IT 167; 127) shapes our commonsense world and creates what Kurt Lewin calls a "hodological space" (cited in IT 167; 127), and it is from this hodological space that the structures of conventional narrative derive.[1] One of Deleuze's central theses is that the modern cinema differs from the classic cinema in its abandonment of the sensori-motor schema. Thus, it is crucial that his conception of the cinematic sign be non-narrative and non-linguistic, and Deleuze sees Peirce as pointing the way toward such a conception.

Nonetheless, Deleuze finds two limitations in Peirce's semiotic theory. First, though Peirce develops a non-linguistic analysis of the components of the sign, he eventually subordinates non-linguistic to linguistic signs by attributing to signs an essentially cognitive function. Signs, for Peirce, render relations efficient—that is, they make possible regular associations of one sign with another, and knowledge gives signs this efficiency. The result is that "if the elements of the sign still imply no privilege for language, this is no longer the case for the sign, and linguistic signs are perhaps the only signs to constitute a pure knowledge" (IT 46; 31).[2] Second, in Peirce's basic tripartite classification of images, he does not account fully for the genesis of his three fundamental images nor for the role played by the perception-image as image through which all the other images are perceived.

Deleuze's first objection might well bear serious consideration, but his second simply shows that his own conception of semiotics is not really Peircean but Bergsonian. Still, it is important to see how Deleuze uses Peirce to generate his own taxonomy of signs. Deleuze rightly states that "Peirce starts from the image, from the phenomenon or that which appears" (IT 45; 30), though the word "image" is not one Peirce uses with any frequency, preferring instead the term "phaneron" for "that which appears." Deleuze then presents Peirce's categories of Firstness, Secondness, and Thirdness as constituting three irreducible and fundamental kinds of images. Deleuze characterizes these categories with reasonable accuracy, saying that Firstness is "something that refers to nothing but itself, quality or potential, pure possibility"; Secondness, "something that refers to itself only through something else, existence, action-reaction, effort-resistance"; and Thirdness, "something that refers to itself only in relating one thing to another thing, relation, law, necessity" (IT 45; 30). But when Deleuze argues that the perception-image is a "Zeroness," it is evident that he is no longer thinking in Peircean terms. Firstness, Secondness, and Thirdness are not simply images but modes of being exhibited by all phenomena in the universe, and all things, from atoms to people to ideas, exhibit Firstness, Secondness, and Thirdness together at the same time, never as separable modes of being.[3] There is no perception "before" these modes of being, for in Peirce's analysis, the simplest perceptual experience always involves a quality of some sort (Firstness), some kind of opposition, resistance, or otherness (Secondness), and a minimal degree of abductive inference (Thirdness).[4]

We need not pursue much further Deleuze's differences from Peirce, but merely note that Peirce's three modes of being serve Deleuze primarily as tools for developing and extending Bergson's three types of movement-images. Deleuze starts with the triad of perception-image, action-image, and affection-image and then observes parallels between the affection-image and Peirce's Firstness (in that both involve *qualities*) and between the action-image and Secondness (in that both involve *actions-reactions*). Rather than tying the perception-image to Thirdness,

Deleuze posits the existence of a fourth movement-image corresponding to the category of Thirdness, the relation-image (which we will
examine later), and then treats the perception-image as a species of
image that lies outside Peirce's classification scheme (a Zeroness). We
might graphically represent the relation between the Bergsonian and
Peircean schemas as follows:

$$
\begin{array}{lcl}
\text{Perception-image} & = & \text{[Zeroness]} \\
\text{Affection-image} & = & \text{Firstness} \\
\text{Action-image} & = & \text{Secondness} \\
\text{[Relation-image]} & = & \text{Thirdness}
\end{array}
$$

Once he formulates these four types of movement-images, Deleuze
identifies two additional types, one midway between the affection-
image and the action-image (the *impulse-image* [*image-pulsion*]), the other
between the action-image and the relation-image (the *reflection-image*
[*image-réflexion*]), for a total of six types of movement-images.

Deleuze claims that Peirce accepts "the three types of images as a
fact, rather than deducing them" (IT 47; 31) and that their deduction
should proceed through an analysis of perception. But this critique
does not really engage Peirce's theory of perception or his concepts of
Firstness, Secondness, and Thirdness so much as it affords Deleuze the
opportunity of relating Bergson's account of perception to the six types
of movement-images. We recall that Bergson "deduces" consciousness
by first positing a universe of billiard ball–like images acting on and
reacting against one another, each responding directly and completely
to the forces around it, and then identifying a special kind of image, a
"center of indeterminacy," which introduces a gap in the interconnected
cause-and-effect networks of acting-reacting images. The billiard ball
images respond to all external actions, and in this sense perceive fully,
whereas living images filter external actions by selectively responding to
some actions and ignoring others. The perception characteristic of living images, then, emerges from the universal field of billiard ball perception, and it comes into being through the creation of an interval or
gap in the universal movement of acting-reacting billiard balls. Thus,
the perception-image, or that image characteristic of the perception of
a living being, may be related first to its *genesis* from the field of billiard
ball perception, that is, to its coming-into-being as a center of indetermination, or interval, within the matter-flow of universal actions and

reactions. But the perception-image may be related as well to its *composition*, or basic makeup, as a function of the specific interval each living image introduces in the field of universal actions and reactions. Since the perception-image is a species of movement-image, and every movement-image manifests movement as both a translation of parts and an expression of the whole, the *composition* of the perception-image has two poles, one related to the movement specific to the interval of a given perception-image, the other related to the movement of the whole: "Perception will have two poles, depending on whether it is identified with movement or its interval (variation of images all in relation to all *or* variation of all images in relation to one among all the images)" (IT 47; 31). Put another way, if the open whole is the entirety of the spiraling flight of a bird, and the interval is the moment between each beat of its wings, the perception-image may be approached either in terms of the bird's spiraling flight that is indirectly expressed in the perception-image or in terms of the moment between any two beats of the bird's wings, that is, the interval that defines any living being and that is basic to every perception-image.

The perception-image, then, may be differentiated in three ways: by its genesis; by its composition as function of the interval; and by its composition as function of the whole. Deleuze argues further that the perception-image extends into the other species of movement-images, for whenever affections, actions, relations, and so forth, occur, there is always an accompanying *perception of* affections, *of* actions, *of* relations. For this reason, the perception-image's triple differentiation is found in each of the other five species of movement-image, and it is on the basis of this triple differentiation that Deleuze defines the sign. "We thus take the term 'sign' in an entirely different sense than does Peirce: it is a particular image that refers to a type of image, either from the point of view of its bipolar composition, or from the point of view of its genesis" (IT 48; 32).

We are now prepared to examine each of the six kinds of movement-images and their related signs. In order to keep track of Deleuze's terminological distinctions, readers may wish to refer to tables 1 and 2 as the analysis proceeds. Table 1 is a chart of the images and corresponding signs of the movement-image. Table 2 is a comparison of the listing of images and signs found in the glossary of *Cinema 1* and the recapitulation of images and signs Deleuze provides in chapter 2 of *Cinema 2* (IT 48–49; 32–33).

Table One: Images and Corresponding Signs of the Movement-Image

Images	Signs of Composition	Signs of Genesis
Perception-Image	Dicisign Reume	Gramme (Engramme, Photogramme)
Affection-Image	Contour Icon (Quality) Trait Icon (Power [*Puissance*])	Qualisign (Potisign) Of discontinuity Of vacuity [*Espace quelconque*]
Impulse-Image	Good Fetish (Relic) Evil Fetish (Vult)	Symptom (originary world)
Action-Image (Large Form)	Synsign (or Englobing) Binomial	Imprint (respiration-space)
Action-Image (Small Form)	Index of Lack Index of Equivocity	Vector (line of the universe) (skeleton-space)
Reflection-Image (Transformation Image)	Figure of Attraction (Theatrical/ Scenographic Figure; Sculptural/Plastic Figure) Figure of Inversion	Figure of Discourse (Discursive Figure)
Relation-Image	Mark Demark	Symbol

THE PERCEPTION-IMAGE

In the classic cinema, we become aware of a visual image as a perception when it is treated as a representation of a subjective point of view—a blurred chandelier as the groggy detective's view upon waking from a mickey-induced sleep, or an elongated hallway as the schizophrenic's vision of the passage to the electroshock therapy room. But what makes the subjective image noticeable is its difference from a corresponding "objective" image—the chandelier or hallway as it is "normally" seen. The objective image one might roughly define as a scene viewed from the outside, the subjective as an image whose point of view, whether distorted or not, issues from within the scene. Yet such an account is

Table Two: Comparison of the *Cinema 1* Glossary and *Cinema 2* Recapitulation of Movement-Image Signs

Cinema 1 Glossary		*Cinema 2* Recapitulation	
Images	Signs	Images	Signs (c: sign of composition; g: genetic sign)
Perception-Image (the thing)	Dicisign Reume Gramme (Engramme or Photogramme)	Perception-Image	Dicisign (c) Reume (c) Engramme (g)
Affection-Image (quality or power)	Icon Qualisign (or Potisign)	Affection-Image	Icon (c) Qualisign or Potisign (g)
Impulse-Image (energy)	Symptom Fetish	Impulse-Image	Fetishes of Good or Evil (c) Symptom (g)
Action-Image (force or act)	Synsign (or the englobing) Binomial Imprint Index (of lack or of equivocity) Vector (or line of the universe)	Action-Image	Synsign (c) Index (c) Imprint (g)
Transformation Image (reflection)	Figure (scenographic or plastic image; inverted image; discursive image)	Reflection-Image	Figures (of attraction or of inversion) (c) Discursive figure (g)
Mental Image (relation)	Mark Demark Symbol	Relation-Image	Mark (c) Demark (c) Symbol (g)

hardly adequate, for the so-called "objective" image is usually not so much outside the scene as somehow shifting in and out of the setting, amid the actors, along with them, now from an angle aligned with one character's vantage, now from a reversed angle aligned with another's, such that "objective" and "subjective" images tend to shade into one another as the camera's point of view changes from shot to shot. Jean Mitry suggests that the cinematic image in fact is neither objective nor subjective, but always "semi-subjective," representing "the anonymous point of view of someone unidentified among the characters" (IM 106; 72). Deleuze endorses this intuition, though he reframes it in terms of the concept of "free indirect discourse," as extended by Pasolini from linguistics to the cinema.

A number of linguists have discussed passages from fiction in which a narrative voice slides imperceptibly into a character's voice, such that one cannot distinguish clearly between "indirect discourse" (As she looked out the train window, she thought that her loneliness was unbearable) and "direct discourse" (As she looked out the train window, she thought, "this loneliness is unbearable"), but must speak of a "free indirect discourse" (She looked out the train window, such loneliness was unbearable). Pasolini, following Bakhtin's analysis, argues that this is not a simple mingling of two fully constituted subjective voices, a narrator's and a character's, but, as Deleuze phrases it, a "differentiation of two correlative subjects in a system itself heterogeneous," an "assemblage of enunciation [*agencement d'énonciation*], putting into effect at the same time two inseparable acts of subjectivation" (IM 106; 73).

This process of double subjectivation, or generation of two subject positions within a heterogeneous system, Pasolini finds in certain films of Antonioni, Bertolucci, and Godard (to which Deleuze adds Rohmer and Pasolini himself). In *Red Desert,* for example, Antonioni "looks at the world by immersing himself in his neurotic protagonist," says Pasolini, but he does so only by simultaneously substituting "in toto for the world-view of a neurotic his own delirious view of aesthetics" (Pasolini 179). Antonioni presents the world as if seen through the neurotic protagonist's eyes, but he also makes the camera noticeable through what Pasolini calls "obsessive framing." Characters enter and leave the frame, but the shot seems to continue too long, the now-uninhabited landscape betraying an insistent, obsessive camera consciousness. Similarly, a scene first framed from one perspective, and then reframed for no apparent reason from a slightly different angle, makes one "feel" the camera. The neurotic protagonist's subjective view of things and the camera's obsessive framing of things emerge at once, the subjective view corresponding roughly to the character's voice in free indirect discourse, the obsessive framing to the narrator's voice. But the neurotic character's view and the obsessive camera's view are not really separable, for the camera's framing transforms the character's view. From a single shot issue two "subjects" of a sort, the neurotic character and the obsessive camera, whose views are "subjective" in that they noticeably differ from an anonymous "objective" view, but whose perspectives do not belong to any autonomous "subject." In the "free indirect subjectivity" of such a shot we find "a correlation between a perception-image and a camera-consciousness that transforms it" (IM 108; 74), an image that is noticeably perceptual *as taken by* a perceiving camera—a perception (obsessive camera framing) of a perception (neurotic character view). This is the essence of the basic perception-image, "a perception in the *frame* of another perception" (IM 291; 217). Such an image Deleuze calls a *dicisign*. The "free indirect subjectivity" of Antonioni, Godard, and Pasolini, of course, does not represent standard cinematic practice, but its obsessive framing of a noticeable perception makes patent the latent structure of every perception-image as perception of a perception.

Pasolini's "free indirect subjectivity" renders problematic the notions of "subjectivity" and "objectivity," but this opposition Deleuze still finds useful, though only when formulated in terms of the Bergsonian concept of the interval, or center of indeterminacy. A subjective perception is one in which images vary in relation to a central and privileged image (i.e., a living image, or center of indeterminacy), and an objective perception is one in which images vary all in relation to all (the perception in things of billiard ball–like images interacting on all sides and surfaces one with another). This definition has the curious effect of reversing the standard sense of *subjective* and *objective,* in that what we usually think of as subjective shots and sequences—dreams, hallucinations, visions—are the classic cinema's most striking approximations of what Deleuze calls the objective "perception in things," in which an "eye in matter" traces the acentered undulations of a single vibratory flux. The dicisign is a "perception in the *frame* of another perception" (IM 291; 217), but Deleuze specifies further that its frame isolates and solidifies the image, and hence the term *dicisign* he reserves for the perception-image that belongs to a single "center of indeterminacy." The perception-image that tends toward a perception "in things" he calls a *reume* (from the Greek *rheume*, "that which flows"), a liquid perception no longer constrained by bodies, in which the image flows "across or under the frame," part of "a matter-flow" (IM 116; 80). This liquid perception Deleuze finds in the French school of the 1920s and early 1930s, especially in Renoir, Grémillon, L'Herbier, and Vigo, with their affinity for images of water and the dynamics of fluids.

The reume tends toward a perception "in things," but only in a third perception-image, the *gramme* (or *engramme* or *photogramme*), is that perception fully manifest. The gramme reveals "a molecular perception, proper to a 'cine-eye' " (IM 116; 80), a gaseous perception "in matter, such that any point whatsoever in space itself perceives all the points on which it acts or which act on itself, no matter how far its actions and reactions extend" (IM 117; 81). The gramme is the "genetic sign" of the perception-image, in that the universal matter-flow of interacting molecular images (which we have loosely characterized as billiard ball–like images) is the element from which any interval, gap, or center of indetermination emerges. The dicisign, by contrast, is a perception-image fully constituted by a specific interval or center, and hence it is a "sign of composition." We have, then, two poles, a perception determined by a single, fixed center of indetermination (the dicisign) and a universal perception in things (the gramme). Between these extremes lies the reume, a perception that tends toward the gramme but remains tied to the dicisign (for which reason the reume is also a "sign of composition"). What this means in practical, cinematic terms is that the dicisign is a perception-image understandable from a specific, commonsense point of view; the reume, a perception-image comprehensible from a floating, flowing perspective that remains, however, assimilable within commonsense coordinates; and the gramme, a perception-image that defies assimilation within a commonsense perceptual framework.

Deleuze's primary examples of the gramme come from Vertov's *Man with a Movie Camera*. In his theoretical writings, Vertov celebrates the documentary "kino-eye" as "the conquest of space" and "the conquest of time," a means of "comparing and linking all points of the universe in any temporal order" (Vertov 87–88). Kino-eye is "the microscope and telescope of time," the "negative of time," the "possibility of seeing without limits and distances" (41). The kino-eye "gropes its way through the chaos of visual events, letting itself be drawn or repelled by movement, probing, as it goes, the path of its own movement. It experiments, distending time, dissecting movement, or, in contrary fashion, absorbing time within itself, swallowing years" (19). "Free of the limits of time and space," says Vertov, "I put together any given points in the universe" (18). This documentary "kino-eye," which connects all spatial points with one another in any temporal sequence, is "the eye of matter, the eye in matter, which is no longer subject to time" (IM 118; 81), says Deleuze, and in *Man with a Movie Camera* Vertov's kino-eye aspirations are most fully realized, multiple material spatio-temporal events being interconnected through the film's juxtapositions of moving trolleys, carriages, industrial machines, athletes, motorcyclists, theater audiences, theater seats, and so forth, now in slow motion or stop action, now on split screens or in superimpressions, linked in varying montage rhythms that at times slow and at others accelerate toward a stroboscopic blur.

But what Deleuze finds most significant in *Man with a Movie Camera* is Vertov's discovery of the "genetic element of the image, or the differential element of movement" (IM 120; 83). The photogramme, or individual still frame on the motion-picture film, functions for Vertov not as an immobile slice of time but as a generative cell of movement. When Vertov freezes the movement of a carriage horse and then plays with still shots of the street crowd, the faces of an old woman, a young factory worker, and three children at a magic show, intercutting shots of an editor splicing the film, reanimating the still close-ups and eventually bringing the crowd and horse back to life, he is making visible a new sense of the photogramme. It is no longer the moment when motion stops, but the instant when motion changes—slows, accelerates, reverses—or prolongs the preceding moment into the next. The photogramme does not " 'terminate' the movement without also being the principle of its acceleration, of its slowing, of its variation. It is the vibration, the elementary solicitation of which the movement is comprised at each moment" (IM 120; 83). It is movement compressed into a micro-interval, one might say, a differential moment in the mathematical sense (an infinitesimal difference between two consecutive values of a variable quantity) and a genetic moment in a biological sense (a locus of generative differentiation such as a seed or ovum). If in the Vertovian photogramme "cinema goes beyond human perception toward another perception, it is in the sense that it attains to the *genetic element* of all possible perception, that is, to the point that changes, and that makes perception change, the differential of perception itself" (IM 120; 83).

The gramme, then, is perception "in things," any point connected with any other point, and each point itself a vibratory locus of genetic, differential movement. In the gramme, the interval is reconceived in two ways, the montage interval linking any "two distant images (incommensurable from the point of view of our human perception)" (IM 118; 82), the photogramme functioning as the embodiment of the interval itself, a concentration of movement's "energetic material element" (IM 121; 84) in a single image. Perception becomes fully molecular, each molecule a genetic, differential vibration, all molecules freely interacting with one another. Thus, "if one starts from a solid state in which the molecules are not free to displace themselves (molar or human perception), one then passes to a liquid state, in which the molecules displace themselves and slide one against another, but one finally arrives at a gaseous state, defined by the free movement of each molecule" (IM 121; 84). The solid dicisign and the liquid reume remain the perception-image's signs of composition, but the gaseous gramme is its genetic sign, "an 'other' perception, which is also the genetic element of every perception" (IM 123; 85).

THE AFFECTION-IMAGE

As we saw earlier, the affection-image occupies the interval between an incoming perception and an outgoing action. Bergson notes that in amoebas the body surface is both a perceptual and a motor organ, whereas in many other creatures there is a specialization of functions, some body parts serving as immobile receptors of outside movement (e.g., eyes, ears) and others as vehicles of locomotion (e.g., legs). In humans, the primary concentration of immobile receptors is found in the face, and it is here that various affections are registered. From Bergson Deleuze derives a definition of affection as " 'a sort of motor tendency on a sensitive nerve,' that is, a motor effort on an immobilized receptive plate" (IM 96; 66). The face converts external movements in space into movements of expression (in the very literal sense of "facial expressions" as well as Deleuze's specialized sense of "expression"), and the two basic elements of the face's expressive movements are its immobile surface and its active features (brows, nostrils, lips, etc.). Deleuze notes two tendencies in portrait painting, one emphasizing the unifying contour of the face, the other the individual features. In the first instance, the face is "a surface of facefication [*visagéification*]" (IM 126; 88), from which the features emerge as unified components of a single contour; in the second, the features are "traits of faciality [*visagéité*]" (IM 126; 88) whose intensive movements suggest a violent struggle to escape the surface. To this opposition of unifying surface and intensive traits Deleuze draws a parallel between Descartes and Le Brun's opposition of the passions of *admiration* (best translated as "wonder" or "astonishment") and *désir*. *Admiration* marks "a minimum of movement for a maximum of reflecting and reflected unity on the face," whereas desire manifests itself in small agitations that "compose an intensive series" (IM 127; 88).[5] The face of *admiration* is a "reflective or reflecting face" that brings the individual features under the domination of a single quality, "immutable and without becoming, eternal in a way" (IM 128-29; 89–90). The face of desire is an "intensive face" whose features "escape the contour" and "form an autonomous series that tends toward a limit or crosses a threshold" (IM 128; 89). The function of the series of intensive movements is to shift from one quality to another, and that passage Deleuze calls a "Power" (*Puissance*). Hence, the intensive face "expresses a pure Power, that is, it is defined by a series that makes us pass from one quality to another," whereas the reflective face "expresses a pure Quality, that is, a 'something' common to several objects of different natures" (IM 129; 90). Deleuze sums up his analysis of the face with the following table of oppositions:

Sensible nerve	Motor tendency
Immobile receptive plate	Micro-movements of expression
Facializing contour	Traits of faciality
Reflecting unity	Intensive series
Wonder (admiration, astonishment)	Desire (love-hate)
Quality	Power [*Puissance*]
Expression of a quality common to several different things	Expression of a power that passes from one quality to another

In cinema, the close-up is the shot most often associated with the face, but Deleuze goes further, asserting that *"the affection-image is the close-up, and the close-up is the face*" (IM 125; 87). The close-up is often said to turn the face into a "partial object," but Deleuze counters that the close-up "abstracts" the face from all spatio-temporal coordinates (IM 136; 96) and thereby converts it into a complete Entity that expresses an affect (whether quality or power). The close-up deterritorializes the face, separating it from what Deleuze identifies as its three conventional functions: "it is individuating (it distinguishes or characterizes each person); it is socializing (it manifests a social role); it is relational or communicating (it assures not only communication between two persons, but also, within a single person, the internal accord between one's character and one's role)" (IM 141; 99). Rather than being a body part in a determinate spatio-temporal setting, or a marker of an identity, a role or a relation, the face in close-up is an autonomous object, an immobile surface with motor tendencies. Once removed from social codes and the commonsense coordinates of space and time, the face becomes an affection-image: an image expressing an affective quality or power (or a combination of quality and power, or passage of one into the other, for the qualities of the reflecting face and the powers of the intensive face are poles of a continuum, not exclusive categories). Deleuze calls the combination of "the expressed" (affect, or that which is expressed) and "its expression" (the face, or that which does the expressing) an "Icon," and he concludes that "there are thus trait icons [*icônes de trait*] and contour icons [*icônes de contour*], or rather every icon has these two poles: this is the bipolar sign of composition of the affection-image. The affection-image is power or quality considered for itself, as an expressed" (IM 138; 97).

The *trait icon* and the *contour icon,* then, are the affection-image's two signs of composition (or two poles of a single sign of composition—the distinction does not seem to concern Deleuze overmuch), the one emphasizing an individual interval of movement (the passage of one quality to another in the movement of a given facial feature), the other the interrelated movements of multiple elements (brought together in the reflective quality of a unifying facial contour). The close-up, in abstracting the face from its spatio-temporal coordinates and personal markers, allows an affect (quality/power) to appear in itself, separated from its contextual determinants. The affection-image thus makes visible what Peirce calls Firstness, a quality when considered without regard to its actual manifestation in a specific situation (its concrete actualization being an instance of Secondness). In this differentiation between Firstness and Secondness, between a quality as pure possibility or potential and a quality as actualized in a concrete situation, Deleuze finds a parallel to the Stoic opposition of incorporeals and bodies, or virtual events and actual states of affairs.[6] Hence, Deleuze distinguishes between "two states of qualities-powers, that is affects: insofar as they are actualized in an individuated state of things and in the corresponding *real connections* (with this particular space-time, *hic et nunc,* these characteristics, these roles, these objects); insofar as they are expressed for themselves, outside spatio-temporal coordinates, with their proper ideal singularities and their *virtual conjunctions*" (IM 146; 102).

The close-up extracts from the face a pure quality, but Deleuze argues that the close-up may extract such a quality from any object, making visible, say, the "glistening" of a leaf, the "sharpness" of a knife, the "luminescence" of a glass of milk. The close-up *is* the face in that the close-up *facializes,* or converts a concrete entity into a decontextualized immobile surface with motor tendencies that expresses an affective quality/power. Affect, thus, is not strictly human. In Pabst's *Pandora's Box,* the close-ups of Jack the Ripper and Lulu extract from their faces various shifting qualities and powers, but the close-ups of the knife also extract qualities that communicate through virtual conjunctions with the qualities expressed by those face surfaces, the interacting qualities pertaining no longer to specific human beings or objects but existing in themselves, impersonal yet determinate, each a singular "indivisible quality, which will only divide by changing in nature (the 'dividual')" (IM 140; 98–99).

The close-up, however, is not the sole means of creating an affection-image, Deleuze argues. Dreyer is a master of the close-up, his *The Passion of Joan of Arc* being one of the great studies in the affective handling of the face, but in his later films, especially *Ordet* and *Gertrud,* he uses few actual close-ups yet finds a way to treat all shots as equivalents of that shot. The close-up in general tends to decontextualize by depriving the image of spatial coordinates, especially those of a perspectival depth. In his later films Dreyer develops a technique he refers to as a "flowing close-up," whereby the camera pans slowly from an initial close-up of a face to a medium-shot focus on a scene or long-shot framing of a setting, but what Deleuze finds significant is that the medium-shot scenes and long-shot settings themselves lack depth and are deprived of perspectival coordinates, as if all the images were flattened into a thin surface, the medium shots and long shots functioning as close-ups in their absence of depth. As a result, each of Dreyer's late films tends at its limit to operate as a single flowing close-up shot sequence. This suggests to Deleuze that the affection-image finally may not necessarily be restricted in its manifestation either to faces or to the close-up. If qualities/powers may be extracted from any entity, and if medium shots and long shots may function as close-ups, perhaps affects in themselves may be made visible in ways that are unrelated to the specific objects presented or the type of shot employed.

In Bresson's *Pickpocket* Deleuze finds evidence that this is the case. When Bresson shows his thief at work in the Gare de Lyon, Bresson situates the thief within a fragmented space, the various elements of the train station disconnected from each other, the elements themselves framed as incomplete parts of objects. No common measure reconciles the heterogeneous elements. The montage of parts provides no clear orientation for their interconnection. "Space itself has departed from its proper coordinates and its metric relations. It is a tactile space" (IM 154; 109). Borrowing a term from the anthropologist Marc Augé, Deleuze calls this space an *espace quelconque,* an "any-space-whatever," and he defines it as "a perfectly singular space, which has simply lost its homogeneity, that is, the principle of its metric relations or the connection of its proper parts, so that the linkages may be made in an infinite number of ways. It is a space of virtual conjunction, grasped as pure site of the possible" (IM 155; 109). If the close-up extracts affects by decontextualizing the face, the *espace quelconque* extracts affects by decontextualizing space itself. Space becomes tactile, as if the eye were a hand grazing one surface after another without any sense of the overall configuration or mutual relation of those surfaces. It is a virtual space, whose fragmented components may be assembled in multiple combinations, a space of yet-to-be-actualized possibilities.

The *espace quelconque* is "the genetic element of the affection-image" (IM 156; 110). If the *icon* is the sign in which a quality-power is expressed by a face or its equivalent, the *qualisign* (or *potisign*) is the sign in which a quality-power is expressed by an *espace quelconque.* Just as the *gramme* of gaseous perception makes visible the perception "in things" of a universal matter-flow, so the *qualisign* makes visible qualities-powers in an acentered, non-oriented space-flow. Like the *gramme,* the qualisign is at

the limit of the sensori-motor schema, the point at which images cease
to be interrelated according to commonsense spatio-temporal grids.
The qualities-powers expressed across the *espace quelconque* are the
genetic "matter" from which local configurations of qualities-powers
(such as those expressed by faces) may be composed. The icon retains a
limited connection to commonsense coordinates; the qualisign, none.

   Deleuze describes three ways of constructing an *espace quelconque*.
The first is via shadow, the masters of German expressionism best exem-
plifying this practice. In the struggle between light and dark that
informs expressionist films, shifting shadows, zones of brightness, striations, and fogs break the contours of objects, imbue them with a non-
organic life, and thereby "potentialize space, making it something
unlimited" (IM 157; 111). The second is through the "lyrical abstraction" of such directors as Dreyer and Bresson, which Deleuze characterizes as an alternation between the actual and the virtual which
"expresses an alternative between the state of things itself and the possibility, the virtuality, that goes beyond it" (IM 158; 112). In Bresson,
especially, one sees an actual moralized space of white (our duty, our
power of acting), black (our impotence, our desire for evil) and gray (our
indecision, our indifference). But a virtual, spiritual space, an *espace quelconque,* emerges when the protagonist "chooses to choose" when he or
she becomes conscious of making a choice of faith. Black no longer
imprisons white or tints it gray, but a black, white, and gray become in
the *espace quelconque* potential components of a newly constructed
world. "*Space is no longer determined, it has become the espace quelconque identical with the power [puissance] of the spirit,* with the always renewed spiritual decision: it is this decision that constitutes the affect, or the
'auto-affection,' and which takes upon itself the linkage of parts" (IM
165; 117). And the third means of constructing an *espace quelconque* is
through color, which in certain directors works by "absorption," a color
quality absorbing heterogeneous objects into an affective medium, for
example, the mauve and gold of Varda's *Happiness* absorbing characters,
settings, and landscapes within color spaces that function as decontextualized affects-in-themselves. In Antonioni this color space tends
toward the void; all his films explore the empty frame, the deserted
landscape, the world effaced of its inhabitants, with an absorbent
palette extracting from things the atmospheric color quality of a space
in the process of vanishing. Hence, Deleuze argues there are two kinds

of *espaces quelconques,* either disconnected or emptied [*vidés*], and "two sorts of 'qualisigns,' qualisigns of disconnection and of vacuity. But of these two states that always imply one another we should only say that one is 'before' and the other 'after.' The *espace quelconque* retains a single and same nature: it no longer has coordinates, it is a pure potential, it exposes only pure Powers and Qualities, independently of the states of things or milieus that actualize them" (IM 169; 120).

THE IMPULSE-IMAGE

Affection-images arise from a virtual *espace quelconque* of affects, of pure qualities and powers. When treated as elements actualized within concrete, determinable states of affairs, such qualities and powers are subsumed within the realm of action-images. But between the virtual *espaces quelconques* of affects and the actual milieus of actions Deleuze identifies a domain that belongs clearly to neither, one of "originary worlds" and "impulses" (*pulsions,* which may also be translated as "drives" or "instincts," as in *pulsions de mort,* the French translation of Freud's *Todestriebe,* rendered in English as "death drives" or "death instincts"). This is the domain of the impulse-image, *l'image-pulsion,* which Deleuze associates with naturalism and finds best exemplified in the films of Erich von Stroheim, Luis Buñuel, and Joseph Losey.

Naturalistic writers such as Emile Zola, Frank Norris, and Theodore Dreiser generally portray human beings as animals driven by brute instincts in a primal world of implacable and violent material forces. Most often, their characters are victims of internal drives and external forces whose stories trace paths of decline, degradation, and destruction. Stroheim might well seem a naturalist in this sense, especially in *Greed,* his cinematic rendition of Norris's *McTeague,* and perhaps Buñuel and Losey in certain of their films,[7] yet Deleuze's point is not that these directors narrate naturalistic plots but that everything in their films—settings, characters, stories—issues from a peculiar kind of vision, one that sees a primordial world of drives and forces immanent within and inseparable from the real world of concrete particularities. For these directors, the real is haunted by an "originary world," comprised of "non-formed matter, sketches [*ébauches,* rough forms, vague outlines] or fragments [*morceaux*], traversed by non-formal functions, acts, or energy dynamisms that are not even related to constituted subjects" (IM 174; 123). A realm of fragments and impulses (the impulse is simply "the energy that seizes fragments in the originary world" [IM 174; 124]), the originary world is a kind of primal swamp from which the material world arises and an ultimate garbage dump into which all matter eventually passes. At once "radical beginning and absolute end" (IM 174; 124), the originary world has an inherent temporality of decline, a cruel passage from primal origin to ultimate destruction that adheres to a law "of *the greatest slope*" (IM 174; 124). In Stroheim impulses follow a course of entropic dissipation, in Buñuel a cycle of repeated descents (especially in *The Exterminating Angel* and *The Discreet Charm of the Bourgeoisie*), and in Losey an implosive "turning against the self" (IM 192; 137), but in all a fundamental temporality of degradation prevails, a destiny dictated less by psychological motivations than a physical law of gravity.

Deleuze cites as manifestations of originary worlds the Death Valley expanse at the end of *Greed,* the African swamp of *Queen Kelly,* the drawing room of *The Exterminating Angel,* the column-filled desert of *Simon of the Desert,* the gravel square of *The Servant,* and the velodrome of *Mr. Klein.* These spaces, however, are not "pure" originary worlds, for in the impulse-image "the originary world does not exist independently of the historical and geographic milieu that serves as its medium" (IM 175; 124). Rather, these are concrete sites where the originary world's presence within the real becomes most evident. Conversely, the most mundane spaces in the films of Stroheim, Buñuel, and Losey "communicate from within with originary worlds" (IM 174; 123), for in the impulse-image the real milieu "has the status of a 'derived' milieu which receives from the originary world a temporality as destiny" (IM 175; 125). What Deleuze senses, it would seem, is a peculiar atmospheric consistency in films such as *Greed, The Exterminating Angel,* and *The Servant,* whereby spaces, objects, and actions belong at once to a real environment and to a primordial domain of fragments and impulses. Death Valley is merely one end of a continuum of spaces from McTeague's dentist office through the couple's increasingly abject dwellings, each communicating in varying degrees with an originary world. The littered, chaotic drawing room at the close of *The Exterminating Angel* seems the inevitable result of a degradation inherent in the initially pristine salon, just as the violent vectors of the eerie, shadow-distorted staircase late in *The Servant* seem simple intensifications of a potential latent throughout the house from the beginning.

The originary world is midway between an *espace quelconque* and an actual milieu. It is fragmented and disconnected like an *espace quelconque,* but it is inseparably tied to an actual milieu, though in such a way that the milieu itself is altered, as if it were "derived" as a secondary effect of a turbulent substrate (hence the surreal tendencies within naturalistic films, especially those of Buñuel). Likewise, impulses are midway between affects and actions—they are affective energies embedded in real situations, yet distinct from actualized emotions; they are proto-actions that may take on various concrete forms in diverse contexts (e.g., the sex drive of Monteil in Buñuel's *Diary of a Chambermaid,* which plays through his several proposals of *amour fou* to the maids in the house). Characters tend to resemble animals in naturalistic films—one thinks of the brute close-ups of McTeague, the jackal movements of *The Exterminating Angel*'s aristocrats, or the predatory prowl of Losey's servant—but only because the impulses they embody proceed from an originary world, in which there are no clear differentiations between the animal and the human, simply energies permeating fragments and pieces. "Impulses and fragments are strictly correlative" (IM 174; 124), and thus the frequent appearance of fetishistic objects in these films also points to an originary world immanent within actual milieus. Such fetishes may be either Good or Evil, either "relics" or, "in the vocabulary of sorcery, vults or voodoo objects" (IM 183; 130), but whether relics or vults, they remain fragments wrested from actual milieus by impulses.

Deleuze identifies two signs of the impulse-image: symptoms and fetishes (or idols). "Symptoms are the presence of impulses in the derived world, and idols or fetishes, the representation of fragments" (IM 175; 125). It would seem that symptoms and fetishes would be the signs of composition of the impulse-image, and that a third sign corresponding to the originary world would constitute the impulse-image's genetic sign. But in his recapitulation of the signs of the movement-image, Deleuze states that "the impulse-image, intermediate between affection and action, is composed of *fetishes,* fetishes of Good or of Evil: these are fragments wrested from a derived milieu, but which refer genetically to *symptoms* of an originary world operating underneath the milieu" (IT 49; 33). The bipolar signs of composition, then, are the Good fetish (relic) and Bad fetish (vult), and the genetic sign is the symptom. Deleuze does not elaborate on the logic of this classification, but perhaps fetishes as discrete objects are more closely tied to the derived milieu than are symptoms, whereas symptoms as more abstract traces of energetic proto-actions have a greater affinity with originary worlds than do fetishes. In *Cinema 1*'s glossary Deleuze does say that the symptom "designates qualities or powers related to an *originary world* (defined by impulses)" and that the fetish is a "fragment wrested by the impulse from a real milieu, and corresponding to an originary world" (IM 292; 218). Yet whatever the logic behind this differentiation of compositional from genetic signs, it is clear in any case that as the *espace quelconque* is "the genetic element of the affection-image" (IM 156; 110), so is the originary world the genetic *element* from which the impulse-image arises.

THE ACTION-IMAGE

Of all the movement-images, the action-image has the greatest affinity with narrative. Much of Deleuze's discussion of this image seems at first glance to focus on plot, but again, the point is that narratives presuppose and issue from configurations of movement-images, and not the reverse. If the affection-image involves *espaces quelconques* and affects (qualities and powers), and the impulse-image originary worlds and elementary impulses, the action-image concerns determinate milieus and actual behaviors (*comportements*, both a general term for "comportments," or "manners of behaving," and the technical psychological term for "behaviors"). The action-image is the domain of realism, of qualities and powers actualized in a concrete, specific space-time (a milieu), and of affects and impulses incarnate in discrete actions (behaviors). Hence, "what constitutes realism is simply this: milieus and behaviors, milieus that actualize and behaviors that incarnate. The action-image is the relation between the two, and all the varieties of this relation" (IM 196; 141).

Bergson, we recall, argues that with the emergence of a living image (or point of indeterminacy), its surrounding space "curves," forms an enclosing sphere oriented around the living image as central point. In this sense, then, the milieu "effects a global synthesis, it is itself the Ambience or the Englobing [*l'Englobant,* that which encompasses, includes, or, to use a rare English word, 'englobes,' i.e., 'encloses in, or as in, a globe' (OED)]" (IM 197; 141). The milieu constitutes a surrounding configuration of forces that impinge on the living image and instigate the living image's actions and reactions. Hence, the action-image always entails an encompassing milieu of forces and the related actions/reactions of an individual or individuals. As the domain of the concrete and the actual, the action-image exemplifies Peirce's category of Secondness. Peirce argues that a real existent thing can appear only through a reaction with another thing. In this regard, the actual always implies two-ness, dyads, oppositions, reactions and resistances. Thus, Deleuze asserts that the action at the center of a surrounding milieu "is a duel of forces, a series of duels: duel with the milieu, with others, with oneself" (IM 197; 142). One of the fundamental structures of the action-image, what Deleuze calls "the Large Form" action-image, consists of a milieu of forces that constitutes an initial Situation (S), a duel of forces that comprises an Action (A), and a consequent modification of the Situation (S'): S-A-S'. This structure may be thought of as an hourglass-shaped convergence of two spirals, the broad spiral of a situation (S) narrowing and contracting into a specific action (A), which then issues in the expanding spiral of a new situation (S'). The sign associated with the milieu Deleuze calls a *synsign*, which he defines as "an ensemble of qualities-powers as actualized in a milieu, in a state of things or a determinate space-time" (IM 198; 142). The sign associated with the specific action he labels a *binomial*, which designates "every duel, i.e., that which is properly active in the action-image" (IM 198; 142). The synsign and binomial are the signs of composition of the Large Form action-image.

The Large Form is dominant across a wide range of genres of the classic cinema. One finds it in documentaries, such as Flaherty's *Nanook of the North*, with its hostile milieu converging on Nanook in his tug-of-war with the harpooned seal (a duel that does not so much transform an initial situation, Deleuze concedes, as allow basic survival in an implacably unchanging environment). Westerns perhaps most schematically exemplify the Large Form, with wind, sky, mesas, canyons, and deserts providing an ambient field of forces within which range wars, showdowns, shoot-outs, and ambushes take place. But Deleuze also discerns the Large Form in the psycho-social dramas of King Vidor, in the films noirs of Hawks and Huston, and in the historical films of Griffith and DeMille. In all these genres, Deleuze finds at work five laws, which together constitute a kind of physics of the Large Form action-image. The first is structural and concerns the requisite disposition of milieu forces as components of an organic whole—the particular configuration of the landscape both as impinging force and as setting within which individual forces meet; the specific curvature of the milieu and affinities of various characters for certain elements of the environment; the rhythms of the milieu's "respiration," the tempi of alternations between interior and exterior shots, primary and secondary situations, panoramas and close-ups. The second law concerns the passage from milieu to action. According to this law, "the synsign must contract into a binomial" (IM 210; 152): the milieu forces must converge in a climactic duel, and most often this convergence takes the form of an alternating montage of interrelated actions (such as the parallel manhunts of police and criminals in Lang's *M*, which converge once the criminals capture and begin to try the child killer and the police break in on the criminals' tribunal). The third law is that of the "forbidden montage," which requires that convergent forces eventually meet in a single shot, that the alternation of separate actions lead to a scene in which conflicting forces are simultaneously present to one another (e.g., the dueling sheriff and outlaw finally framed in a single shot). Fourth is the law of the "nesting [*emboîtement*] of duels one within another" (IM 212; 153), no duel standing alone, but each connected to a series of duels within duels like a set of Chinese boxes or Russian dolls. And the fifth is the law of the "great gap" (*grand écart*) (IM 212; 154) between the englobing milieu and the climactic action, which dictates that a distance separate the initial situation from the concluding duel. The surrounding milieu calls forth a future action, but only gradually does the hero become capable of that action, at which point the "great gap" is filled.

These five laws structure the synsigns of the surrounding milieu and the binomials of the englobed actions, but the genesis of synsigns, binomials, and their structural relations is marked by a third sign, which Deleuze calls the imprint (*empreinte*, "stamp," "impression"). The engendering of the Large Form action-image takes place as "the situation deeply and continuously impregnates the character" and "the impregnated character explodes into action, at discontinuous intervals" (IM 214; 155). It is in certain "emotional objects," says Deleuze, that the impregnating situation and the explosive action come together. In such objects, one sees the external sign of the internal genetic connection between milieu and character. Kazan is a master of the realist cinema, and it is no accident that he exploits to the full the talents of those trained in the Actors' Studio, for the Method is designed to externalize internal emotions at the point where milieu and character coincide. The method actor's technique of discovering an inner emotional analog to an external situation and establishing a link between the two by manipulating a milieu object (a glove, knife, ball, etc.) is consonant with the realist cinema's invention of images of emotional objects. The imprint, or emotional object, belongs at once to the milieu and its related action, and thus it is "a genetic or embryonic sign for the action-image"; it is "the internal link, but visible, between the impregnating situation and the explosive action" (IM 219; 159).

If S-A-S′ is one form of the action-image, it would seem logical that the configuration A-S-A′ might also be possible, and indeed Deleuze asserts that this is the action-image's other fundamental form, what he calls the Small Form. Here, the movement is from an equivocal action (A) to a clarified situation (S) that makes possible a modified or new action (A′). Perhaps the difference between Large Form and Small Form is most evident in the contrast between the crime film and the detective film (*film policier*). Whereas the crime film situates criminals within an underworld milieu and then follows their actions, the detective film commences with mysterious, fragmented actions and then traces the clues to disclose the situation from which the actions arose. Thus, Hawks's *Scarface* and Huston's *Asphalt Jungle* are Large Form, Hawks's *The Big Sleep* and Huston's *The Maltese Falcon* Small Form. Other Large Form genres have Small Form counterparts as well, Deleuze shows, the neo-Westerns of such directors as Mann, Boetticher, Daves, and Peckinpah often exploiting the Small Form, many "costume dramas" supplying Small Form examples of the historical film, and the English school documentaries of Grierson, Rotha, Wright et al. providing Small Form alternatives to Flaherty's Large Form models. But above all, comedy—especially burlesque—exploits the Small Form, with much of the humor of comedy arising from the equivocal nature of the characters' actions.

In Lubitsch's *Design for Living*, for example, a woman's suitor sees his tuxedo-clad rival at his beloved's abode in the morning, from which he mistakenly concludes that his rival and she have spent the night together. In *The Idle Class*, we see Chaplin with his back to the camera, apparently shaking with tears after his beloved has abandoned him, but when he turns to the camera we find he is shaking a cocktail. In each case, the humor is generated by the sign of an equivocal action—a tuxedo in the morning, a shaking body. Borrowing from Peirce, Deleuze calls such a sign an *index*. (For Peirce, an index is a sign of the existence or occurrence of some concrete singular entity or state external to the sign—smoke, for example, being an index of fire.) In the Lubitsch example, the index is an action from which an as yet unknown situation must be inferred. Deleuze calls this an "index of lack" (*indice de manque*), since it "implies a hole in the story" (IM 221; 160), a missing situation that is only gradually revealed. The gesture in the Chaplin example Deleuze labels an *index of equivocity,* an action that simultaneously points toward two different situations—bemoaning a lost love and preparing a cocktail. Here, "a very small difference in the action or between two actions induces a very great distance between two situations" (IM 222; 162). The index of lack and the index of equivocity constitute the two signs of composition of the Small Form action-image.

Deleuze calls the genetic sign of the Small Form the *vector,* and he introduces it by contrasting the Large Form's *respiration-space* and the Small Form's *skeleton-space* (*espace-ossature, ossature* meaning "the disposition of the skeleton's bones" as well as "any framework of elements structuring a whole"). Deleuze develops the distinction from Henri Maldiney's discussion of Chinese painting, which centers on Hsieh Ho's sixth-century advice that the painter first "reflect the vital breath; that is, create movement" and then "seek the skeleton [*ossature* in Maldiney's French translation]; that is, know how to use the brush" (Maldiney 167). The vital breath (*chi* in Chinese) that issues from the primordial void unifies the world in a systolic and diastolic respiration, and the painter's primary aim is to manifest the movement of this breath through the "appearing" or "coming into presence" of things. But the painter must also capture individual details in distinct brush strokes, delineate the structuring *ossature* of things, and render them in their "disappearing," like the mountain whose peak vanishes in the clouds. The first principle finally dominates and informs the second, but Deleuze sees in them two contrasting means of constructing space, the first via a global conception of an encompassing, ambient whole within which individual elements are already situated and structured (Large Form space), the second via a local operation whereby an individual element is connected to a neighboring element and then to another, and so on, as an open space of related but heterogeneous elements is constructed (Small Form space). The local skeleton-space consists of fragments, appearances and disappearances, which, however, manage to communicate with one another. Heterogeneous elements, without intermediaries, "leap from one to another or interconnect directly [*de plein fouet*]" (IM 231; 168). The elements are like points connected by a zigzag line, a temporal vector of force passing from one element to another and thereby forming "a line of the universe [*ligne d'univers*], across the holes" (IM 231; 168; the *ligne d'univers* is clearly a version of Worringer's Gothic line we met earlier in Deleuze's account of German expressionist space— see chapter 2). The vector, the genetic sign of the Small Form action-image, "is the sign of such a line" (IM 231; 168).

Mizoguchi's films provide the clearest examples of the construction of a *skeleton-space,* especially in his use of extended, slow-paced horizontal pans and tracking shots (most fully utilized in the pre-War *Sisters of Gion* and *The Story of the Late Chrysanthemums*).[8] Often Mizoguchi pans and tracks across a house, passing from outside walkways to diverse interiors framed by open sliding screens, with partitions and posts marking qualitative changes in the individual spaces linked by the camera's continuous movement. Sometimes he adds subtle dissolves to the camera's pan such that the eye traversing an architectural space flows across a wall into a forest or field. The camera's movement traces a line of the universe that "connects or joins heterogeneous elements, while maintaining them as heterogeneous" (IM 264; 194). Space is constructed piece by piece; each space has its own internal geometric coordinates, its own temporal rhythms, and its own dramatic intensities, as "each scene, each shot . . . brings a character or an event to the summit of its autonomy, of its intensive presence" (IM 262; 193). The space is not totally fragmented and disconnected (as an *espace quelconque* may be), but neither is it unified as an englobing whole. It manifests "the paradox of a successive space as space in which time affirms itself fully, but in the form of a function of variables of that space" (IM 262; 193). Midway through *Ugetsu,* for example, a medium shot frames the potter and his demon lover in a palace room. The camera slowly moves left, across a partition and into a forest, until it frames the potter and lover at a bathing pool. When the potter appears in a close-up and the lover is heard entering the water and giggling, the potter swims out of the frame and the camera gradually tracks left in close-up across rocks, then over open ground, then by means of a dissolve over the raked soil of a garden. As the horizontal movement finally slows, the camera rises to disclose a panorama of the potter and lover on a large cloth beside a lake. Three distinct spaces—palace room, woodland pool, lakeside meadow—each with its own rhythms, trajectories, and moments of dramatic climax, are linked in a meandering line that connects as it moves along from place to local place, that "creates space instead of presupposing it" (IM 262; 193).

The imprint, the genetic sign of the Large Form, brings together outer milieu and internal action through the emotional object, and in its own way the vector does the same. In Mizoguchi, each scene has its spatio-temporal rhythms as well as its dramatic culmination. In the Small Form, each action reveals a situation and passes into a succeeding action, and the connection between elements of the Small Form is as much a linking of intense actions as a joining of heterogeneous spaces. This point is implicit in Deleuze's brief reference to the Westerns of Anthony Mann, which according to Philippe Demonsablon are characterized by an absence of smooth transitions in story lines as well as an absence of transitions in the movement from one locale to another. In his review of Mann's *The Far Country,* Demonsablon notes Mann's disdain for the well-made plot, arguing that "the abrupt offhandedness of the scenario is the shortest path which traces the necessary connections between scenes, assuring to each scene its virtue of immediacy, of a becoming restricted to the closest future moment: that of the instant about to follow, where everything will be played out anew. . . . Each [of these peripities] is a present moment sharpened to its extreme point" (Demonsablon 53). Citing Demonsablon, Claude-Jean Philippe observes that Mann's "sudden anfractuosities" of plot, which conjoin moments of an "exacerbated present" (Philippe 292), have as their counterpart a discontinuous handling of space. No stylistic unity informs Mann's treatment of the landscape (as in Ford or Hawks), Philippe claims, but each natural setting has an individual atmospheric presence that communicates with the characters occupying that space. Citing Demonsablon and Philippe, Deleuze emphasizes the link between intensive actions that structures Mann's films, in which, he says, there is "a 'shortest path' which is not the straight line, but which brings together actions or parts, A and A', each of which retains its independence, each of which is a heterogeneous critical instant, 'a present sharpened to its extreme point' " (IM 231; 168). But the connection between actions entails as well a connection between spaces, Mann's conjunction of diverse landscapes forming a *skeleton-space* of heterogeneities. Deleuze describes the vector primarily in terms of the line of the universe that traverses a skeleton-space, but in *Cinema 1*'s glossary, he also defines the vector as "the jagged line that unites singular points or remarkable moments at the summit of their intensity" (IM 292; 218). Each of Mann's films, says Deleuze, "is like a knotted climbing rope, which twists at each take, at each action, at each event" (IM 231; 168). The vector, then, connects both spaces and actions. A line of the universe links heterogeneous, local spaces to one another, and that same line passes from intensive action to intensive action, from knot to knot along the twisting rope. In the vector, each scene is an action-space passing into another action-space, intensive actions filling each space, each space connecting to a contiguous space, each climactic intensity leaping to the next. The vector is the genetic sign of the Small Form in that it combines action and situation while generating the skeleton-space traversed by a jagged line of the universe.

THE REFLECTION-IMAGE

The reflection-image (*image-réflexion,* also referred to as the "transformation image," *image à transformation,* in the *Cinema 1* glossary) is situated between the action-image and the relation-image. In the action-image, action and situation are directly related in two basic structures, the Large Form S-A-S', and the Small Form A-S-A'. The reflection-image allows a passage from the Large Form to the Small Form, a "transformation of forms" (IM 243; 178). Deleuze calls the signs of the reflection-image *figures,* and he defines the figure as "the sign of such deformations, transformations or transmutations" (IM 244; 178) of the action-image. The reflection-image "is composed when action and situation enter into indirect relations" (IT 49; 33). In its most basic guise, the reflection-image establishes "an indirect reflexive relation" (IM 247–48; 181) between the Large Form and the Small Form; in this case, the sign, "instead of referring to its object, reflects another" (IM 292; 218). This indirect relation of reflection, as we shall see shortly, introduces a third element between action and situation. Peirce identifies Thirdness as the category of relations, and in this sense the reflection-image has affinities with the relation-image, which Deleuze treats as "an image that takes relations for its object" (IM 268; 198). Unlike the relation-image, however, the reflection-image remains tied to the action-image as a deformation, transformation, or transmutation of the action-image, and hence the reflection-image is "the intermediary between action and relation" (IT 48; 32).

Eisenstein provides Deleuze with two instances of the reflection-image that help clarify the concept. Both, in Deleuze's analysis, are instances of what Eisenstein referred to in his first published essay as a "montage of attractions," an insertion of a special image that seems to interrupt the flow of the action.[9] In *Ivan the Terrible, Part 2,* Ivan treats his cousin Vladimir to a lavish banquet, during which Ivan feigns affection for his simple-minded cousin. Eventually Ivan coaxes from the drunken Vladimir indications that Vladimir's mother plans to assassinate the czar and put her son on the throne. Sensing imminent danger, Ivan has Vladimir dressed in the czar's official regalia and sends him into the cathedral at the head of a procession. In the cathedral, Vladimir is mistakenly assassinated by an agent of his mother. During the banquet, however, before Vladimir has revealed the assassination plot, a group of Ivan's bodyguards stages a premonitory "infernal clown and circus spectacle" (IM 247; 181), a dance and pantomime in which the bodyguards hint that the czar intends to execute his enemies ("Strike with the axes," they shout). Here, a theatrical or scenographic representation prefigures a future action. Instead of the sequence S-A (Ivan confronting his enemies–death of Vladimir), one sees an intervening A′ (fictive theatrical action) between S and A. The circus spectacle (A′) is an indirect reflection of the death of Vladimir (A). It is also an "index of the real action A which is being prepared" (IM 248; 182), in that it is an equivocal sign whose precise sense is only fully confirmed with the future death. The S-A sequence (Ivan confronting his enemies–death of Vladimir) belongs to the Large Form action-image (S-A-S). A′, as *index,* belongs to the Small Form. Hence, "the small form is, as it were, injected into the large form through the intermediary of the theatrical representation" (IM 248; 182).

A complementary example comes from the famous milk separator sequence of *Old and New* (*The General Line*), which Eisenstein discusses at length in *Nonindifferent Nature* (38–59). To express the joy of the peasants at the successful operation of the separator as it begins to extract cream and spew forth milk, Eisenstein follows a shot of a fountain of milk with a shot of a fireworks explosion of light. In this case, a "plastic representation" (IM 248; 182) indirectly reflects a real situation.

Primary here is the Small Form sequence A-S (operation of the separa-tor and reactions of the peasants [A]-joy of the village [S]), the action only gradually unveiling the implicit situation. The fireworks explosion (S') is a "grandiose" situation "that englobes the implied situation"; hence, it serves as a "synsign or englobing element of the real situation S" (IM 248; 182). Since the synsign is a Large Form sign, one may say that in this case "the large form is injected into the small form, through sculptural or plastic representation" (IM 248; 182). In both examples, then, an intervening sign indirectly reflects its object (spectacle>assassi-nation, fireworks>village joy) and transforms Large Form and Small Form by injecting an element of one form into a sequence of the other. The injected image is a third element in a binary sequence, a sign of a relation (a dramatic, indexical prefiguration in the first instance, a plas-tic, englobing figuration in the second), and thus an image that carries "situations and action to an extreme limit," that raises them "to a third that goes beyond their constitutive duality" (IM 249; 183): an image that pushes the action-image toward the relation-image, and hence serves as the "intermediary between action and relation" (IT 48; 32).

Besides these two figures (sculptural/plastic and theatrical/ scenographic), Deleuze identifies two additional reflection-image signs, *figures of inversion* and *discursive figures* (or *figures of discourse*). These four signs he categorizes through a somewhat playful reference to Fontanier's taxonomy of figures in his classic *Les Figures du discours* (1818–30).[10] Eisenstein's plastic figure corresponds to Fontanier's "trope properly speaking" (substitution of one word for another, as in metaphor, metonymy and synecdoche) in that one image is substituted for another (fireworks explosion–fountain of milk). Eisenstein's theatrical figure corresponds to Fontanier's "trope improperly speak-ing" (substitution of a group of words for another word, as in allegory, hyperbole, and irony), since the theatrical scene is a sequence of actions standing in for a future action. Fontanier's third category of non-trope "figures properly speaking" includes the stylistic figure of inversion (a substitution involving a simple alteration of word order, e.g., "to the battle he came" for "he came to the battle"), and to this category Deleuze parallels the cinematic figure of inversion. Fontanier's fourth category, that of "figures improperly speaking," or "figures of thought," which entail no change in the words themselves but a change in the way one thinks about them or imagines them (e.g., prosopopoeia, in which an

absent, dead, or imaginary person is represented as speaking), has as a
cinematic counterpart the "discursive image."[11] In his *Cinema 2* recapitulation of signs, Deleuze collapses the four classifications of reflection-
images into three, identifying the reflection-image's signs of composition
as the figure "of attraction" (Eisenstein's plastic and theatrical figures)
and the figure "of inversion," and its genetic sign as the "discursive" figure
(IT 49; 33).

The figure of inversion Deleuze treats only briefly in a paragraph on
Howard Hawks. The landscapes of Hawks's Westerns retain the "respiration" of the Large Form, Deleuze claims, but Hawks's use of inversion
induces a "topological deformation of the large form" (IM 228; 166).
Whereas in the standard Large Form Western an englobing milieu
shapes the action of a coherent collectivity, in Hawks's Westerns the
milieu tends to lose its organic vitality—a purely functional prison in
Rio Bravo, a diagram-like town in *Rio Lobo*—and the group engaged in
action often is a simple makeshift alliance of individuals pursuing
a temporary task. In the Large Form Western, the milieu offers a disruptive challenge to the ordinary activities and plans of the community,
whereas in Hawks, "the unexpected, the violent, the event arrive from
the interior, while the exterior is instead the place of customary or pre-
meditated action, in a curious inversion of the outside and the inside"
(IM 227–28; 166). Outside and inside take on interchangeable functions, a situation that allows a conversion of one into the other, and
hence a transformation of Large and Small Forms through a play of
inversions. Throughout Hawks's films Deleuze finds "the constant
mechanism of inversions" (IM 228; 166), inversions of male-female and
adult-child roles (in the comedies especially), as well as inversions in
high speech–low speech, love-money, and so on. Inversion is common in
burlesque and comedy, but in Hawks "the mechanisms of inversion rise
to the state of an autonomous and generalized figure" (IM 250; 183),
though precisely how this autonomy is achieved Deleuze does not spec-
ify further.

The genetic sign of the reflection-image, the "discursive figure" or
"figure of discourse," Deleuze approaches via Chaplin's later comedies
(*The Great Dictator, Monsieur Verdoux, Limelight, A King in New York*).
Throughout his career, Chaplin is the master of burlesque, the quintessential Small Form genre, but in his talkies he manages to transform
burlesque, for there he gives sound "a radical original usage: Chaplin

uses it to introduce into cinema the Figure of discourse, and thus to transform the initial problems of the action-image" (IM 236; 172). The essence of Chaplin's Small Form burlesque is in the equivocal action, a single sign (a shaking body) that may belong to two divergent situations (weeping and preparing a cocktail). *The Great Dictator* in its entirety, one might say, is structured in a similar fashion, Chaplin's moustache belonging to two radically different situations, that of the Jewish barber and that of the Hitlerian dictator. That Chaplin plays both the Jewish barber and the dictator may suggest that there is a Hitler in each of us, but Chaplin's point, Deleuze argues, is that the social order creates situations that engender dictators, and that it can and should create situations that foster liberty, tolerance, and goodness. Herein lies the significance of the conclusion of *The Great Dictator,* when the barber, disguised as the dictator, delivers his impassioned and enlightened speech. The barber/dictator's discourse makes explicit the implicit differences that have organized the film's two basic social worlds, the two possible societies that we may inhabit (the humanitarian community versus the inhuman totalitarian state). The situations (the S's of the film's various Small Form A-S-A' sequences) are transformed by the discourse, which gives the situations "a totally new dimension, and constitutes 'discursive' images" (IM 235; 172). The infinitesimal differences in Small Form actions (say, the twitching of a moustache) point toward enormous differences in situations, two "states of life" and "two states of society" (IM 236; 173). Through the discursive figure, Chaplin pushes "the small form burlesque . . . to its limit, which makes it rejoin the large form, and which no longer has need of the burlesque, all the while retaining its powers [*puissances*] and signs" (IM 236; 173).

The discursive figure, then, is a reflection-image in that it pushes the action-image to its limit and transforms Small and Large Forms. But in what sense is it a genetic sign? The reflection-image, we recall, arises when "action and situation enter into indirect relations" (IT 49; 33). In Eisenstein's figures (theatrical/scenographic or sculptural/plastic) the sign, "instead of referring to its object, reflects another"; in Hawks's figures, the sign "reflects its proper object, but by inverting it"; whereas in Chaplin's discursive figures the sign "directly reflects its object," as Deleuze says in his *Cinema 1* glossary (IM 292; 218). Thus, the discursive figure is the *direct* reflection of an *indirect* relation between action and situation, the explicit presentation of what is implicit and presupposed in all the figures of the reflection-image. Put another way, the reflection-image's condition of possibility, that which is necessary for the generation of theatrical/plastic figures or figures of inversion, is made manifest in the discursive figure.[12]

The subcategorization of reflection-images, however, is ultimately only a secondary concern for Deleuze. What interests him most is the general process of transformation whereby action-images are pushed to their limits, a process that in some cases brings about a conversion of Large and Small Forms, but in others allows a continuing separation of the two forms. Indeed, in Kurosawa and Mizoguchi, argues Deleuze, one finds "a clear distinction between the two forms, rather than a complementarity that converts one into the other" (IM 261; 192), and yet in both directors the action-image is transformed as situation and action are brought into indirect, "mental" relations with one another. Kurosawa is a master of the Large Form, in whose films one encounters the fullest embodiment of an englobing "respiration-space." A "very pure SA formula" organizes his works—"one must know all the givens before acting and in order to act" (IM 256; 188). Yet throughout Kurosawa's films, the givens of the situation are less important than "the *givens of a question* that is hidden in the situation, enveloped in the situation, and that the hero must disengage in order to be able to act, in order to respond to the situation" (IM 257; 189). In *The Seven Samurai,* "the question is not, 'can one defend the village,' but 'what is a samurai, today, precisely at this moment of History' " (IM 260; 191). In *Ikiru,* the question is "How should one live?" In some films, the hero responds only to the situation rather than its implicit question, and as a result perishes (*Throne of Blood,* in which the Macbeth figure misconstrues the witch's predictions). In others, the hero adopts a new course of action once the question emerges from the situation (*Red Beard*). In *Ikiru,* the protagonist initially responds only to the facts of his situation—that he has only six months to live—by seeking sensual pleasure. Through the young woman who formerly worked in his office he begins to articulate the question in a new fashion, especially when she tells him of the meaning she derives from making mechanical rabbits that give joy to children across the city. When the hero finally responds to the question, he devotes himself to building a park for a group of poor citizens, thereby altering the givens of the world, "making something circulate . . . in such a manner that, through these new or renewed givens, questions that are less cruel, more joyous, closer to Nature and to life may emerge and multiply" (IM 260–1; 192). Through this response, the hero has "given breath back to space," he has "rejoined breath-space," he has "become park" (IM 261; 192).

The question in Kurosawa transcends the situation, but emerges from it and remains tied to it (and hence its status as a reflection-image, midway between the concrete action-image and the mental relation-image). It is a kind of Idea enveloped in an englobing world. "Kurosawa is thus a metaphysician after his own manner, and invents a broadening of the large form: he goes beyond the situation toward a question, and raises the givens to the level of givens of the question, no longer those of the situation" (IM 258; 189). What counts is not the question *per se,* but "this form of disengagement of any question whatever, its intensity more than its content, its givens more than its object" (IM 258; 189). The question "haunts the situation" (IM 259; 190), and the hero who manages to respond to the question reaches "a new limit: the one who is impregnated with all the givens will only be a double, a shadow in the service of the master, of the World" (IM 259; 191). The protagonist of *Ikiru* rejoins the respiration-space, "becomes park." He himself becomes an *imprint,* a genetic sign of the link between action and the impregnating situation. In all these ways, "Kurosawa, by his technique and his metaphysics, submits the large form to a broadening that functions as a transformation on the spot [*une transformation sur place*]" (IM 261; 192).

If Kurosawa broadens the Large Form by unfolding metaphysical questions from enveloping situations and by creating protagonists who become cosmic imprints, Mizoguchi subjects the Small Form to "a lengthening, a stretching that transforms it in itself" (IM 261; 192) and traces vectors along an unlimited "line of the universe." Mizoguchi is an exemplary practitioner of the Small Form, as we have seen. He constructs a skeleton-space of heterogeneous parts put together piece by piece, step by step in an ongoing movement from place to contiguous place. But through his masterful handling of continuities—using a single angle for shots of contiguous spaces so that the spaces seem to slide into one another across the cuts; shooting from a mid-distance that allows sweeping, circling movements within scenes as the camera follows various characters in their complex trajectories; linking diverse sites through extended horizontal pans and tracking shots, as we discussed earlier— Mizoguchi develops "a metaphysics as much as a technique" (IM 263;

193), a vision of an unlimited cosmos with a "very special homogeneity" (IM 263; 194) created by a single line of the universe that passes through diverse places, both real and fantastic, and through various characters, both living and dead. He gives the Small Form "an unequaled amplitude" (IM 264; 194), one that makes visible a metaphysical Idea of an unlimited cosmic skeleton-space. Yet Mizoguchi also shows the breakdown of this cosmic order, for the connections between spaces, social classes, states of being, and so on are always made by women in his films, whereas the hierarchical male world constantly blocks these connections. The men benefit from the women's transgression of social boundaries (one thinks especially of *The Sisters of Gion, The Story of the Late Chrysanthemums,* and *The Story of Oharu*), but the men punish the women and often force them into lives of prostitution. "The lines of the universe are feminine, but the social state is prostitutional," and in the confrontation of the two worlds, "Mizoguchi thus reaches an extreme limit of the action-image: when a world of misery undoes all the lines of the universe, and brings forth a reality that is no longer anything but disoriented, disconnected" (IM 265; 195). When the cosmic connections of an endless line of the universe are severed, the movement-image as a whole begins to collapse, for the unified sensori-motor schema that underlies the movement-image is threatened with the emergence of a disoriented, disconnected space. Deleuze notes that in Kurosawa a similar failure of a cosmic vision at times takes place, but in such cases the Large Form's englobing sphere cracks and yields a dispersive space (as in the chaotic junkyard landscape of *Dodeska'den,* interconnected solely by the retarded boy who plays at driving a streetcar through the dump). Such a dispersive space, like Mizoguchi's disconnected space, is a symptom of the breakdown of the sensori-motor schema, and hence of the dissolution of the movement-image in general.

THE RELATION-IMAGE

Deleuze identifies the relation-image with Peirce's category of Thirdness, one of the most difficult concepts in Peirce's philosophy. Thirdness is the category of continuity, regularity, habit, rule, law, interpretation, representation, and thought. Peirce says, "Third is the conception of mediation, whereby a first and a second are brought into relation," a statement Gallie helpfully glosses as follows: "Here by relation Peirce means *intelligible* relation; and his main aim in all his accounts of his Third category is to show that the ideas of natural or operative law and of continuous development are different facets of one supremely general form of mediation, whose prototype is the action of a sign mediating between its object and its interpretant" (1966, 198). For Peirce, everything in the universe has a tendency to form habits—to move from pure chance and indeterminacy to regularity, continuity, and generality. Such habit-forming is an attribute of mind, and for Peirce brute matter is simply "mind whose habits have become so fixed that it loses the powers of forming and losing them" (Sheriff 1994, 15). Hence, scientific laws are merely increasingly rigidifying habits rather than fixed, inexplicable facts, and as active processes, they form part of a general evolutionary development of the cosmos from chaos toward regularity. Habit-forming requires mediation, the connection of two things by a third. In the numerical series 2, 4, 6, 8, . . . , the first two numerals might also belong to the series 2, 4, 8, 16, . . . , but the third numeral establishes the rule, the general formula, whereby regularity, continuity, and habit may be formed. For human minds, signs are fundamental to all thought and all habit formation, and in semiosis mediation is evident in the basically triadic nature of the sign. The sign mediates between the object and the interpreter, for which reason Peirce defines the sign as a relation between a representamen (the sign vehicle), an object, and an interpretant (that which interprets). Further, every interpretant is a sign pointing to another sign, the process of sign formation being an open, developing process of interpretation (what Peirce calls "infinite semiosis"). Habit as a generalizing tendency, and semiosis as an open-ended, continuing activity, go hand in hand, not simply for humans, but for animals, plants, and presumably all matter. "The essential function of a sign," says Peirce, "is to render inefficient relations efficient,—not to set them into action, but to establish a habit or general rule whereby they will act on occasion" (Peirce/Welby 31).

Deleuze rightly notes that for Peirce Thirdness is "the mental" (says Peirce, "If you take any ordinary triadic relation, you will always find a *mental* element in it. Brute action is secondness, any mentality involves thirdness" [Peirce/Welby 29]). And what Deleuze finds central in Thirdness is the concept of relation. The relation-image is a mental image, a "figure of thought" in which the mental is introduced into the image. Deleuze does note that to some extent the mental is implicit in other images, in the consciousness revealed through an affection-image, say, or in the goals, choices, and calculations inherent in action-images. But what sets the relation-image apart from the other five movement-images, what makes it a mental image, an instance of Thirdness, is that *"it is an image that takes for its object, relations,* symbolic acts, intellectual feelings" (IM 268; 198). When treated from the perspective of Thirdness, the basic elements of the movement-image—perceptions, actions, and affections—are transformed. Perceptions are revealed as interpretations, signs mediated by other signs in a chain of semiotic relations. Actions are shown to "include necessarily the symbolic element of a law (to give, to exchange)" (IM 267; 197). As Peirce points out, an instance of "giving" is not that of A placing B on a table and C picking B up, but an irreducibly triadic relation of A giving B to C according to the regular practice of a habit or law. (Giving, says Peirce, "consists in A's making C the possessor according to *Law.* There must be some kind of law before there can be any kind of giving" [Peirce/Welby 29].) And affections, under the aegis of Thirdness, are presented as "intellectual feelings of relations, such as the feelings that accompany the use of the logical conjunctions 'because,' 'although,' 'so that,' 'thus,' 'now,' etc." (IM 267; 197).

Deleuze regards Hitchcock as the director who most fully develops the potential of a cinema of the relation-image. In Hitchcock's films, "all is interpretation, from the beginning to the end" (IM 270; 200). Here Deleuze cites Jean Narboni, who observes that there is an "interpretative passion and a fever of decipherment" (Narboni 31) in the great films of Hitchcock, a perception pervaded by signs that force themselves on characters, compelling interpretation of the relations they obliquely intimate. Further, this interpretative passion is registered above all on the faces of the characters, says Narboni, faces that reveal the affects aroused in the process of decipherment. In Deleuze's terminology, the affection-images of Hitchcock's faces disclose "intellectual feelings of relations" (IM 267;197), the affects of "if," "hence," "although," and so on. But above all, Deleuze asserts, the *action* in Hitchcock is structured around mental relations. Each of his films is conceived in terms of what Hitchcock calls a postulate, a set of relations, which then undergoes logical development. "What counts is not the author of the action, what Hitchcock calls with scorn the *whodunit,* but neither is it the action itself: it is the set of relations within which the action and its author are held" (IM 270; 200).

Countless are the thrillers, suspense films, and tales of murder and espionage that have filled the screen, but for Deleuze what sets Hitchcock's films apart is the insistent presence of Thirdness. Murder seems a simple enough action, involving a dyad of killer and victim, but in Hitchcock "the criminal has always committed his crime *for* another" (IM 271; 201), either on behalf of another, or in relation to a third party. In *Strangers on a Train,* Bruno proposes that Guy and he swap murders, and in *Dial M for Murder,* a tennis player blackmails an adventurer into murdering his wife. In *I Confess,* the murderer "gives" his crime to the priest in the confessional; the young men in *Rope* offer their murder as a gift to their teacher. Jane Wyman becomes entangled in her childhood friend's murder in *Stage Fright,* James Stewart gets involved in the murder across the courtyard in *Rear Window.* Everywhere, the mediation of a third term intervenes in the action, structuring it as a relation. Yet the characters themselves do not directly reveal the relations that structure them, though they do decipher signs and eventually uncover truths. Rather, it is the camera—its shots, framings, movements—that discloses relations, and as a result, often the audience knows more about the relations than do the characters. Hence the significance of Hitchcock as a master of suspense: "In the history of cinema, Hitchcock appears as the one who no longer conceives of the constitution of a film as a function of two terms, the director and the film to be made, but as a function of three: the director, the film, and the public which must enter into the film" (IM 272; 202).

Hitchcock creates a cinema of mental images, which means for Deleuze that "he makes the relation itself the object of an image, which is not simply added to perception-, action- and affection-images, but frames them and transforms them" (IM 274; 203). Hitchcock also fashions special "figures of thought," signs specific to the relation-image. Deleuze observes that philosophers have often distinguished between natural relations and abstract relations, and he builds his classification of relation signs upon this opposition.[13] Via natural relations, the mind moves easily from one object to another in order to form a series of interconnected elements (e.g., as one listens to a piano sonata, the mind passes from the composition to the performer, to the concert hall, to previous concerts, etc.). Such a series is formed by a habit (natural relations in this context designating simply usual, customary, or ordinary mental relations, not necessarily relations intrinsic to the natural world and its scientific laws). Abstract relations, by contrast, link elements that are not naturally (i.e., habitually) connected in the mind. Via abstract relations, a whole is constituted, as opposed to a series.

The signs of composition of the relation-image are the *mark* and the *demark*. The mark is the sign of a natural relation. It is "a term that refers to other terms in a customary series such that each can be 'interpreted' by the others" (IM 274; 203). A demark is a term that breaks from such a series, an unsettling, anomalous element that disrupts the habitual movement of the mind from one thing to another. Hitchcock is famous for his demarks—Deleuze cites the windmill turning against the wind in *Foreign Correspondent,* the cropduster descending over an already harvested field in *North by Northwest,* the glowing glass of milk in *Suspicion,* the key that does not fit the lock in *Dial M for Murder.* But the extraordinary demark would never be noticed if it were not part of an ordinary series of marks. Both the mark and the demark, then, are elements defined by a series, the one perpetuating habitual connections of terms in the series, the other disrupting such connections.

The genetic sign of the relation-image is the *symbol,* which is the sign of an abstract relation that constitutes a whole. In Hitchcock's early film *The Ring,* for example, a bracelet given to a married woman by her lover symbolizes their adulterous affair, but when her husband playfully slips it on her finger it becomes a "ring" symbolic of their marriage, and later it is visually associated with a coiled serpent, and hence with sin (see Rohmer and Chabrol 13–14). Similarly, the wedding ring Grace Kelly finds in the killer's apartment in *Rear Window* serves as a symbol of the killer's marriage, his crime, the detection of the crime, and Grace Kelly's desire to marry James Stewart (see Truffaut, 1967, 166). In both cases, an image invites a "comparison of terms independently of their natural relations" (IM 293; 218). The symbol is the genetic sign of the relation-image in that it reveals the condition of possibility of all mental relations—the conjoining of any term whatever with any other. In this regard, the mark and demark may be seen simply as specialized instances of the general domain of relations indicated by the symbol. Hence Deleuze's summary characterization of the signs of the relation-image: "the two signs of composition will be the *mark,* or the circumstance through which two images are united according to a habit ('natural' relation), and the *demark,* the circumstance through which an image is wrested from its relation or natural series; the genetic sign will be the *symbol,* the circumstance through which we are made to compare two images, even arbitrarily united ('abstract' relation')" (IT 49; 33).

At a minimum, the signs of the movement-image are fourteen: dicisign, reume, gramme; icon, qualisign; symptom, fetish; synsign, index, imprint; figure; mark, demark, symbol. At most, they number twenty-three: dicisign, reume, gramme; contour icon, trait icon, qualisign of discontinuity, qualisign of vacuity; good fetish (relic), bad fetish (vult), symptom; synsign, binomial, imprint, index of lack, index of equivocity, vector; theatrical/scenographic figure, sculptural/plastic figure, figure of inversion, discursive figure; mark, demark, symbol. But obviously, the tally is insignificant, for Deleuze is no ordinary system builder. Whether the contour icon and the trait icon constitute two separate signs or two poles of the same sign is for him an indifferent matter. His taxonomy is a generative device meant to create new terms for talking about new ways of seeing. But if the minute terminological differentiations are unimportant, the concepts and the logic of their formation are crucial, for they articulate the objects of analysis and their interconnections. From the movement-image to perception-action-affection, to the six movement-images, to the fourteen/twenty-three signs, a proliferation of distinctions emerges, each embedded in a network of dyadic and triadic relations that afford means of thinking about the interplay of images in film. And though the branchings of Deleuze's schema may resemble a Porphyrean tree, his complex discussions of specific images and signs ensure their inter*play* in acentered, rhizomic combinations.

Nor is Deleuze a conventional semiotician, despite his frequent use of Peirce, not simply because he categorizes with a decidedly playful *élan,* but also because the *sign,* in its usual sense, is not really his object of interest. For most semioticians, there is nothing beyond signs; if they study cinema, they study the *signs* of cinema, and nothing else. For Deleuze, however, cinematic signs are simply specialized images within a broader domain of images. In describing Deleuze's relation-image, for example, one cannot merely divide it, like Gaul, into three parts—mark, demark, symbol. Rather, the relation-image is much more like France, and the mark, demark, and symbol like Lyon, Marseilles, and Paris. Each of the six kinds of movement-images allows Deleuze to explore different ways of seeing, different ways of handling the materials of film. The various signs allow a further investigation of the potential of those materials. For Deleuze, cinematic images constitute the "signaletic matter" (IT 43; 29) that directors, like sculptors, mold, bend, smooth, scrape, gouge, cut, paste, and weld to form light-and-sound sculptures in time. And Deleuze's taxonomy is merely a tool for inventing a language adequate to those sculptures and the creative processes that generate them.

Each of the six movement-images has its own signaletic matter—gaseous perceptions, *espaces quelconques*, originary worlds, respiration-/skeleton-spaces, metaphysical respiration-/skeleton-spaces, mental "relation spaces." And in each case Deleuze's effort is to conceive of seeing in a new way. Gaseous perception is seeing from all perspectives at once, as if one were a scattered cloud of eyes, and this mode of seeing pervades the other five movement-images as the limit toward which all movement-images tend. In an *espace quelconque,* one sees an affective space, a domain of qualities and powers (powers being passages from one quality to another) abstracted from specific coordinates yet still enmeshed in a material, sensual medium. Originary worlds allow one to see impulses and energies permeating and possessing settings and characters. In a respiration-space an englobing vision lets one see a rhythmic contraction and dilation of milieu and action; in a skeleton-space, one sees "vectorially," step by step, zig by zag, from intensity to intensity. A metaphysical respiration- or skeleton-space renders visible both an action world and an Idea immanent within it—in Kurosawa, we see situations *and* questions; in Mizoguchi, vectors *and* an ideal, unlimited line of the universe. And in a mental "relation space" we see relations within a concrete, tangible world. In each case, Deleuze invites us to imagine other ways of seeing, ways that make sensible within the visual what common sense regards as invisible—affects, energies, rhythms, vectors, ideas, and mental relations. Deleuze then shows us that these ways of seeing actually exist—that from the inception of the cinema, directors have been inventing these ways of seeing while making their films, and we, in watching their films, have been seeing in these strange ways all along.

Six images and some fourteen to twenty-three signs help map the movement-image. But a different set of terms must be used to chart the territory beyond. When the sensori-motor schema collapses, a new species of image emerges—the time-image. Yet that image, as we shall see, has been haunting the cinema from the beginning.

Chapter Four

HYALOSIGNS: CRYSTALS OF TIME

The movement-image is "matter itself"; the six kinds of movement-image are the elements "that make of this matter a signaletic matter"; and the fourteen to twenty-three signs of the movement-image are "the features of expression [*traits d'expression*] that compose these images, combine and ceaselessly recreate them, borne or carried along by matter in movement" (IT 49; 33). Through montage, the movement-image offers an indirect image of time as the open whole, but Deleuze argues that beyond the movement-image is a separate category of images and signs that provide a direct manifestation of time—the time-image. The first indications of the time-image in film occur in pure optical and sonic images that break with the sensori-motor schema (what Deleuze calls opsigns and sonsigns). Memory-images and dream-images (mnemosigns and onirosigns [IT 358; 273]) interconnect opsigns and sonsigns. But only in the time crystal, or crystal-image, with its corresponding *hyalosigns,* does "time in person" begin to "surge forth" (IT 358; 274). Our concern for the moment is with crystal-images and hyalosigns, but in subsequent chapters we will examine other forms of the time-image: *chronosigns,* which present either coexisting relations and simultaneous elements of time (the order of time) or a before-and-after in a single becoming (the series of time); *noosigns,* which reveal a new relation between thought and images; and *lectosigns,* which manifest a new relation between the visual and the sonic.

OPSIGNS

In the classic cinema of Hollywood, an integrated system of practices develops that ensures a seamless and continuous presentation of action within a single time and space. A commonsense, rational sensori-motor schema informs the Hollywood system, and it is on this basis that Hollywood directors fashion their "well-made films." But after World War II, Deleuze observes, indications of a collapse of the sensori-motor schema begin to appear in American films, both outside and inside Hollywood. Deleuze identifies five symptoms of the sensori-motor schema's disintegration. In films like Altman's *Nashville,* the englobing, synthesizing milieu of the Large Form action-image gives way to a dispersive situation, in which the links between actions and milieus are not entirely severed but are stretched and relaxed, loosely and casually constructed. Correlatively, in works like Cassavetes's *Too Late Blues* and *The Killing of a Chinese Bookie,* the continuous "line of the universe" of the Small Form action-image tends to break apart, and gaps in the action arise; reality becomes "lacunary as much as dispersive," linkages and connections are made "deliberately weak" (IM 279; 207). And in other films, an aimless wandering affects the action (e.g., Scorsese's *Taxi Driver*); the sensori-motor schema is replaced by "the stroll, the *balade* [ramble, jaunt], and the continual round-trip journey [*l'aller-retour continuel*]" (IM 280; 208). Besides these three deformations of the action-image, Deleuze finds two additional indications of the sensori-motor schema's demise, one in the parodic handling of the modern world as a realm of clichés (again, Altman's *Nashville* and Scorsese's *Taxi Driver* provide good examples), the other in stories of diffused conspiracies, anonymous plots, and ubiquitous technological surveillance (e.g., Coppola's *The Conversation*). For when the sensori-motor schema begins to disintegrate, and with it the interconnecting links that hold action and situation together, the only totality remaining that can provide the coherence and coordination of space and time is either a network of circulating clichés or a conspiratorial system of surveillance. These, then, are the "five apparent characteristics of the new image: *the dispersive situation, the deliberately weak links, the balade-form, the consciousness of clichés, the denunciation of the conspiracy*" (IM 283; 210).

Yet such breakdowns in the sensori-motor schema alone are not sufficient to bring forth a new image, and in the American films Deleuze cites he sees primarily a negative critique of the Hollywood system and an unproductive parody of the modern world of clichés. The collapse of the sensori-motor schema makes possible a new image—the time-image—but its positive creation requires more than dismantling and mockery. The earliest instances of the time-image in Western cinema Deleuze finds in Italian neorealism (ca. 1945–53).[1] Neorealism is often characterized by its social themes, but in Deleuze's view it should be defined by the "rise of purely optical situations, which are essentially distinct from the sensori-motor situations of the action-image of the old realism" (IT 9; 2). In De Sica's *Umberto D,* for instance, the story of the retired civil servant's poverty and loneliness is interrupted by an extended sequence of a young servant girl stirring about in the kitchen—moving pots and pans, washing ants from the kitchen sink, grinding coffee—that culminates when she stops to contemplate her pregnant stomach. In the midst of an everyday series of motor actions, a sudden moment of pure seeing arises, unassimilated within the ongoing action, as the girl stares at her body. Likewise, in Rossellini's *Europa 51,* a wealthy housewife undergoes a series of purely optical moments as she learns to see the realities of poverty and misery—when she visits the housing projects and stares at the grim buildings and razed wastelands; when she helps a poor woman by taking her place at a factory for a day and gazes with incomprehension at the crowds of workers and the towering factory, at its massive rollers, cavernous expanses, labyrinthine passages and stairways, whirring conveyor belts; and when she contemplates the faces of her fellow inmates in the asylum at the film's conclusion. Of course, these images are eventually assimilated within a coherent narrative, but what counts is that at these crucial moments the housewife becomes a spectator rather than an active participant, someone whose seeing is detached from her doing, and what she sees we also see—visions, purely optical situations disconnected from the common-sense coordinates of their standard usages and practices.

Such pure optical images Deleuze calls *opsigns* (their sonic counterparts being *sonsigns*), and their appearance he finds throughout Italian neorealism, in De Sica and Rossellini, but also in Visconti, Fellini, and Antonioni. In a brief survey of the early works of the last three directors, Deleuze cites instances of the collapse of the sensori-motor schema—

dispersed or disconnected space, aimless wandering—as well as examples of pure optical situations. He notes further that though such situations may be classified as either objective or subjective, real or imaginary, physical or mental, opsigns put these polar opposites in communication with one another and tend "toward a point of indiscernibility (and not confusion)" (IT 17; 9). Fellini's opsigns are often clearly to be taken as memories or dreams, yet within the memory or dream, a practical staging frequently takes place, as if the mental world were a rehearsal for a play. At the same time, the real world itself resembles a spectacle, and ultimately the images of the mental, subjective, imaginary world and those of the physical, objective, real world tend to form a single continuum of interrelated stagings (8½, though post-neorealistic, best illustrates this tendency). Conversely, Antonioni's neutral presentations of blank objects and empty landscapes eventually take on a peculiarly mental aspect, as if the real had assumed "a strange invisible subjectivity" (IT 16; 8). Opsigns, then, may emerge from and ultimately be resolved within a common-sense narrative—as with a housewife's growing alienation from her privileged milieu in *Europa 51*—but in themselves, opsigns disrupt such stories by tending toward a point of indiscernability between the subjective/objective, imaginary/real, and mental/physical.

Opsigns mark the occurrence of "something intolerable, unbearable," something "too powerful [*trop puissant*] . . . that exceeds our sensori-motor capacities" (IT 29; 18). (Note that the distinction is not merely quantitative—extreme pain and suffering may be tolerated and borne, in the sense that they may be integrated within a sensori-motor schema, and conversely, the most anodyne moment may disrupt that schema and become intolerable and unbearable.) In this regard, opsigns are necessarily opposed to clichés, since "a cliché is a sensori-motor image of the thing" (IT 32; 20). As Bergson argues, within our sensori-motor world objects become both more and less than they are otherwise. We perceive objects through our accumulated experiences of them, through our memories, fears, desires, and plans, loading them with characteristics that extend into complex patterns of association and anticipation. But we also perceive selectively, ignoring those aspects of the object that do not interest us. (Bergsonian consciousness, we recall, is *subtraction*, not addition.) Hence, the world of clichés may become intolerable in two ways: when objects are stripped of their customary associations, or when those characteristics we habitually ignore are restored. And directors manage to create opsigns in both ways, "to rarefy the image, by suppressing many things that have been added," or "to restore the lost parts, to rediscover everything that one does not see in the image, everything that one subtracts in order to make it 'interesting' " (IT 33; 21). Yet again Deleuze insists that the battle against clichés entails more than critique or parody. It is not enough to "perturb the sensori-motor links," but one must "*combine* the optical-sonic image with immense forces" (IT 33; 22). Three "growing powers [*puissances*]" (IT 34; 22) must be joined to the image: it must "be tied directly to a time-image"; it must "enter into internal relations that force the entire image to be 'read' no less than viewed, readable as much as visible"; and it must take on "the functions of thought" (IT 34–35; 22–23). In short, the pure optic image must "open itself to powerful and direct revelations, those of the time-image, the readable image [*l'image lisible*] and the thinking image [*l'image pensante*]" (IT 35; 23), and Deleuze's task throughout *Cinema 2* will be to show how opsigns may be developed into "chronosigns" (time-images), "lectosigns" (readable images), and "noosigns" (thinking images).

MNEMOSIGNS AND ONIROSIGNS

Deleuze's first goal, then, is to indicate how the opsign may "open itself" to the time-image, and he does so in three stages, examining initially memories and dreams, then crystals of time, and finally full-fledged chronosigns. Throughout, the basic question is, if the opsign is dissociated from the sensori-motor schema—and hence from its correlate, commonsense chronological time—how might one opsign be linked to another? What may connect one moment to the next, if not a simple succession of causally related present instants? Memory provides a convenient starting point for such an investigation, since the onward flow of present instants would seem to be reversed in the recollection of a past event. As we saw earlier, Bergson finds in memory the key to a proper understanding of *durée,* and Deleuze's treatment of memory images is framed in the terms Bergson uses to analyze the phenomena of recognition and attention in *Matter and Memory.* To recognize an object is to revive a past memory of it and note its resemblance to the present object. Such recognition is most often automatic and unconscious, unlike the recognition that occurs when we consciously pay attention to an object and its various characteristics. Automatic recognition is "a recognition of which the body alone is capable, without the intervention of any explicit memory. It consists of an action, and not of a representation" (1959, 238; 1911, 109–10). To recognize an object in this sense "is above all to know how to use it" (1959, 239; 1911, 111). When I first walk through a city, everything is strange and unfamiliar, but after living in the city for years, I unconsciously recognize its streets and buildings as I automatically find my way from home to the office, the store, and so forth. My recognition is part of a sensori-motor pattern that I act as much as I think, so much so that my perception of the city and my recognition of the city—my automatic recollection of it—become one. In attentive recognition, when I consciously pay attention to an object, I summon up a remembered image of the object and superimpose it on the perceived object. Such recognition presupposes "a *reflection,* that is, the external projection of an image, actively created, identical or similar to the object, and which comes to mold itself on the contours of the object" (1959, 248; 1911 124). But *all* perception involves a similar projection of remembered images, Bergson argues. Perceiving is like reading a text. We do not read letter by letter, but phrase by phrase, detecting physical traits on the page yet simultaneously anticipating words to come. Reading "is a veritable work of divination, our mind gathering here and there characteristic traits and filling every interval with memory-images which, projected onto the paper, are substituted for the characters actually printed on the paper and give us the illusion of being there" (1959, 249; 1911, 126). Walking familiar city streets is no different; it involves both a reception of stimuli and a projection of memory-images. "Our distinct perception is truly comparable to a closed circle, in which the perception-image directed onto the mind and the memory-image launched into space run one after the other" (1959, 249; 1911, 126). Indeed, in the automatic recognition of everyday perception the perception-image and memory-image occur in the same instant (1959, 238; 1911, 109).

Attentive recognition, then, does not differ qualitatively from automatic recognition. In both cases, we summon up a memory-image and project it onto the object. In attentive recognition, the object and each memory-image we summon up together form a circuit, "as in an electric circuit" (1959, 249; 1911, 127). As we pay closer attention to the object, we summon up memory-images from broader and more distant past contexts, each wider context encompassing the narrower. In his diagram **113** of the process (Fig. 1), Bergson labels the object O and the memory-image "closest to immediate perception" A. Memory-images B, C, and D form increasingly larger circuits with O, each larger circle encompassing the smaller. The memory-images B, C, and D are projected onto the object O, thereby forming B′, C′, and D′, which are "situated behind the object, and virtually given with the object itself" (1959 250; 1911, 128). (There is no A′ corresponding to A, since the most immediate memory-image is inseparable and indistinguishable from the object itself.) The process of attentive recognition thus "has the effect of creating anew, not simply the perceived object, but the more and more vast systems to which it can be connected; such that, as the circles B, C, D represent a higher expansion of memory, their reflection attains in B′, C′, D′ deeper layers [*des couches plus profondes*] of reality" (1959, 250; 1911, 128).

Deleuze uses Bergson's analysis of automatic and attentive recognition in two related ways, first as a means of approaching opsigns, and then as a framework for dealing with the cinematic flashback. In attentive recognition, the sensori-motor schema is relaxed. The habitual linkage of memory and perception within action, such as the automatic mingling of memory-images and perception-images when I read a page or walk a

Figure 1

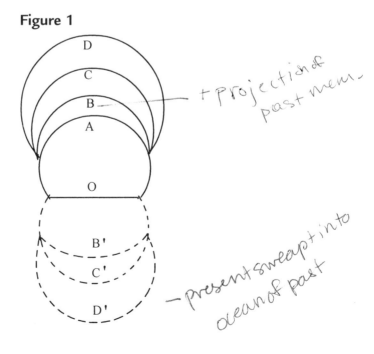

familiar street, ceases for a moment, and a present object O forms circuits with memory-images B, C, and D, which are then projected onto the object and "virtually given with the object itself" (1959, 250; 1911, 128). Similarly, Deleuze argues, in the pure optical situation the sensori-motor schema is suspended, and an object gives rise to a virtual image—often, a memory, a dream, or a thought. In *Europa 51,* the heroine looks at the factory and registers a look of incomprehension. Later, she says that at that moment she thought she saw crowds of condemned prisoners. In the alternation of images of the factory and shots of the heroine's reactions, then, we see the circuit of an actual image and a virtual thought. Of course, one may object that the heroine's face is as much an actual object as the factory, and indeed we may say that in one sense the montage of factory and facial expressions is simply a *representation* of the circuit of actual object and virtual thought. But the factory is presented in a way that complicates this view. It is shot as an abstract composition of dynamic geometrical forms, whose functions and purposes are largely unclear. The factory in this regard is an impoverished object, deprived of the characteristics that might make it a complete, understandable entity, but at the same time, it is an object full of potentially noteworthy characteristics, if we simply knew what to make of it. It has a singular, insistent presence to it, an arresting palpability, but it also seems somehow strange and unreal, dreamlike, hallucinatory. Bergson says that in recognition, actual perception-images and virtual memory-images "run one after another" and in fact occur simultaneously in any instant of action-perception (such as reading a sentence or walking a street). Likewise, in the pure optical situation the actual and the virtual "run one after another" (IT 65; 46) and "tend *at the limit* to become confused in falling into a same point of indiscernibility" (IT 65; 46). In Fellini and Antonioni, Deleuze finds an alternation of virtual and actual (subjective/objective, mental/physical, imaginary/real) tending toward a point of indiscernibility, and that same tendency can be seen in the coalescence of actual/palpable and virtual/hallucinatory qualities of *Europa 51*'s factory images.

Bergson's diagram of attentive recognition also serves Deleuze as a model of the flashback, which is "precisely a closed circuit that goes from the present to the past, then brings us back to the present" (IT 67; 48). In films like Carné's *Daybreak* (*Le Jour se lève*), the story is told through flashbacks, a present narrative of a murder (AO, in Bergson's diagram) alternating with past memories of the events contributing to the hero's jealous act of rage (in this case, the past memories proceeding chrono-logically toward the present: AO-D-AO-C-AO-B) such that the present situation attains "deeper levels of reality" (B′, C′, D′). In the standard flashback, past memory-images are integrated with present action-images in a single narrative, but Deleuze discerns in the apparently con-ventional narratives of *Daybreak* and the films of Joseph Mankiewicz a creative use of flashbacks that points toward the development of a gen-uine time-image. As Bazin shows at length, the flashbacks of *Daybreak* form part of a realistic story, but they also have their own logic. The music, with its alternation of lyrical strains and insistent, percussive rhythms, the *mise en scène,* the objects in the hotel room that serve as mementos of past events (the brooch, the teddy bear), the dialogue pat-terns linking past scenes to one another, the gestures of the actors, the actors themselves (especially Jean Gabin, known to his audiences for his roles as an explosive, elemental type)—all contribute to a sense of inevitability. "The realism of the *mise en scéne,* the characters, the intrigue, the décor, the dialogue is only a pretext" (*Le Cinéma français* 68) for a destiny that structures the past and compels it into the present. It is destiny, says Deleuze, "that exceeds determinism and causality, that traces a super-linearity, that gives at once a necessity to the flashback and a mark of the past to the memory-images" (IT 67; 48).

In Mankiewicz, "the greatest flashback *auteur*" (IT 68; 48), memory-images are also given their own "necessity," their own mode of connection—that of a "bifurcation of time" (IT 68; 49). In one of Deleuze's favorite stories, Borges's "Garden of Forking Paths," the narrator tells of a tem-poral labyrinth in which time diverges into branching paths at each point that individuals make decisions. A path of events is traced as per-son A stabs person B, but down a complementary forking path A does not stab B, and the two paths coexist, each path forking into other divergent paths until a labyrinth of all possibilities is formed. Mankiewicz's flashback films, *All About Eve, Letter to Three Wives,* and *The Barefoot Contessa,* like Carné's *Daybreak,* may be subsumed within a con-ventional narrative chronology, but implicit (and only implicit) within their flashback scenes is a bifurcating time. In each film, past memories are distributed among multiple narrators (two in *All About Eve,* three in *Letter to Three Wives* and three in *The Barefoot Contessa*), and each narrative strand proceeds by a branching path. These are commercial Hollywood films, of course, and hence no mutually contradictory paths are shown, but the crucial events in the films are bifurcations, unpredictable breaks in the straight lines of causality. In *Letter to Three Wives,* the points of rupture are imperceptible as the three wives ask themselves at what juncture their marriages went wrong. In *All About Eve,* the breaks are clear: Eve's initial meeting with the great star Margo Channing, her attempted seduction of Margo's fiancé, her alliance with the critic Addison, her manipulation and blackmail of Karen, her seduction of Karen's husband. Eve's driving ambition provides the events with narrative continuity, but each event is an improvisatory moment, a zigzag movement toward stardom, "a new rupture of causality, which itself bifurcates with the preceding, in a collection of non-linear relations" (IT 69; 49). What we see in the flashbacks are the residual traces of a branching time, the actual paths taken of a virtually forking labyrinth of coexisting paths. It is this bifurcating maze of time that gives the flashbacks their inner logic, their "necessity," their "reason" (IT 68; 49).

In conventional flashbacks, a commonsense chronology integrates past and present, and in this regard they are like all memory-images as Bergson conceived them. When we remember, we figuratively leap from the actual present into a virtual past, find a virtual memory-image, and then bring it into the actual present. For the most part, only those memory-images that have a practical value enter consciousness, and they do so on the condition that they become assimilated within our ongoing sensori-motor actions. But in dreams, argues Bergson, we have glimpses of the true nature of memory and the virtual past. When we are asleep, our sensori-motor system is at its most relaxed, and our mental world is filled with images from various moments of our past, all coexisting in a single domain. For Bergson, then, actual memories and dreams mark the ends of a continuum through which we encounter the virtual past. At one end, that of actual memory, the past contracts into a present moment; at the other, that of dreams, the past dilates into a broad expanse.

In the classic cinema, Deleuze observes, occasional experiments with dream images can be found, various special effects or unconventional editing techniques signaling their appearance, a general logic of substitution leading from one image to the next (city lights dissolving into stars into candles on a cake). At times, the dreamer's movements seem to extend into the surrounding world, as when the walls of a street rush forward as the dreamer runs in terror. And at such moments, we find "a sort of 'worlding' [*mondialisation*] or 'societing' [*mondanisation*], depersonalizing, pronominalizing of lost or impeded movement" such that "the world takes upon itself the movement the subject can no longer or cannot execute" (IT 80–81; 59). Yet for the most part dream-images, like flashbacks, are eventually integrated within a common-sense, waking time-space. In Hollywood musicals, however, dreamlike images are a constitutive part of the form, Deleuze argues. In the dance sequences and musical numbers of Busby Berkeley, Stanley Donen, and Vincent Minnelli, narrative time is suspended, objects and people are conjoined in improbable combinations and configurations, and space is frequently metamorphosed as one setting flows into another. Here, movement is depersonalized and pronominalized on a broad scale. The dancer "passes from a personal motricity to a super-personal element, to a movement of the world that the dancer traces" (IT 83; 61). The dancer enters the dance as one enters a dream, and in the alternation of dramatic action and music/dance the world tends to take on the appearance of one gigantic dream. If we return to Bergson's diagram of attentive recognition, we can say that the ongoing dramatic action corresponds to AO, and the music/dance sequences to oniric world-movements marked by the circuits B, C, and D. And in the great musicals—Deleuze is particularly fond of Minnelli—the alternation of AO-B-AO-C-AO-D tends toward "a point of indiscernibility of the real and the imaginary" (IT 87; 64).

HYALOSIGNS

Conventional flashbacks and dream sequences may tend toward a point of indiscernibility, but seldom do they arrive there. Indeed, they generally are subsumed within a structure that separates the actual and the virtual. But in some images, claims Deleuze, we see the point of indiscernibility itself—in what he calls time crystals, whose corresponding signs are hyalosigns (from Greek *hyalos,* glass). Bergson once again provides Deleuze with much of the scaffolding for his analysis. In a 1908 essay titled "The Memory of the Present and False Recognition," Bergson examines the uncanny phenomenon of déjà-vu and concludes that this uneasy and vague sense of having already experienced a present event stems from the fundamental nature of time, perception, and memory. Memories are commonly thought of as mere faded perceptions, either quantitatively or qualitatively impoverished versions of actual present sense experiences (i.e., versions either less intense or with fewer qualities). If this were the case, however, we would be unable to distinguish actual faint or sketchy perceptions from the weaker or less complex versions of intense or rich perceptions that constitute memories, which is absurd. Bergson thus argues that memories and perceptions must be qualitatively different from one another. He then asks, When is a memory formed? And his conclusion is that such an event must take place in the present—in the future makes no sense, and if at some juncture in the past, there would remain a memoryless "dead zone" between the present and whatever point in the past one should choose as the initial moment of memory formation. There must, then, be a "memory of the present," a virtual memory-image that coexists with each perception-image in the present, a virtual double that is like a reflection in a mirror: "our actual existence, as it unfolds in time, is thus doubled [se double] by a virtual existence, by a mirror image" (1959, 917; 1920, 165). The present "doubles itself at every instant, in its very gushing forth [dans son jaillissement même], into two symmetrical streams [jets, as in jets or streams of water], one of which falls back toward the past while the other leaps forward toward the future" (1959, 914; 1920, 160). The present divides into two parts—indeed, it "consists of that splitting [scission] itself" (1959, 917; 1920, 165). The present is that "fleeing limit between the immediate past that is no longer and the immediate future that is not yet," a "mobile mirror that ceaselessly reflects perception in memory" (1959, 917-18; 1920, 165). And that memory of the present cannot logically be anything other than "the totality of what we see, hear, experience, everything that we are with everything that surrounds us" (1959, 918; 1911, 166).

How might we intuitively grasp this effect of doubling? Bergson takes the example of a school lesson he once learned by heart but had long forgotten, which one day he is suddenly able to repeat in a nearly mechanical manner. He finds himself divided into two individuals, one of whom observes the other as if he were on a stage. The self that repeats the lesson is like "an actor who recites a role," the other, "conscious of his liberty, becomes a spectator independent of a scene that the other plays in a mechanical manner" (1959, 920; 1920, 169). In such experiences, as observers we feel free and real, whereas as actors we are converted "into automata," transported "into a theater-world or a dream-world" (1959, 920; 1920, 169-70). This sensation of oniric automatism, of being an actor playing a role, is frequently mentioned in accounts of déjà-vu, and Bergson concludes that the sensation stems from the very real doubling of the present—in perception, which forms part of our ongoing, largely unconscious sensori-motor action (the automaton/actor), and in memory, which is mental, reflective, free from the constraints of action, but also passive (the spectator). We must note, however, as Deleuze insists, that Bergson's virtual domain of memory, though mental and reflective, is not that of a personal subjectivity. In his first book, Bergson does conceive of memory in terms of an individual consciousness, but in *Matter and Memory* and *Creative Evolution* he argues that the past preserves itself by and in itself ("En réalité, le passé se conserve de lui-même, automatiquement" [1959, 498; 1913, 5]), that the past coexists as a single domain and hence as a kind of gigantic memory. Memory is not inside the individual mind, but each mind is inside memory, like a fish in the ocean. The ocean of memory is the virtual past, which gushes forth at each present moment in a perpetual foundation of time. In this sense, as Deleuze phrases it, "time is not inside us, but just the contrary—time is the interiority in which we are, in which we move, live and change" (IT 110; 82).

In Bergson's schema of attentive recollection, the smallest circuit is labeled AO, and the absence of an A' is explained by the fact that perception, when seized in this narrowest instant of the present, allows of no clear separation of A from O. The present is immediately double, an actual present perception and a virtual memory of the present, a mobile mirror that *is* the ongoing splitting and coexistence of the actual and virtual, physical and mental, present and past. Though expressed as two terms, AO is a two-in-one, a *point* of indiscernibility. Like a mirror image that joins actual object and virtual reflection, the point of indiscernibility is an "objective illusion," not something simply "in our heads"; it is a real doubling in which virtual and actual are distinct but unassignable, in a relation of "mutual presupposition" or "reversibility" (IT 94; 69).

How might we recognize a cinematic point of indiscernibility? What is this "coalescence of the actual image and the virtual image," this "bifaced image, actual and virtual at the same time" (IT 93; 69)? In a first approximation, Deleuze says, "it is as if an image in a mirror, a photo, a postcard came to life, became independent and passed into the actual, even if the actual image went back into the mirror, took up its place in the postcard or the photo, following a double movement of liberation and capture" (IT 93; 68). Such an image Deleuze likens to a description of an object in a Robbe-Grillet *nouveau roman*, which, in Robbe-Grillet's words, "is accomplished in a double movement of creation and erasure" (Robbe-Grillet 1962, 127). In what Deleuze calls an "organic" description, such as one finds in nineteenth-century realistic fiction (and in its counterpart, the classic cinema), the object described is presumed to exist independently of the description. A "crystalline" description, by contrast, is one "which counts for its object, which replaces it, creates it and erases it at the same time, as Robbe-Grillet says, and ceaselessly gives way to other descriptions that contradict, displace or modify the preceding ones" (IT 165; 126). Crystalline descriptions "reflect [*renvoient à*] purely optical and sonorous situations, detached from their motor continuation" (IT 166; 126). The crystal-image, one might conclude at this juncture, is simply another name for the opsign—the purely optical situation—but Deleuze specifies that if the opsign is detached from the sensori-motor schema, it does not necessarily bring virtual and actual together in a single point of indiscernibility. The crystal-image is the "genetic element," the " 'heart' of opsigns and their compositions," whereas opsigns "are nothing more than the shattered splinters [*des éclats*] of the crystal-image" (IT 93–94; 69).

The crystal-image, then, is the genetic element of opsigns, something like an animated mirror-reflection, photograph or postcard, an image detached from the sensori-motor schema in which there is no means of distinguishing the object from its description. It would seem at this point that Deleuze is confusing two questions, one of "objective illusions," such as mirror images, and one of "representation," or the relationship between an object in the world and its semiotic representation, such as that of a photograph, postcard, painting, or prop on a stage. But the second question presumes a clear distinction between objective reality and its description, and that distinction is made possible only by the existence of a sensori-motor schema. With its collapse, Deleuze argues, there is no means of differentiating presentation from re-presentation; the object and its appearance—whether in a visual image, mirror image, photo, postcard, painting, or stage prop—are one. No longer are there objects and their mechanical or artistic representations, but simply images. Hence, as Deleuze develops the concept of the crystal-image he moves insensibly from optical illusions to artistic illusions, speaking first of objects and their mirror reflections, and then of actors and their roles, as means of understanding the coalescence of virtual and actual in a single image.

Bergson says that the "memory of the present" is a virtual reflection of the actual present, and that in the rare moments when we encounter the present's doubling of virtual and actual we are like actors watching ourselves on a stage. Deleuze suggests that in the crystal-image we are not simply *like* actors, but we *are* actors—that all the world is a stage, not in the traditional sense of baroque *desengaño* (the disillusioned recognition that life is a dream) but in the sense that in the absence of a sensori-motor schema the world becomes a theater/spectacle/film of animated reflections/photos/postcards, a play of images in which virtual and actual are indiscernible because they coexist in the real (and not just "in our heads"). This rapprochement of optical mirrors and mimetic enactments, we should note, leads Deleuze to treat the elements of crystal-image films as "reflections" in the broadest sense of the term. At times he speaks of actual mirror images in such films, at others of mechanical reproductions of images in photos, films, or video clips. But he also treats paintings and theatrical performances as reflections of objects, extending the notion as well to include simulations, mimings, and the enactment of roles as so many mirror images. Finally, he treats resemblances and correspondences between objects, settings, characters, and actions as reflections—perhaps prismatically distorted, tinted, bleached or clouded, but reflections nonetheless.

The simplest model of the crystal-image is that of a reflection in a mirror. When Garbo looks at herself in the mirror, she is the actual image, her reflection the virtual image, and the two are co-present. The image on the screen, of course, is itself an "animated photo," a celluloid "reflection" of Garbo before the mirror, one in which Garbo and mirror (the actual) and the celluloid stock (the virtual) were at one point co-present. She is also an actress playing a role (say Ninotchka). Garbo the finite, physical human being is in this regard the actual image, her role a virtual image that she is actualizing in the film. And again, virtual and actual, Ninotchka and Garbo, are co-present. Further, the role she is playing is part of a fictional world that reflects the real world, the fictional world being initially virtual in relation to the actual real world, but becoming actual as it is performed and recorded on film. The situation is quite mundane, and my account of it hopelessly naïve—as long as the sensori-motor schema is in place. Once it collapses, however, the distinctions between object and reflection, physical entity and its celluloid recording, actor and role, real world and fictional world become indiscernible—not muddled, but unassignable in the sense that one can no longer determine definitively the category to which a given image belongs. Thus, in Deleuze's analysis, when directors systematically play with the relationship between acting and being, stage world and real world, film and reality, they are not simply questioning art's function as a re-presentation of reality. They are seeing the world as a proliferation of *reflections,* objective illusions that are coalescences of the actual and the virtual produced by the perpetual scission of time into the Bergsonian actual present and the virtual "memory of the present" that extends into the entirety of the virtual past.

Though the mirror image provides us with a figure of the *simultaneity* of the virtual and the actual, there is a temporality inherent in the presentation of the virtual and the actual. When we see Garbo's mirror reflection on the screen, her virtual reflection is the actual image before us. Perhaps we see the back of her head as well as her reflected image, but to see the "real Garbo" from the same vantage as she appears in the reflected image requires a reverse shot directly focused on her face. We could put her between two mirrors, of course, and thereby capture two views at once—the front and back of her head—but this would simply multiply the mirror reflections ad infinitum (as well as compound the problem of right-left inversion created by mirror images). The "actual" Garbo image and her virtual reflection, thus, must succeed one another in time. Yet if we follow a direct shot of Garbo's face (actual) with a shot of her reflection (the virtual corresponding to that initial actual shot), in the reflection shot the actual image before us is the mirror image, and she has become the virtual, off-camera counterpart of the image. What was actual has become virtual, and vice versa; the two have become reversed. An exchange of virtual and actual has taken place, and the sequence of direct-shot and reflection-shot constitutes a circuit of exchange, a back-and-forth passage from image to image.

Yet in the crystal-image there is no "originary" Garbo from which the reflection arises, but simply another image, another reflection. Garbo between two mirrors, rather than before a single mirror, is in this regard a more accurate way to envision the crystal-image's exchange circuit of virtual and actual, each reflection leading to another in an open-ended sequence of reflections. Even better, if we were to increase the number of mirrors to, say, twelve, position them to form a dodecagon with Garbo and the invisible camera eye in the middle, we would see a proliferation of reflections images (as in the famous funhouse sequence at the end of Welles's *The Lady from Shanghai,* in which the images of Bannister and his wife are multiplied in dozens of thin vertical facets as the two characters confront one another within the hall of mirrors). Form a three-dimensional dodecahedron with the twelve mirrors, and we would have a crystal, with multifaceted mirror surfaces capable of multiplying and interrelating images in countless complex patterns and structures.

This is one reason Deleuze speaks of a crystal-image rather than a simple mirror image. But the crystal figure serves two additional purposes. The surfaces of a crystal may be reflective, yet they may also be glasslike and transparent; they may refract light or reflect it, filter, tint, cloud, or block it. The crystal's facets thus may be said to possess varying degrees of limpidity or opacity, the state of a given facet varying with its surrounding conditions (such as temperature), becoming transparent one moment and opaque the next. Thus, in the crystal-image, "when the virtual image becomes actual, it is then visible and limpid," as when we see Garbo's reflection-image on the screen. But "in turn the actual image becomes virtual, sent elsewhere, invisible, opaque and shadowy," like the invisible off-camera Garbo. As a result, "the actual-virtual couple thus immediately extends into the opaque-limpid, the expression of their exchange" (IT 95; 70). Finally, the crystal figure suggests a genetic dimension to the unfolding of the virtual and the actual. Certain liquid solutions may be crystallized by the introduction of a "seed crystal," a single crystal that initiates a process of crystal formation which extends until the entire solution is solidified in myriad replicated versions of the initial seed. And some such solutions may lend themselves to more than one form of crystallization, depending on the nature of the seed crystal introduced. Deleuze argues that crystal-images may likewise be regarded in terms of their genesis, certain images functioning as seeds that proliferate in a milieu. The seed-image serves as a virtual that is actualized in a given milieu, but at the same time the milieu is a virtual domain of potential crystallization that may or may not be conducive to a given seed's power of actualization.

Deleuze concludes that "exchange or indiscernibility thus proceeds in three ways in the crystalline circuit: the actual and the virtual (or two mirrors face to face); the limpid and the opaque; the seed and the milieu" (IT 96; 71). Given that crystalline circuits involve temporal sequences of images, it is not surprising that the examples Deleuze offers of these circuits are not those of isolated moments. Indeed, as one considers Deleuze's examples, it becomes evident that his object in developing this triad of actual/virtual, limpid/opaque and seed/milieu is not so much to describe individual shots and sequences as to treat entire films as crystals. Each film, we might say, is like an astronaut film crew's exploration of a multifaceted, gemlike planet. The crew members orbit the planet, taking various shots of its surfaces. They land, traverse different planes, then penetrate the planet's outer surfaces and film shimmering and shifting prismatic reflections from within the planet, the facets changing tints, growing foggy, opalescent, silvery, or transparent. They follow the process of crystallization as a seed crystal spreads into a milieu; they record the shattering of a facet, the powdery disintegration of another, the liquid dissolution of a third. And the record of this journey (creatively edited to problematize spatio-temporal continuities, of course) is the completed film, a set of images that as a whole comprise a giant crystal-image.

One such crystal planet that Deleuze describes is Fellini's *And the Ship Sails On*. From the beginning we see a world of appearances and semblances, representations and performances. The initial images are like a silent-era newsreel recording the arrival of an opera company at a dock; a still photographer and motion-picture cameraman who record the event themselves appear in the footage. When the company arrives, the sound of the clicking silent-film projector is supplemented by music as the opera soloists break into song, and the crowd joins in as if it were a chorus in a musical. The gray and sepia tones gradually give way to color images, the passengers ascend the gangway, and the ship-world comes to life. In the kitchen, the cooks and waiters perform a frenetic dance, the fast-motion images accompanied by the second theme of the Nutcracker Suite's Dance of the Reed Pipes; as the waiters enter the dining room, the ballet gradually retards as the graceful opening theme of the Reed Pipes plays over the slow-motion shots of the diners sipping soup in synchronized motions. A reflective correspondence is established between the artistic and aristocratic passenger audience and the proletarian crew performers, between the limpid stagelike dining room and the backstage kitchen, with an obscure, infernal engine room fleetingly disclosed below. When the opera singers visit the engine room, the

virtual depths become actual and the performer-audience relation
between crew and passengers is reversed, as the tenors and divas proudly
compete in singing above the din of the clanging engines while the stok-
ers listen and applaud. With the appearance on deck of the Serbs, who
had been rescued from a shipwreck, a new reflective circuit emerges, one
between the rich paying passengers and the destitute refugees, the two
entering into a back-and-forth exchange of positions when the passengers gradually join the Serbs in a late-night Balkan dance; "here again,
the exchange takes place between the actual and the virtual, the limpid
and the opaque, in a musical arrangement à la Bartók" (IT 99; 73). The
Serbs also function as a seed-crystal, an incipient socio-political element
that gradually expands to connect the floating pleasure ship to the historical world when the Austro-Hungarian flagship appears on the horizon with a demand for the surrender of the refugees.[2] The somber,
granular-greenish warship and the glittering liner mirror one another,
and as they near and open a circuit of semaphore communications, an
accelerating exchange of shots brings the two together in shifting combinations of limpidity and obscurity. When the cruise ship eventually
shatters and sinks under the warship's bombardment, the crystalline
liner dissolves into the sea, "an eternally amorphous milieu" (IT 99; 73).
Amid the smoke and clouds of the sinking ship, a reverse tracking shot
reveals Fellini's crew filming the simulated disaster in the studios of
Cinecittà, followed by a closing iris shot in sepia tones of the film's narrator in a lifeboat seated by a rhinoceros saved from the liner's hold.

CRYSTALLINE STATES

And the Ship Sails On combines several standard techniques for rendering
indiscernible the division between art and life: the film within the film
(the newsreel footage), the film in the making (Fellini's crew on the
sound stage), the world as theater (the engine-room concert), as narrative (Orlando, the journalist-cum-narrator, directly addressing the camera), as ritual (the funeral service for Edmea Tetua, the count's stateroom
shrine for the late diva), as dance (the dining room ballet, the topside
folk dance). Within this hall of mirrors, various elements reflect one
another—passengers and crew, performers and audience, artists and
aristocrats, official passengers and refugees, warship and cruise ship.
Throughout, virtual reflection and actual image exchange positions,

one growing limpid as another becomes obscure, a seed image now spreading to a larger milieu, a crystal now dissolving into an amorphous solution. The film itself is a massive crystal-image, and its construction proceeds along various circuits of exchange among indiscernibles. Though the pathways are multiple, "it is the same circuit that passes via three figures, the actual and the virtual, the limpid and the opaque, the seed and the milieu" (IT 100; 74).

Besides these three "figures" Deleuze differentiates as well several "states of the crystal." In his review of time-images at the close of *Cinema 2*, Deleuze indicates that "crystalline signs or hyalosigns concern properties (the three aspects of the exchange)," whereas "crystal-images" properly speaking "concern states of the crystal" (IT 358; 333). The distinction between sign and image here is evidently one between components and kinds of crystals. The three hyalosigns—actual/virtual, limpid/obscure, seed/milieu—are constituents of every crystal; in this sense, they are properties or "elements of the crystal" (IT 110; 82). Crystal-images, by contrast, may be of various types—like amethysts, azurites, malachites, tourmalines—differentiable as "states of the crystal." Among an open-ended number of such "states of the crystal," Deleuze isolates four, and each of these "crystalline states . . . we can now call a *crystal of time*" (IT 110; 82). Crystalline states are crystals of *time* not simply because they disclose the coexistence of actual present and virtual past in every moment—hyalosigns do this, too—but because they reveal different ways in which the whole of that great ocean of the virtual past may be related to the ongoing actualization of time in a present moving toward a future.

If Deleuze paints with broad strokes in characterizing hyalosigns, treating whole films as crystals, his strokes are even broader in delineating the four crystalline states, each state being exemplified by a director's entire oeuvre. The first state is that of the perfect crystal, represented by the cinema of Max Ophuls. Ophuls's vision of the world as spectacle and theater is perhaps most evident in *La Ronde*, which opens with a character shrouded in fog, mounting the steps of what seems a theater stage with proscenium arch, but what proves to be a semicircular soundstage platform, along which he walks until he passes imperceptibly from a patently artificial street scene set into a "realistic" Viennese arcade. As he strolls, he asks, am I the narrator or the author? "I am you," he says, "I see everything because I see completely [*parce que* rator providing spoken or written titles for each story, playing various minor roles within each episode, and between scenes singing of the *ronde* of love as he tends to the machinery of a spinning merry-go-round. With the final tale, he reverses his steps along the Viennese arcade, across the arched soundstage and into the fog. Each episode reflects the other, each a variation of the round of love, and all are scenes from the great operetta of life.

A similar seamless interchange of spectacle and reality informs *Lola Montès,* the narrative presented through an alternation of past scenes from the scandalous dancer's life and present tableaux of those episodes in a circus pageant starring Lola herself. Circular movements dominate the circus tableaux, Lola often seated at the center of a rotating plat-form with animals and players circling in the reverse direction, the var-ious scenes of Lola's life at one point being presented as a circle of wagon-platforms, each mounted with a model of a city's landmark. The past "real" episodes and present tableaux echo one another, the real past proving to be a mere repetition with variations of a pageant perform-ance. In both *La Ronde* and *Lola Montès* we see a perfect crystal, a self-contained series of reflections: "the actual image and the virtual image coexist and crystallize; they enter into a circuit that constantly takes us from one to the other; they form a single and same 'scene' in which the characters belong to the real and yet play a role. In short, it is the real as a whole, the entirety of life, that has become spectacle" (IT 112; 83–84). Time in this crystal is circular, rolled in upon itself, perpetually repeat-ing itself. In *La Ronde* the repetition is genial, but in *Lola Montès* it is grim, the inescapability of her destiny being inscribed in the structure of time, shown here as a double movement—of flashback events, each a discrete unit of the past unfolding in its own present, tending toward an inevitable circus future; and of a coexisting past, collected and retained in the circling tableaux of the present circus pageant.

If in Ophuls the crystal is perfect, in Jean Renoir it is "cracked" (*fêlé*) with "a fault, a line of flight, a 'flaw' " (IT 113; 85). Like Ophuls, Renoir is intrigued by spectacle and the theater, and much of his work tends toward "a theatricality in its pure state" (IT 113; 84). This is perhaps no more evident than in *The Golden Coach,* the story of a commedia dell'arte troupe's arrival and establishment in a primitive Spanish colony in Latin America. The film opens with credits over a painting of a theater curtain, which dissolves to a similar real curtain, which in turn rises on what seems a theater scene, but is shown to be the grand staircase of the viceroy's palace. Throughout the film, the troupe's burlesque stage antics parallel the real-world comic plot, in which three suitors, an aristocrat soldier, a bullfighter, and the viceroy, pursue Camilla, the troupe's principal actress. Late in the action, Camilla asks, "Where does the theater end and life begin?" And at the film's close, the camera pulls back to the opening grand staircase, framed by a proscenium arch, the citizens of the colony posed on the upper landing, the commedia troupe dancing on the lower. As the curtain drops behind Camilla, the troupe's leader tells her, "Don't waste your time in the so-called real life. You belong to us, the actors, acrobats, mimes, clowns, mountebanks." Yet in Renoir, unlike Ophuls, though world and stage mirror one another, there is life beyond the theater, Deleuze insists. By the end of *The Golden Coach,* though Camilla remains a commedia player,[3] the three suitors have found their proper functions in the world. The roles of our stage world ultimately are means of rehearsing, experimenting, and testing various possibilities, but only so that we may escape theater and enter life. And the point of entry is through a crack, a line of flight, in the crystal of time.

That crack is not always apparent, Deleuze observes, for there is a pessimistic streak in Renoir. *The Rules of the Game,* for example, seems a perfect, self-contained crystal. There, the aristocrats' amateur vaudeville stage is but a miniature of the larger social stages of the chateau and the allegorical hunting fields. Actual and virtual coexist in multiple reflections, living beings reflected in automata (the mechanical figures on the marquis' giant music machine), humans reflected in animals (the rabbits and pheasants of the hunt), the aristocrats reflected in the servants and the servants in the aristocrats (most evident in the parallel chases of upper-class and lower-class couples and rivals during the vaudeville performance). In this complex of reflections, no escape seems possible, save that of death. The Marquise Geneviève manages to leave with neither Jurieu nor Octave, but returns to the chateau and her husband, while Jurieu is mistakenly shot and killed by the jealous Schumacher. The characters are trapped by "the rules of the game," the weight of the past embodied in social norms and conventions. Yet in other films, a movement beyond the theater of custom and fixed roles seems possible—in *Grand Illusion* de Boïeldieu and Von Rauffenstein remain within the aristocratic past, but Maréchal and Rosenthal escape the prison camp to freedom, and in *The River* the adolescent Harriet matures by going beyond the conventional poses of love and surrendering her infatuation with Captain John. For Renoir, the past accumulates, congeals, stultifies, and fixes. "Everything that is past falls back into the crystal, and stays there: it is the collection of frozen, fixed, readymade, too-conforming roles that the characters try on one after another, dead roles or roles of death, the *danse macabre* of memories of which Bergson speaks" (IT 116; 87). Yet this crystal of inter-reflecting roles is split, like the Bergsonian present, that "scission" in which two jets of time come gushing forth, a virtual past that preserves itself as a great ocean of memory, and an onrushing present pushing into a future. The virtual past is a force of death for Renoir, a theater of frozen and imprisoning roles, but in rehearsing different roles a character on occasion is able to emerge into an unfixed future, a genuine life beyond the theater. "Time in the crystal is differentiated into two movements, but one of the two takes charge of the future and freedom, on condition that it leave the crystal. Thus, the future will be created at the same time that it escapes the eternal recurrence [*renvoi*] of the actual and the virtual, of the present and the past" (IT 117; 88).

In Fellini Deleuze finds a third crystalline state, that of the crystal "grasped in its formation or its growth, related to the 'seeds' that compose it" (IT 117; 88). From *8½* on, Fellini's world seems a grand carnival of sideshow attractions, a universal exposition of pavilions and displays, spectacles and parades, tableaux, pageants, pantomimes, and clown shows.[4] Each scene or setting is like the entrance to a different pavilion, a different world in the making, and yet one that communicates in a topologically enigmatic way with the ensuing pavilion. The entrance to each pavilion is a seed-crystal in the process of expanding into a milieu, and in the film's sequence of pavilions we see elements of a larger crystal in formation. The pavilions disclose different spaces (geographical, archaeological, theatrical) in various modes (perception, memory, fantasy, hallucination, fiction), and each film collects and connects its pavilions to form a separate world's fair, a single crystal which "is only the ordered collection of its seeds or the transversal of all its entrances" (IT 118; 89). Be it a city of women or a floating opera, a literary/mythological site (the ancient Mediterranean of *Satyricon*), a phantasmagoric historical milieu (*Casanova*'s debauched eighteenth-century

Europe), a circus of performance, memory, and dream (*The Clowns*), or a modern dreamscape of desire and anxiety (the complex of spa/launching pad/purgatorial corridors and catacombs of *8½*, the amalgam of boudoir, convent pageant, and oniric panoramas of *Juliet of the Spirits*), each film is a collection of inter-reflecting images in gestation and dissemination: "It is a crystal always in formation, in expansion, that crystallizes everything it touches, and that gives its seeds an indefinitely increasing power. It is life as spectacle, and yet in its spontaneity" (IT 119; 89).

If in Renoir the retentive virtual past is death and the propulsive present a force of life, in Fellini "it is the present, the parade of presents which pass, that constitutes the *danse macabre*" (IT 121; 91). Fellini's galleries of monsters and grotesques, his merciless images of sagging skin and spreading wrinkles, his various studies in corporeal decline and decay, all attest to a universal, headlong rush of time into the grave. If there is escape from this omnivorous propulsive present, it lies in the virtual past. Yet that escape occurs within the crystal of interrelated reflections, not outside it, and it takes place through an impersonal "pure memory," not through nostalgic reminiscence. Fellini frequently returns to childhood memories, Deleuze insists, not to recapture once-lived moments that have passed, but to create a dimension of coexisting pasts in which we are contemporaries with the children we have been, and the children themselves contemporary with other times past and to come. The time of Fellini's crystal-in-formation, thus, is one of a "present that passes and goes toward death," and a "past that conserves itself and retains the seed of life," and the two "ceaselessly interfere, cut into one another" (IT 122; 92).

Deleuze's fourth crystalline state is that of the crystal in dissolution, exemplified by the later films of Visconti. The world explored in these works is a self-enclosed, aristocratic domain of inherited wealth, an artificial realm cut off from history and nature. As in Ophuls, Renoir, and Fellini, we see here life as spectacle, especially in such scenes as the formal dance of *The Leopard,* the ritualized family dinner and theatricals of *The Damned,* the extended coronation ceremony of *Ludwig,* and the salon concert of *The Innocent*. The sumptuous visual compositions, the painterly handling of color, light, and shadow, and the near-balletic conception of music as continuous accompaniment to the images (one thinks especially of Visconti's use of Mahler in *Death in*

Venice and Wagner in *Ludwig*) emphasize the stylized, ritual, ceremonial nature of this rarefied world. Though elegant and refined, however, these crystalline milieus "are inseparable from a process of decomposition that undermines them from within, that renders them somber, opaque" (IT 125; 94). A time of decline and decay permeates these realms, an inherent decadence of bodies and souls. History impinges on this world, but only from without. The Prussians make war on Bavaria, yet they only hasten the process of dissolution internal to Ludwig and his kingdom. In *The Damned,* the S.S. troops massacre the S.A. revelers, but the revelers are already engaged in an orgiastic descent and decline when they are slaughtered.

In rare moments, it does seem possible that this process of dissolution might be suspended, that this artificial world might be connected to nature and history, as when the old prince dances with his nephew's fiancée and the two exchange glances of love in *The Leopard,* or when Aschenbach has his vision of sensual beauty in the adolescent Tadzio in *Death in Venice.* Yet such revelations always come too late, and indeed they form the most important element of the temporality of Visconti's time-crystal, for "the too-late is not an accident produced in time, it is a dimension of time itself" (IT 126; 96). Just as dissolution is inherent to this world, so too is the revelation of escape that always arrives after the fact. Amid the declining world's general deepening and darkening of colors and tones (quite literally manifest in the sequence of scenes charting Ludwig's decline), the revelation appears as "a sublime clarity, which is opposed to the opaque, but whose property it is to arrive too late, dynamically" (IT 127; 96). Like Ophuls's crystal, Visconti's is self-enclosed, but its time is unidirectional rather than cyclical. The onrushing present provides no line of flight, as in Renoir, and no disposition of the virtual past overcomes the present's inevitable decline, as in Fellini. Yet Deleuze sees in this temporality of dissolution and the perpetually too-late a final dimension that transforms it—the dimension of art. In this regard, Visconti is like Proust, who views every paradise as necessarily lost since it can be grasped only after it has happened, but who finds access through art to a *temps retrouvé.* In this sense, "the Beautiful truly becomes a dimension in Visconti" (IT 128; 97), a fourth dimension of the cinematic object.

In post-War American films Deleuze finds several symptoms of the sensori-motor schema's collapse—dispersive and disconnected space, wanderings, clichés, conspiracies—but only in Italian neorealism do pure optical and sonic situations emerge. These opsigns and sonsigns are moments uncharted within the coordinates of Newtonian space and chronological time. The flashbacks and dream scenes of the classic cinema suggest possibilities for interconnecting these pure optical and sonic situations, but only in rare instances—Mankiewicz's flashbacks and Minnelli's dream-world musicals—are virtual memories and dreams linked to an actual present through a time unrelated to some sensori-motor schema. In Mankiewicz and Minnelli, the virtual and actual alternate in circuits that tend toward a point of indiscernibility. That point, however, at which the actual present and its own virtual past coexist is visible only in time crystals, prismatic reflections in which actual and virtual are unassignable, each mirror image actualizing another virtual mirror image, each theater reflecting, filtering, or refracting another theater. Points of indiscernibility are simultaneously virtual and actual, but their manifestation is through three circuits of exchange: between actual and virtual, limpid and obscure, seed and milieu. These circuits characterize the three hyalosigns, and their interrelation and co-presence are apparent when entire films are regarded as crystals. Then, too, one can differentiate various crystalline states, or "crystal-images" properly speaking, each of which reveals a distinct way of envisioning the Bergsonian present's scission of time into the ocean of the virtual past and the onrushing stream of the actual present. In Ophuls's perfect crystal, a circular time provides a seamless connection of past and present; in Renoir's split crystal, the living present offers potential escape from the stultifying weight of the dead past; in Fellini's crystal in formation, the *danse macabre* of the present is countered by the non-personal memory of the past; and in Visconti's crystal in dissolution, past and present combine in an inexorable decline and an always-too-late revelation of other possibilities.

One might object that in Ophuls, Renoir, and Visconti, if not Fellini, we meet practitioners of the classic cinema, in that their films generally have coherent narratives that may be reconciled with the time-space of the sensori-motor schema. But narrative versus non-narrative is not the determining factor in separating classic and modern films, for in Deleuze's analysis even the narratives of the classic cinema are secondary products of a primary sensori-motor schema. What Deleuze identifies in Ophuls, Renoir, Fellini, and Visconti is a particular vision of the world-as-reflection, as infinite mirrorings, stagings, performances, spectacles, rites, and ceremonies. More than a mere theme, the world-as-reflection is a way of seeing and one that issues from a particular conception of time. Every moment forms a crystal as it perpetually splits into a virtual past and an actual present, and "the visionary, the seer, is the one who sees in the crystal, and what is seen is the gushing forth of time as doubling, as scission" (IT 109; 81). The world-as-reflection and the treatment of past and present may seem separate matters, but Deleuze argues that in these directors the two are one, that "seeing in the crystal" at once produces a vision of unassignable virtual/actual reflections and a vision of time as a particular mode of relating the virtual past and actual present as they emerge in the perpetual split of the ongoing present instant. The narratives of their films issue from this conception of time, and in each of their films we see a crystal with interreflecting facets of unassignable virtual/actual images and unassignable virtual/actual durations. In each crystal, we see a specific image of time.

Chapter Five

CHRONOSIGNS: THE ORDER OF TIME AND TIME AS SERIES

Hyalosigns are "mirrors or seeds of time" (IT 358; 274) that make present direct images of time. They render visible "the hidden foundation of time, that is, its differentiation into two streams, that of presents that pass and that of pasts that conserve themselves" (IT 129; 98). In these crystalline signs, the actual present and virtual past enter into circuits of exchange between the actual and virtual, real and imaginary, seed and milieu, such that the pairs of terms become indiscernible. Chronosigns, too, render visible direct time-images that combine past and present, virtual and actual, but such that "what is in play is no longer the real and the imaginary, but the true and the false" (IT 359; 274). In chronosigns, past and present, virtual and actual, are not indiscernible but "undecidable or inextricable" (IT 359; 274). Deleuze distinguishes two kinds of chronosigns, those that concern *the order of time* and those that concern *time as series* (IT 359; 274–5), and in both kinds, the true and the false are rendered undecidable or inextricable, in the one case through a coexistence or simultaneity of different times, in the other through "a becoming as potentialization, as series of powers [*puissances*]" (IT 360; 275). The task before us is to make sense of this complex of distinctions and see what bearing it might have on the classification and analysis of specific films.

As we have seen, the Bergsonian virtual past is a single dimension in which all past events coexist. The virtual past is produced at every present moment as a "memory of the present," a virtual double of each actual present. Bergson visualizes the virtual past as a cone, with its point representing the past's coincidence with the present, and its widening volume representing the ever-growing expanse of coexisting past events. In that our past is preserved within itself and surges forward into the present, we can say that each present moment is a contraction of the past, a concentration of the entire cone in the point of its apex. Conversely, the endless expanse of the past may be regarded as a dilation of the present, the cone's spreading volume issuing forth from the apex of each present moment. When we try to remember something, says Bergson, we place ourselves in the past straightaway, and then traverse "a series of different *planes of consciousness*" (1959, 369; 1911, 319) in search of the given memory (see Bergson's diagram, Fig. 2). Each plane is a cross section of the cone of the virtual past, a *nappe de souvenirs* (1959, 184; 1911, 25) or "sheet of memories" (as in a sheet of ice), a region of the past with its peculiar affective "tone" (1959, 308; 1911, 221) and its "dominant recollections, veritable brilliant points around which others form a vague nebulosity" (1959, 310; 1911, 223). These planes of the virtual past Deleuze calls

Figure 2

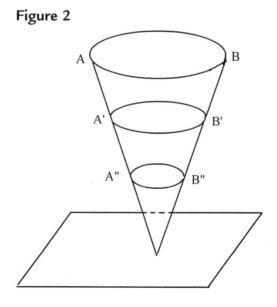

nappes de passé, "sheets of the past," and *gisements,* geological "layers" or "strata." "Between the past as pre-existence in general [i.e., the entire cone of the past that pre-exists every present moment] and the present as the infinitely contracted past [i.e., the apex of the cone], there are thus all the circles of the past [i.e., circular cross sections of the cone] which constitute so many stretched-out or shrunken *regions, layers, sheets:* each region with its proper characteristics, its 'tones,' its 'aspects,' its 'singularities,' its 'brilliant points,' its 'dominants' " (IT 130; 99). Hence, in the virtual past we find three basic paradoxes of a non-chronological time: "the pre-existence of a past in general" (the cone as a whole), "the co-existence of all the sheets of the past" (the cross sections), and "the existence of a most contracted degree" (the apex) (IT 130–31; 99).

With the concept of the virtual past, the past "counts for [*vaut*] the totality of time" (IT 129; 98), in that all dimensions of time may be characterized as different aspects of the past—the past itself as a "dilated past," the present as a "contracted past," the future as a "projected past."[1] But Deleuze argues that the present may also count for the totality of time. In developing this idea, Deleuze turns from Bergson to the phenomenologist Bernhard Groethuysen for inspiration. In a lengthy essay on the time of narration, Groethuysen argues that the past is the domain of facts, or "that which has been done," and hence the domain of knowledge, whereas the future is the domain of action, "that which will be done" and which cannot be known until it happens. The present in this sense is merely the meeting point of future actions and past facts, the juncture at which "things to do" become "things already done." Such a present "now" Groethuysen calls a "dialectical *nunc.*" But Groethuysen finds another function for the present besides that of a mere link between past and future, one fulfilled by an "intuitive *nunc.*" The present is the domain of vision, he claims. Seeing is always in the present. We see one object, then we see a second, and in this way the contents of seeing change, but the seeing itself remains unchanged. The changing objects of vision belong to the dialectical *nunc* and its succession of future-present-past occurrences, whereas the unchanging vision reveals an intuitive *nunc,* which "remains in a way outside the order of succession" (Groethuysen 168). The intuitive *nunc* is like a dramatic scene; it is an "event," delimited by a beginning and an ending, but existing as an indivisible whole. If measured from the outside, the events of the intuitive *nunc* would seem variable in length, for an event may embrace a microscopic chronological duration (a sudden fall) or a broad expanse of metric time (one's childhood, or even one's life, taken as a whole). But from within, the event of the intuitive *nunc* is a single present, in which there is no distinction between subject and object, but simply a unified lived experience. That experience is a kind of dramatic "act," preceded and followed by "entr'actes," or pauses between acts. When we narrate events, say those of a day, we do not account for every minute of duration, for we sense that there is a time when things happen (the events), and a time between when nothing happens. The time of the event is a "full time," a "living time," and its beginning and ending are marked by a preceding and following "empty time," a "dead time" in which nothing happens. In this regard, "every event is, so to speak, within the time in which nothing happens" (188). But the event is "within the time in which nothing happens" in a second sense. The event is lived from within as a unified experience, and hence unknowable as it is occurring, but it can be known when *relived* in a reminiscence (*un souvenir*, by which term Groethuysen means a personal memory of a lived experience as opposed to a mere recollection of an externally viewed sequence of occurrences). Reminiscence takes place when we disengage ourselves from the present, when we "de-actualize" *l'actualité* (the French word for the present-day, everyday world of current events, or *actualités*). We reminisce within an empty, dead time in which nothing happens. Hence, it is "within this empty time that we in a sense disaggregate the present, so that it may be reborn in new forms in the reminiscence. It is finally within this empty time that reminiscences, once they are formed, will be placed, and will rejoin the present-day world [*l'actualité*]" (194).

Deleuze does not regard the present of the "event" in phenomenological terms, as a personal lived experience, as does Groethuysen, but he does see it as a de-actualization of *l'actualité*. For Deleuze, of course, the actual is opposed to the virtual, and what Groethuysen calls a dialectical *nunc* and an intuitive *nunc* Deleuze would label an actual present and a virtual present. The present, says Deleuze, "is actually distinguished from the future and the past" (IT 131; 100) when something is replaced by something else. Such an actual present is viewed from outside as a moment in a sequence of past-present-future occurrences. It is a present seen from a "longitudinal pragmatic view" (IT 131; 100), that is, as a point on a time line ("longitudinal") integrated within the sensori-motor schema ("pragmatic"). But when de-actualized, the present may be grasped from within and apprehended through a purely optical vision, vertical or rather in depth (IT 131; 100). The actual, horizontal, commonsense time of the sensori-motor schema may be suspended, in which case a virtual event emerges in an empty time when nothing happens. The virtual event takes place in a non-chronological, vertical present unrelated to the horizontal line of actual, chronological time.

Like Groethuysen, Deleuze sees the event as of variable dimensions, capable of including within it an episode, a season, a life, or even the world as a whole.[2] But Deleuze exploits this characteristic of the virtual event to emphasize the paradoxes inherent in a non-chronological time. We may think of the time of virtual events as a single present, elastically shrinking or expanding as the dimensions of various events change, but we may also look on it as a simultaneous coexistence of multiple presents. If, for example, we consider the event of "finding a lost key," we may focus narrowly on the instant when we discover the key, but we may also regard "having the key," "losing the key," and "finding the lost key" as all part of the same event. If so, we may then speak of three different present moments within the same event, which we may distinguish as a "present of the past" (having the key), a "present of the present" (losing the key), and a "present of the future" (finding the lost key).[3] Though distinct, the three presents are contained within the same event, inextricably enfolded, or "implicated," within a non-chronological present of presents. Each of these presents may be referred to as a "peak of the present" (*une pointe de présent,* with *pointe* designating such things as the point of a pin, the apex of a cone, the peak of a mountain, etc.), the three peaks "implicated in the event, rolled up in the event, hence simultaneous, inexplicable" (IT 132; 100). The paradox of such an implicated time is that within it mutually exclusive occurrences may take place at the same time. In ordinary life, I may have a key, lose it, and then find it again, but I cannot be in the state of having the key, losing the key (not having it), and finding it (having it again) *at the same time.* Each of the three moments is a possible state of affairs, but their simultaneous occurrence within a single universe is, in Leibniz's word, "incompossible." Yet when time as a whole is viewed as an enfolding of peaks of the present, such incompossibles do simultaneously coexist, inextricably rolled up within the event, "inexplicable" (unexplainable in rational terms) and "non-unfoldable" (incapable of being unfolded).

The whole of time, then, may be regarded in two different ways, as "the coexistence of sheets of the past," or as "the simultaneity of peaks of the present." Hence, we have "two sorts of chronosigns: the first are *aspects* (regions, layers [*gisements*]), the second are *accents* (peaks of view [*pointes de vue,* with a pun on *points de vue,* "points of view"])" (IT 132–33; 101). Deleuze finds in the films of Alain Robbe-Grillet the clearest instances of "accents," or "peaks of the present." In the films *L'Immortelle, Trans-Europ Express, L'homme qui ment,* and *Le jeu avec le feu,* as in many of his novels, Robbe-Grillet creates what have been called "generative fictions,"[4] works in which the process of generating the story—experimenting with different combinations of characters, testing various possible actions and outcomes—is incorporated into the work itself. Frequently, variations of the same scene are presented, in one of which, say, a woman is stabbed, while in another she is merely interrogated, as if the author or narrator was trying out various narrative options. As a result, incompossibles abound in Robbe-Grillet's films, mutually contradictory states of affairs that exist simultaneously in the same story. The murderer does and does not commit the crime, the victim does and does not die, the detective does and does not apprehend the killer, and all at the same time—that is, within a single simultaneous present. Rather than treat these contradictions as mere signs of the fictional nature of the work—as Robbe-Grillet himself tends to do—Deleuze regards them as evidence of a different conception and presentation of time. What we see in the various scenes of a Robbe-Grillet film are "peaks of the present," presents of the past (e.g., the day before the murderer kills), presents of the present (the day he kills), presents of the future (the day after he has killed), the film as a whole constituting the "event" that enfolds the peaks within a single simultaneous present (in which the murderer does and does not kill, has already and has not yet killed).

In *Last Year at Marienbad,* written by Robbe-Grillet and directed by Alain Resnais, Deleuze again discovers peaks of the present, but he argues that sheets of the past are also evident in this instructive hybrid of a film. In his introduction to the published script, Robbe-Grillet says that the whole film "is the story of a persuasion: it deals with a reality which the hero creates out of his own vision, out of his own words" (Marienbad 10). X, the narrator/hero, attempts to persuade A, the woman, that they met the previous year at Marienbad, that they had an affair, and that now she should abandon M (possibly her husband) and go away with X. Scenes are repeated as X tries out various story options, A initially denying any memory of X, but eventually surrendering to X's accumulation of diverse plot suggestions until she departs with him at the end of the film. What Deleuze finds fascinating is that A seems to leap from peak to peak in a perpetual present, whereas X explores multiple sheets of the past, seeking out the "brilliant points" of each memory space that might magnetically draw A into his story. Two conceptions of time coexist in the film, one of which Deleuze attributes primarily to Robbe-Grillet (peaks of the present), the other to Resnais (sheets of the past).

When *Marienbad* first appeared, Robbe-Grillet claimed that he and Resnais were as one in their understanding of the film, but years later Robbe-Grillet remarked that the two differed in their sensibilities and that Resnais had imposed on the film greater continuity than Robbe-Grillet would have liked. Resnais was too concerned with memory and temporal regularity; he tried too hard to please the audience and smooth over violent events and abrupt shifts from scene to scene. (Robbe-Grillet found especially telling Resnais's replacement of the script's rape scene with an overhead shot of the angelic reclining heroine and Resnais's choice of a pleasing, seamless score for the jolting, fragmented music Robbe-Grillet would have preferred.)[5] Yet this difference in sensibility, in Deleuze's analysis, arises not from a somewhat conventional filmmaker's treatment of an avant-garde writer's script, as Robbe-Grillet implies, but from different conceptions of time and its rhythms. Robbe-Grillet's incompossible peaks of the present lend themselves to abrupt breaks and shifts, to stark juxtapositions of conflicting events. A's contradictory responses to X's suggestions, her alternating denials, qualifications, and acceptances of his accounts of their past, mark discrete states of the present that succeed one another by fits and starts, leaping from one state to another like subatomic particles passing from one quantum state to the next. X's memory suggestions, by contrast, are explorations of diverse sheets of the past, each a continuous time-space plane over which X wanders. The continuities Resnais extracts from Robbe-Grillet's script are those not of a chronological time and a personal memory, but of a malleable, non-personal virtual past, the various sheets of the past abutting one another at strange angles, repeating one another with slight variation, in such a way that each sheet seems a topological metamorphosis of the preceding.[6] Hence, Deleuze can say of Robbe-Grillet's and Resnais's methods that "what the one obtains through the discontinuity of peaks of the present (leaps), the other obtains through the transformation of continuous sheets of the past. There is a statistical probabilism in Resnais, which is very different from the indeterminism of the 'quantum' type in Robbe-Grillet" (IT 157; 120).

Robbe-Grillet's apparent misapprehension of Resnais's aims is understandable, for unlike peaks of the present, with their overt disruptions of narrative regularity, sheets of the past can easily be mistaken for mere psychological variations of a chronological time (personal memories, fantasies, dreams, etc.). The films of Orson Welles, for example, seem relatively conventional narratives, but Deleuze sees them as the earliest instances of a systematic exploration of sheets of the past. *Citizen Kane* may be read as a straightforward biography, the various memories of Kane reported by discrete individuals, coordinated within a single chronological sequence of events, and united in their focus on the figure of Kane. Yet the film may also be treated as an extended search within a transpersonal memory space for the elusive Rosebud, each character's reminiscence of Kane revealing a region of the past within which a period in Kane's life takes shape, the various regions coexisting within a single film consciousness, but a consciousness finally that belongs to no individual and that is unified only by the image of the burning sled, which is witnessed solely by the camera eye. Likewise, *Mr. Arkadin* may be taken simply as an investigation into the dark secrets of Arkadin's past, but Van Stratten's interviews with Arkadin's former associates may also be regarded as encounters within different sheets of the past, each interview a failed reminiscence that is wiped away as Van Stratten leaves (and Arkadin murders Van Stratten's informant). Even *The Trial* may be viewed as a coherent narrative—perhaps as K.'s dream-hallucination—yet K.'s wanderings through the office, court, lawyer's apartment, artist's loft, cathedral, and vacant field may also be read as a quest within the past for the source of K.'s guilt, each site a strange sheet of the past, a warped time-space topologically transformed into the next, with all sites gravitating toward the pit within which K. meets his explosive death.

In each of Welles's films, sheets of the past coexist within a transpersonal memory, but Deleuze argues as well that in individual shots one can actually see characters inhabiting a region of time. Welles is often celebrated for his deep focus shots, which allow foreground, middle ground, and background details to remain in focus within a single image. Bazin especially praises Welles for his use of depth of field, arguing that such complex images enhance the realism of the films, since they allow extended shots without cuts, the relations between characters unfolding within a continuous time-space, while the audience is necessarily drawn into the image and forced to interpret the ambiguities of actions transpiring simultaneously in the various planes of the image.[7] Deleuze observes that others before Welles had used deep focus shots, but usually with the planes of the image remaining relatively isolated from one another. What Welles achieves by contrast is a communication and interpenetration of foreground, middle ground and background, each shot a dynamic space-in-depth.[8] Yet the effect of Welles's handling of depth of field, Deleuze claims, is not to render the shot more realistic but to make time visible. In the famous scene of Kane's discovery of Susan's attempted suicide, a deep focus shot combines the foreground bottle of sleeping pills, the middle ground figure of Susan drugged in bed, and the background entrance of Kane into the room, each plane marking a moment in a temporal sequence. The shot points toward the basic function of depth of field, its "proper element," which is "to reverse the subordination of time to movement, to exhibit time for itself" (IT 143; 109). In the deep focus shot, a space of coexisting times opens up, an in-depth sheet of the past.

Even when such shots do not explicitly juxtapose elements from different temporal moments (as in the shot of the pills-Susan-Kane), they fulfill "a function of remembering, of temporalization: not exactly a recollection [*souvenir*], so much as 'an invitation to recollect' [*une invitation à se souvenir*]" (IT 143; 109).[9] Bergson identifies two distinct moments in the process of remembering: an initial leap from the contracted past of the present (the apex of the cone) into the dilated past of memory (the cone); and an exploration of a plane of the past in search of a given recollection. These two moments, says Deleuze, have their counterparts in the deep focus shot, for "depth of field shows us now the initial act of evocation, now the sheets of the past that one explores in order to find the sought-after recollection" (IT 144; 109). An instance of the first use of depth of field is the high-angle deep-focus shot of the drunken Susan bent over the nightclub table, a present contraction of the past into an initial "invitation to recollect" (with the preceding tracking shot over the roof of the club, through the skylight window and inside constituting a veritable leap into the past); an instance of the second is the shot of Susan toying with a jigsaw puzzle in the foreground while Kane roams the cavernous background depths of Xanadu. In neither instance do we see a memory image per se, but in the one case we see "the actual effort of evocation, through which [the memory image] may be summoned up," and in the other, "the exploration of virtual zones of the past, through which [the memory-image] may be found, selected, and brought back" (IT 145; 110).

Deleuze regards Welles as the first great explorer of sheets of the past and Resnais as his most notable successor. In Welles, the sheets of the past tend to be oriented around a single contracted point in the present (Rosebud, the figure of Arkadin, Joseph K.), but in Resnais the fixed point disappears and "the present starts to float, struck with uncertainty, scattered in the comings and goings of the characters, or already absorbed by the past" (IT 152; 116). Each of his films presents a series of memory spaces unmoored from any secure referent, the sheets of the past forming plural, supraindividual memory worlds.[10] *Marienbad* displays a memory world for two, a single site constructed of the incommensurable and contradictory reminiscences of X and A. In *Hiroshima, mon amour,* two characters inhabit the separate memory worlds of Hiroshima and Nevers, and though the lovers' present tryst seems to function as a point of reference for the diverse sheets of the past, the two characters struggle to disengage themselves from their proper pasts and construct a hybrid Hiroshima/Nevers memory space that belongs to neither. In *Muriel,* Boulogne and Algeria are the sites of separate past events, but here three characters belong to one memory space (Hélène, Alphonse, and Ernest), two to the other (Bernard and Robert), and both spaces harbor uncertain and conflicting recollections, the film's sheets of the past finally becoming a group memory of undecidable alternatives, a jumble of grainy footage of Algeria, blank views of vacant Boulogne, and spare interior shots in the family apartment. With *La guerre est finie,* one might suppose (as many critics do) that Resnais creates a conventional present-tense narrative, but Deleuze sees in the images of Diego's clandestine crossings between Spain and France a juxtaposition of different "ages," the age of the Spanish civil war (still alive in the veterans of the movement), the age of a new terrorism (represented by the committee of young radicals before whom Diego appears), and the age of Diego himself, the disillusioned perpetual revolutionary suspended between the old guard and the new. Three different sheets of the past coexist in the narrative, three ages of Spain that comprise a collective memory, "historical, political, or even archaeological" (IT 155; 118) in its scope. *Mon oncle d'Amérique* merely extends this juxtaposition of "ages," the parallel narratives of René, Janine, and Jean interconnecting different temporal strata from each life, while evolutionary strata are interposed through Professor Laborit's sporadic commentary on animal ethology, with its accompanying images of bears, crabs, mice, and so on.

Throughout Resnais's work, Deleuze finds a memory that is more than psychological, a "memory for two, memory for many, memory-world, memory-ages-of-the-world" (IT 155; 119). Each film presents sheets of the past, time-spaces that are not simple representations of characters' individual internal states, but domains of time that the characters inhabit. Those sheets of the past form a "memory," but only in the Bergsonian sense of a retention of the past in coexisting strata of time, a supra-personal memory cone of past events. Each sheet has a certain continuity, but each is like a malleable square of pastry dough, in metamorphosis and hence in a state of perpetual fragmentation as contiguous points in one sheet become widely separated in a subsequent stretching, folding, and rolling of the surface. Resnais at times seems consumed with psychological concerns, as in his well-known practice of preparing for shooting by developing elaborate biographies of his characters and diagrams of their environs and movements. But the biographies are simply maps of individual sheets of time, according to Deleuze, and each diagram is a combination of maps, "the collection of transformations of the continuum, the piling-up of strata or the superimposition of coexisting sheets" (IT 158; 121). The maps of individual sheets and the diagrams of superimposed sheets "subsist as integral parts of the film" (IT 158-9; 121), appearing even in the sequences of inanimate objects, buildings, and landscapes of which Resnais is so fond. In *Night and Fog*, Resnais's acclaimed documentary on the Nazi death camps, he shows images of the abandoned barracks, guard towers, and gas chambers, but with a voice-over that establishes the "mental functions—cold, diabolic, almost impossible to comprehend—that presided over their organization" (IT 159; 121). In general Resnais discloses through objects and places "the mental function or level of thought to which it corresponds" (IT 159; 121), the sequence of objects or places constituting a map of mental relations. That map, however, is mental in no personal sense, any more than the maps and diagrams of the characters' lives are psychological components of a given film. Resnais maps and diagrams mental worlds, but ones that are apersonal. Each mental time world is like the Bibliothèque Nationale, which Resnais presents in his documentary *Toute la mémoire du monde* as "a gigantic memory, in which humans themselves are only mental functions" (IT 159; 121), the archive's endless rows of shelves like lobes of a brain along which humans pass like speeding neurotransmitters.

Each of Resnais's films maps individual strata of time and diagrams the collective superimposition of strata, but Deleuze insists that Resnais does more than simply display the coexistence of multiple sheets of the past, for he also establishes continuities *between* the various sheets. If Resnais treats the sheets of the past as parallel cross sections of a single cone, he also constructs transverse planes that are perpendicular to the parallel cross sections or slant obliquely across them. Such transverse planes are fashioned through a combination of feelings (*sentiments*) and thoughts. Resnais says that in his films "I would hope that the spectator would not identify with the hero, but only, for a moment, with the feelings of the hero. That there would be moments of identification and also moments of retreat" (quoted in Prédal 163). Deleuze concurs with René Prédal that there is a kind of *Verfremdungseffekt* in Resnais, but one that operates through an un-Brechtian hypnotic fascination, whereby spectators are engaged by a feeling or mood while being simultaneously distanced from the characters. One key to this technique, says Prédal, is in Resnais's use of music, which often establishes a continuity of mood within or between shots but without fully matching up with the visual images, a sudden climactic surge in the score, for example, playing over an innocuous image of a character walking down the sidewalk. Another is in continuities of color that define and interconnect scenes. Still a third is in the poetic, self-consciously "literary" voice-overs that accompany the images. In all cases, a "sort of hypnosis, purely aesthetic in origin, dedramatizes the anecdote, impedes identification with the characters and directs the attention of the public solely toward the feelings that animate the heroes" (Prédal 163).

Resnais frequently comments that feelings interest him more than characters, and Deleuze regards each film's continuities of feelings, established through such aesthetic means as music, color, and poetic rhythms and sounds, as constitutive elements of sheets of the past. These pure feelings, extracted from the characters and set free in a mental time-space of coexisting pasts, become "living realities of a mental theater," "the true figures of a very concrete 'cerebral play' [*jeu cérébral*]" (IT 163; 125). Feelings themselves, in this sense, become characters of a sort; they become dramatic actors on a mental stage, with each feeling establishing the continuity of a given temporal zone. Once extracted from the characters, the feelings function as mental figures, elements available for a thought that interconnects various sheets of the past, thereby forming a transverse plane intersecting parallel cross sections of a cone. Resnais's hypnotic dedramatization "reveals thought to itself. In a single movement, Resnais goes beyond the characters toward feelings, and beyond feelings toward thought, whose characters are feelings" (IT 163; 125). Feelings, hypnotically extracted from characters, delineate sheets of the past; and thought, by connecting and interrelating diverse feelings, forms a transverse plane across multiple sheets. Hence, "if feelings are ages of the world, thought is the non-chronological time to which they correspond. If feelings are sheets of the past, then thought, the brain, is the collection of non-localizable relations between all these sheets, the continuity that rolls them up and unrolls them like so many lobes" (IT 164; 125).

POWERS OF THE FALSE

Hyalosigns, as we have seen, make indiscernible the real and the imaginary. Chronosigns, by contrast, make undecidable or inexplicable the true and the false. A traditional narrative develops according to the regularities of the sensori-motor schema. It is "a veracious narrative, in the sense that it claims to be true, even in fiction" (IT 167; 127). In other words, a narrative's verisimilitude, or truth likeness, depends on its adherence to the commonsense coordinates of space and time. When those coordinates are abandoned, time appears directly, and "if time appears directly, it is in *de-actualized peaks of the present*, it is in *virtual sheets of the past*" (IT 170; 130), at which point the truths of Euclidean space and chronometric time are immediately subverted. Deleuze observes that "time has always put the notion of truth into crisis" (IT 170; 130), and he cites the Stoics' reflections on "future conditionals" as an early instance of such a crisis. If it is true that a battle may take place tomorrow, the Stoics reason, then a paradox necessarily arises the next day. Today, it is possible that the battle may take place, but also that it may not. If tomorrow the battle actually occurs, then one of today's possibilities becomes impossible—that the battle may *not* take place. The conclusion is that either the impossible proceeds from the possible (since what was possible yesterday becomes impossible today) or the past is not necessarily true (since yesterday the battle could have *not* taken place). It is easy to dismiss the argument as a mere sophism, says Deleuze, but what it indicates is the direct relation between truth and the form of time. Leibniz takes the sophism seriously and solves the Stoic paradox by arguing that the battle may and may not take place, but not in the same world. In one world it takes place, in another it does not. Both worlds are possible, but the two are not mutually compatible, or "compossible"; hence, they are "incompossible," and it is "only the incompossible that proceeds from the possible; and the past can be true without being necessarily true" (IT 171; 130). But what if incompossibles belong to the same world, as is the case with simultaneous peaks of the present and coexisting sheets of the past? Then we have a world of "*incompossible presents* related to *not-necessarily true pasts*" (IT 171; 131), and in such a world, narrative falsifies the truths of commonsense space and time. It becomes "a power of the false [*une puissance du faux*] that replaces and dethrones the form of truth, since it poses the simultaneity of incompossible presents or the coexistence of not-necessarily true pasts" (IT 171; 131). Each peak of the present and each sheet of the past offer perfectly distinct possible versions of events, and in this sense they are fully *discernible* possibilities (whereas hyalosigns blur, and hence render indiscernible, the line between the real and the imaginary). Each peak of the present is a distinct possibility, and each by itself may be regarded as true. But the peaks cannot all be true at the same time—and yet they are so enfolded with one another that they cannot be separated. Likewise, any one sheet of the past may be treated as true, in which case other sheets are necessarily false, but we cannot decide which is the true sheet and which the false. In this regard, then, the true and the false, though discernible, are rendered inexplicable or undecidable in peaks of the present and sheets of the past.[11]

Narratives have a falsifying capacity, a "power of the false" [*puissance du faux*], when they unfold in simultaneous presents or coexisting pasts, but the power of the false manifests itself in another way as well, through another kind of chronosign. When we consider a succession of events in a commonsense fashion, each event seems a discrete moment, a point in time, and the sequence of moments forms a uniform line which we tend to view from the outside, as it were, simply observing points A, B, and C, and noting their positions, A before B, C after B. But if we consider the events from "inside," as participants in the events, we sense the dynamic surge of time, the passing of A through B and into C (in Husserl's terms, we sense the present's retention of the past and protention of the future). This dynamic surge is a *puissance,* a power or potency, of time. Within this surge, "before" and "after" are not discrete moments but the two faces of a single *puissance,* a single becoming. The commonsense succession of moments Deleuze calls an empirical sequence (*suite empirique*), but those same moments, when treated as part of a single *puissance,* he labels a *series.* Becoming he defines as "that which transforms an empirical sequence into a series" (IT 359; 275). A series is a transformed "sequence of images" (IT 359; 275), and each series is a *puissance* leading to another *puissance,* a series surging into another series, a "burst of series" (IT 359; 275). It is *time as series* that makes possible a second kind of chronosign, a direct image of time that involves not the *order of time*—that of simultaneous presents and coexisting pasts—but "a becoming as potentialization, as series of *puissances*" (IT 360; 275). The *puissance* of this chronosign is a "power of the false" in that it is a power of becoming, of metamorphosis and transformation that renders fixed, stable, "true" identities perpetually "false."

Deleuze regards Welles not only as the first great explorer of sheets of the past, but also as a primary exponent of the "powers of the false." Deleuze finds a pervasive Nietzscheanism in Welles's cinema, especially in *The Lady from Shanghai, Mr. Arkadin, Touch of Evil,* and *F for Fake.*[12] Three Nietzschean figures may be extracted from these films: the man of truth, who in the name of the ideal judges the world of appearances guilty; the man of vengeance, who no longer believes in the ideal but negates the world of appearances out of self-hatred; and the artist, a joyous forger or falsifier (*faussaire*) who creates value by affirming the becoming of the world. Like Nietzsche, Welles has little use for the man of truth, who at best is a naïve dupe (O'Hara in *The Lady from Shanghai,*

Van Stratten in *Mr. Arkadin*), and at worst an obsessed agent of the law, willing to sacrifice anything to pass judgment on the world (Vargas in *Touch of Evil*). Welles has more sympathy for the man of vengeance, since in his trickery and deception he abandons the "true" and embraces the becoming of shifting, metamorphic appearances. Yet the man of vengeance is an impotent monster, one who betrays the truth but only out of self-loathing and a hatred of life. *The Lady from Shanghai*'s crippled Bannister and *Touch of Evil*'s bloated Quinlan are grotesques, falsifiers whose deceptions ultimately fail to trap their victims, and even the spectacularly wealthy Arkadin proves finally to be powerless in his effort to erase his past and sustain his fake identity. These men of vengeance engage the powers of the false, but only to a limited degree. They do not submit *themselves* to becoming and enter into a metamorphosis that is total and one with the ongoing, transformative processes of life. Only the artist fully embraces such a becoming, and in *F for Fake* Welles explores the gamut of falsifiers that ranges from the con man and trickster to the magician and artist. Here Welles combines the true story of the painter Elmyr de Hory, a forger of modern masterpieces, and Elmyr's biographer Clifford Irving, himself the author of a faked biography of Howard Hughes, with a fictional account of a forger of Picassos. Welles reminisces about his own career as an actor and director, observing that all art is in some sense fakery. Yet what the film ultimately makes evident, says Deleuze, is not that art is mere fraud, but that art is the full expression of the power of the false. Finally, there is a difference between the forger and the artist: whereas the forger is restricted by a reverence for form, "the creative artist alone carries the power of the false to such a degree that it realizes itself, no longer in form, but in transformation" (IT 191; 146). In the artist the opposition of the true and the false no longer pertains, since the transforming, metamorphic power of the false produces truth. Indeed, the artist is above all "the *creator of truth,* for truth is not something to be attained, found or reproduced—it must be created" (IT 191; 146).

ROUCH'S ETHNOFICTIONS

In Welles's cinema, the power of the false is manifest in the characters, "who form series as so many degrees of a 'will to power' [*volonté de puissance*] through which the world becomes a fable" (IT 360; 275). Some might object that Welles's narratives are basically conventional and that Deleuze merely offers a thematic reading of the films, but Deleuze's implicit claim is that the films' characters do more than "represent" Nietzschean themes, for they themselves are metamorphic forces-in-action, images engaged in a process of becoming that transforms them from mere sequences into series. Deleuze finds a similar process of metamorphic character formation in the films of Jean Rouch, and perhaps here the skeptical may find more convincing evidence that the power of the false indeed can engender direct images of time.

Best known as a practitioner of cinéma vérité, Rouch has produced dozens of documentaries over his long career, many of which deal with the peoples of Niger and the Gold Coast.[13] As Stoller demonstrates at length, Rouch's African documentaries are inseparable from his work as an ethnographer, and though many of his films are "docu-fictions," they are always grounded in decades of extensive and prolonged study in the field. An advocate of "participatory ethnography" and "shared anthropology," Rouch recognizes that his presence necessarily alters the object of his investigation, and so he invites the people he lives with to join him in his fieldwork, not as students, but as teachers initiating the ignorant anthropologist into the wisdom of their ways. Rouch's cinema is likewise participatory. Taking his cue from Flaherty, who had shown rushes to Nanook while shooting *Nanook of the North,* early on Rouch adopted the practice of screening his footage for those he was filming, and soon he involved his "actors" in the process of constructing the films themselves. For example, after a 1954 screening of *Bataille sur le grand fleuve* before a Songhay audience, Damoré Zika and Illo Goudel'ize, both of whom appear in *Bataille,* proposed to Rouch that they make a film together about young Nigeriens who migrate to the Gold Coast. Rouch had himself been writing an exhaustive analysis of such migration patterns, but rather than simply provide visual documentation for the written scholarly record, he and his collaborators created the "eth-nofiction" *Jaguar,* which recounts the adventures of three young Nigeriens, played by Damoré, Illo, and Lam Ibrahim (a Fulan herder), as they migrate from Ayoru to the Gold Coast city of Accra. Not only did Damoré, Illo, and Lam play the leads in *Jaguar,* but they also helped plan and stage the action. Shooting was largely improvisatory, as Rouch and his actors followed the route of past migrants, incorporating into the story the chance encounters they experienced on the road. Since synchronous sound cameras did not exist at the time, a sound track had to be generated separately. So Rouch had Damoré and Illo watch the *Jaguar* footage and talk, and from their image-driven conversation he fashioned the film's commentary.

Though a work of fiction, *Jaguar* is informed throughout by Rouch's extensive knowledge of Nigerien migration patterns. His performers are Nigeriens enacting their own people's past, working with Rouch to invent a story that sums up the truth of a group experience. In *Jaguar*, Damoré and Illo exercise what Deleuze calls the *"function of fabulation"* (IT 196; 150), which is neither a fictional nor a factual function. Rather, it is "the becoming of the real character when he himself begins to 'fictionize,' when he starts 'to legendize *in flagrante delicto,'* and thereby contributes to the invention of his people" (IT 196; 150). *Jaguar*'s real characters enact and narrate a fictional story, but one that combines historical experiences in the formation of a new collectivity that emerges through the process of making the film.

The fabulative function of inventing new identities is especially evident in *Moi, un noir*, an ethnofiction suggested to Rouch by Oumarou Ganda, one of Rouch's research assistants in Abidjan, who after viewing footage from *Jaguar* asked Rouch to make a film about real migrants like himself. Rouch and Ganda decided to film Ganda and three other Nigeriens from the Abidjan suburb of Treichville as they led their daily lives. The players all adopted pseudonyms: Edward G. Robinson, Eddie Constantine-Lemmy Caution, Tarzan, and Dorothy Lamour. The sound track was supplied by the actors, who watched the rushes and developed free-form commentaries on the images, interweaving narrative descriptions of the action, reminiscences, anecdotes, and fictions. Like *Jaguar, Moi, un noir* is a form of participatory ethnography, a collaborative effort to create the truth of a lived cultural experience. In this case, however, the experience is not grounded in a traditional past but situated entirely in an unsettling, displaced present. Much more patently than Damoré and Illo, the characters of *Moi, un noir* are engaged in a process of self-invention, melding Western cinematic personas and Nigerien roles in a hybrid urban identity. And the entire voice-over may be considered one prolonged instance of fabulation, an act of "legendizing" caught *in flagrante delicto* as the performers construct selves while contributing to the ongoing construction of the film.

Fabulation's invention of a self entails a "becoming-other," a meta-morphic passage *between* identities, in the case of *Moi, un noir,* a passage between the roles associated with Hollywood, with traditional tribal culture, and with urban Treichville. That process of becoming-other is perhaps nowhere more evident than in *Les maîtres fous,* easily Rouch's most controversial film, which records one of the yearly rituals of the Hauka mediums.[14] The Hauka cult arose around 1925 in colonial Niger, and though its rites were an offshoot of traditional possession practices, many Nigeriens then found and still find them shocking. The mediums Rouch follows are migrants who have settled in Accra, the capital of the colonial Gold Cost. The film opens with scenes of Accra's jumble of European and African cultures and follows the mediums as they travel to the rural compound of Mounkaiba, the Hauka high priest. At the compound, the mediums soon become possessed by the Hauka spirits. They froth at the mouth, set their clothes on fire, plunge their hands in boiling water, ritually sacrifice a dog and drink its blood. The Hauka spirits are parodies of colonial authority—Commandant Mugu, the wicked major; General Malia, the general of the Red Sea; Madame Lokotoro, the doctor's wife; Gommo, the governor-general. Their gestures and actions exaggerate the patterns of British military ritual, and their clothing and adornments (pith helmet, red sash, plume) mock the symbols of British power. The language they speak is their own, a mixture of pidgin English and broken French peculiar to the Hauka possession ceremonies. The film closes with shots of the mediums back in Accra at their workday routines, but clearly the return to normality has not come without a radical dislocation of identities, a passage between tribal and colonial roles by way of a tumultuous, syncretic ritual of possession.

Rouch's camera captures the becoming-other of his subjects, yet never does it merely observe. Rouch insists that his cinema is a form of provocation, not neutral representation, "a tool which will provoke the emergence of a certain reality" (quoted in Yakir 7).[15] What he produces is quite literally cinéma vérité, cinema truth, "a new truth . . . which has nothing to do with normal reality" (Yakir 7–8). In front of the camera, people adopt unnatural roles, become uncomfortable, lie, and invent. And in the process of shooting "we contract time, we extend it, we choose an angle for the shot, we deform the people we're shooting, we speed things up and follow one movement to the detriment of another movement. So there is a whole work of lies. But, for me . . . this lie [is] more real than the truth" (quoted in Eaton 51). In *Les maîtres fous,* the camera's provocation intensifies the becoming-other of the Hauka mediums; in *Jaguar* and *Moi, un noir,* that provocation is reinforced by the inclusion of the subjects' self-invention within the process of the film's construction. And if there is a becoming-other that possesses Rouch's subjects through the provocation of the camera, there is a correlative becoming-other that Rouch himself undergoes as he attempts to abandon his Western presuppositions and enter into the events he is filming. When he shoots, Rouch explains, he walks about with the camera, "taking it to wherever it is the most effective, and improvising a ballet in which the camera itself becomes just as much alive as the people it is filming. . . . It is this bizarre state of transformation in the filmmaker that I have called, by analogy with phenomena of possession, the 'cine-trance' " (Rouch 93–94). In this "cine-trance," the filmmaker is "no longer just himself but . . . a 'mechanical eye' accompanied by an 'electronic ear' " (94). Since Rouch insists that his soundman always be a native speaker of his subjects' language, in his African films an African ear always accompanies his Western eye. Thus when Rouch films his African subjects, he does so as a kind of machine-component of a transcultural sight-and-sound apparatus, immersed through a cine-trance in the reality he is provoking and producing.

The power of the false is a generative force, the potency of time that subsumes a before and an after within an ongoing surge of becoming. In Rouch's cinéma vérité, the characters are real people engaged in a process of self-invention. Their fabulations put fixed identities in disequilibrium, allowing a passage between determinate roles toward as yet unspecified ways of living. In Rouch's ethnofictions, the characters' self-inventions are made part of the construction of the film. From a real situation, studied by Rouch and lived by the people he studies, a fiction is generated that both epitomizes the situation and charts its emergent lines of transformation. The characters' self-invention and the invention of their film story are metamorphic processes, becomings that produce a reality rather than represent it. Rouch himself joins this metamorphic process, becoming other as he enters a cine-trance, provoking a cinema truth through his camera interventions. The standard divisions between the true and the false, reality and fiction, are rendered undecidable, as Rouch and his subjects fabulate their stories, creating truth through a general process of becoming-other.

Rouch's cinéma vérité blurs the line between the real and the fictive, his real actors improvising fictions that produce their own truth. A similar blurring of the real and the fictive has often been observed in the improvisatory films of Shirley Clarke and John Cassavetes, and Deleuze concurs that all three make full use of the powers of the false. Though she consciously distances herself from the label cinéma vérité, Clarke creates her own ethnofictions of a sort, in *The Connection* combining Gelbar's dramatic lines, the improvisations of the Living Theater cast, and the frame of a documentary film shoot to produce a fictive ethnography of a junkie community; in *The Cool World* bringing together actor adults and "real" teens from the street in the improvised construction of the story of an aspiring gang leader; and in *Portrait of Jason* injecting her own story into the portrait of the real prostitute Jason, whose stylized performances and fabulations make him his own real fiction. Likewise, Cassavetes in *Shadows* and *Faces* builds stories from his actors' free-flowing improvisations, and even in his more deliberately scripted films, such as *Woman under the Influence* and *Gloria,* he lets the performers' improvised "real" interactions modify and shape the flow of the narrative. Yet in Clarke and Cassavetes Deleuze also finds evidence of a third power of the false, distinct from the powers manifest in Welles's metamorphic characters or Rouch's fabulations. Here the image of time as series is above all corporeal. The body's routine attitudes and stylized gestures form series that combine "before" and "after" within a single dynamic force, that force providing the generative impetus for the construction of each film. This power of the false informs an entire "cinema of the body," among whose practitioners Deleuze numbers Clarke and Cassavetes, but also Bene, several experimental filmmakers, the New Wave directors Godard and Rivette, and such post–New Wave figures as Akerman, Eustache, Doillon, and Garrel.

Deleuze identifies two poles in the cinema of the body, one of *attitudes* and the quotidian body, and another of *gests* and the ceremonial body. Through attitudes (posture, comportment, bearing) the body incorporates a before and an after into its present. The fatigued body is marked by past exertion, the anxious body by future worries. The body's unconscious poses, rhythms, and movements, its humdrum, unreflective attitudes, put "the before and the after in the body, time in the body" (IT 247; 189), and one way of creating a cinema of the body is to follow the quotidian body, trace its movements, and make visible its history and trajectory. A second way is to stylize the body, "to make it pass through a ceremony" (IT 247; 190) and thereby reveal the gests, or organizing patterns, that interconnect its various attitudes. Deleuze takes the term *gest* from Brecht's brief essay "On Gestic Music," in which Brecht differentiates mere gesture or gesticulation from gest, or action considered in relation to the "overall attitudes" (Brecht 194) it expresses.[16] Brecht's concern in his theater is to convey through "social gests" the social relations inherent in actions, such that when a man chases away a dog, say, it is not as an abstract individual shooing a generic dog, but as an unemployed worker shielding himself from the bosses' watchdogs. From this notion of the "social gest" as a telling gesture that sums up a set of social relations, Deleuze develops a general definition of "gest" as "the tie [*lien*] or knot of attitudes, between them, their coordination with one another, but such that it does not depend on a previous story, on a preexisting plot, or on an action-image. Instead, the gest is the development of attitudes themselves, and, in this regard, the gest effects a direct theatricalization of bodies, which is often very discreet, since it takes place independently of any role" (IT 250; 192).

In Antonioni, the quotidian body is especially evident, the pervasive fatigue, pensive anticipation, disquiet, and despair of his characters conveyed through their postures, glances, and movements. Bene, by contrast, stresses the ceremonial body, establishing a series of ritual spaces within which parodic movements gradually take on an abstract, musical grace. But what interests Deleuze is less the individual poles of the quotidian and ceremonial body than the passage between them, "the imperceptible passage from attitudes or postures to the 'gest' " (IT 250; 192). In Clarke's *The Connection,* for example, the quotidian body is the addicted body, in which the presence of time is particularly marked—past and future fixes visible in the cravings of the strung-out body, past and future cravings and fixes in the euphoria of the stupefied body. The characters perform various actions and trace diverse paths through the apartment, each character embodying addiction in a different way, but midway through the film the bodies take on a general similarity, as a sequence of close-ups shows the anonymous hands of the addicts scratching, drumming, twitching, squeezing and shaking in longing and anticipation. A formal pattern emerges, the gest of an apersonal junkie, a linkage of attitudes that carries over into the lethargic noddings and slumpings of the interchangeable drugged bodies of the last sections of the film.

This passage from attitudes to gests Deleuze sees as central in Cassavetes. Throughout his cinema, Cassavetes "undoes story, plot, action, but even space, to arrive at attitudes as categories that put time into the body" (IT 250; 192). Cassavetes's scripts provide broad outlines for the performers, but the improvisations of his actor-authors generate the action, whose intensity and interest lie more in the performers' volatile and shifting interrelations than in the story they are dramatizing. There is as well a general "dissolution of space" in Cassavetes, as Philippe de Lara points out. "These bodies, these faces, these accumulated gestures provoke a strange imprecision of the places, or rather, of their coordinates" (de Lara 36). It is often difficult to tell how one room is connected to another, where sites are located, or what dimensions an area might have. The result is that the performers do not so much inhabit a coherent, continuous space as they generate a space around themselves, one that is determined by their bodies, faces, and accumulated gestures. Each Cassavetes film, says Deleuze, meets "the exigency of a cinema of the body: the character is reduced to his proper corporeal attitudes, and what must emerge is the gest, that is the 'spectacle,' a theatricalization or a dramatization that is valid for any plot" (IT 250; 192). The actor-authors, in Jean-Louis Camolli's analysis, construct themselves "gesture by gesture, word by word, as the film advances" (Comolli 38), and it is in the linking of attitudes, gesture by gesture, that a "gest" is produced. Early in *Faces,* for example, John Marley and Fred Draper drunkenly flirt with Gena Rowlands, laughing, dancing, stumbling, singing, tugging at her, hanging on her, as she reacts in various ways, now joining their play, now distancing herself, one moment elated, the next bored. Their improvisatory interactions flesh out the basic situation and produce the story of their evening together. Through their movements, postures, and expressions they generate a space and give embodiment to the temporal rhythms of desire, weariness, excitement, depression, anger, or disgust. Each attitude expresses a before and an after, a retention of past states and projection toward future states within a dynamic present. As Marley, Draper, and Rowlands interact, they pass from one attitude to another, linking ennui to irritation to rage to simpering self-pity and so on. The scene becomes a spectacle of attitudes, an intensified distillation of emotions, conflicts, and motivations.

And in this heightened spectacle, each series of interconnected attitudes forms a pattern, a continuous flourish or movement that constitutes a kind of "mega-gesture," or gest. The series ennui-irritation-rage–self-pity takes on a certain cohesiveness, one determined not by a scripted story or character conception but by the process of its own generation. Marley traces one trajectory of shifting attitudes, Draper another, Rowlands a third, the scene taking shape as the three gests unfold. Each attitude is a becoming, each gest a passage from one becoming to another and another. And the scene, like all the other scenes of the film, unfolds as an exploration of the gests that the given situation and configuration of performers may produce.[17]

In Godard Deleuze sees a complex handling of attitudes and gests that ultimately engages a fourth power of the false, one that treats any element of a given film as a component of a series. Godard's method is that of a "generalized serialism" (IT 361; 276), the cinematic counterpart of Boulez's atonal serialism in which all musical elements—pitch, timbre, duration, dynamics, and so forth—are subjected to acentered, systematic permutation and variation. If series are formed in Welles through falsifying characters, in Rouch through fabulating performers and film crew, and in Clarke and Cassavetes through the body's attitudes and gests, in Godard "the series, their limits and their transformations, the degrees of power [_puissance_] may concern any relation of the image whatever: the characters, the states of a character, the positions of the author, the attitudes of the body, but also colors, aesthetic genres, psychological faculties, political powers, logical or metaphysical categories" (IT 360–61; 276).

In each of his films, Godard establishes a set of categories (much like Aristotelian categories, Deleuze suggests), and then puts them in relation to one another, connecting, juxtaposing, separating, modifying them in such a way that they form series, that is, metamorphosing components of a becoming, or _puissance._ One set of categories Godard frequently exploits is that of genre, such as the war film (_Les carabiniers_), sci-fi detective film (_Alphaville_), B movie (_Vivre sa vie_), musical comedy (_Une femme est une femme_), or Bonnie and Clyde crime story (_Pierrot le fou_). Rather than simply follow generic conventions, or even parody them, Godard submits them to a reflective analysis and usage, now juxtaposing genres, now dividing the genre into subgenres, now sliding from one genre to another. But even in the handling of a single genre, what is

essential is that for Godard the genre "constitutes the limit of images
that do not belong to it, but which are reflected in it" (IT 240; 184). In
a traditional musical comedy, for example, all the action is organized
around the song-and-dance numbers, including the dramatic scenes
between numbers. The music and dance naturally issue from the dramatic scenes as their proper expression. In *Une femme est une femme,* by
contrast, the dance occurs abruptly, as if by accident, the dancers per-
forming more for themselves than for an audience. The genre itself
becomes reflexive: the dance displays the limit between dance and non-
dance, and hence the way in which the two elements mutually reflect
and define one another, while also pushing the limit between the two
toward disequilibrium. The sequence of dance images becomes a series,
a dynamic tendency out of and toward non-dance that includes the
thresholds of before and after within a single metamorphic movement.

Genres, then, are not simple conventions in Godard, but problematic categories that "introduce reflection into the image itself" (IT 242;
186), and they do so by constituting series. Genres are only one of the
categories Godard exploits, but all categories are reflexive: classifications that introduce reflection into the image and constitute series. In
some of Godard's films, the categories are explicitly stated, as in the five
titled sections of *Sauve qui peut (la vie):* 0. Life; 1. The Imaginary; 2. Fear;
3. Commerce; 4. Music. In others, the categories are implicit, as in *Les
carabiniers,* a movie, Deleuze insists, not *about* war, but a direct filming
of the categories of war—things of war, ideas of war, feelings of war, phenomena of war, each category revealed through its corresponding series.
As the titles of *Sauve qui peut (la vie)* suggest, categories may be of various sorts—metaphysical (life), phenomenological (the imaginary), emotional (fear), economic/sexual (commerce), aesthetic (music). Each film
establishes a different set of categories, each category delineates a problem, and each configuration of categories forces viewers to determine
the non-conventional yet non-arbitrary relation that brings those categories together (e.g., in *Sauve qui peut (la vie),* what do life, the imaginary,
fear, commerce, and music have to do with one another?).

Godard's categories, it should be emphasized, are not simply organizing themes or concepts, in Deleuze's analysis. Though the name of the
category and the series of images constituted by the category may be
presented separately (the title frame "Fear" followed by images of fear),
the category and the series are inseparable from one another. To "put

reflection into the image" is to render the category itself visible (or audible), and the means of doing so is through the constitution of a series. When we see the category "musical comedy dance" in *Une femme est une femme,* it is not because a label tells us that the ensuing dance sequence is an example of a genre (there is no such label), but because the dance itself reflects the genre by tending toward a limit, by forming part of a series, or a becoming. It is as if the dance image itself were self-conscious, both a concrete instance of dance and the abstract category of dance at the same time. When we see the category of "fear," we see concrete fearful behavior, but such that the fear reflects the limit toward which it tends (toward anger, toward paralysis, toward excitement—the possibilities are open-ended), and it is through this tendency that the category comes to visibility within the image. Hence, when Deleuze says that colors may function as categories in Godard, he does not mean that colors are mere thematic, symbolic, or formal elements, but that images of blue and green things, say, form series tending toward a limit (perhaps that of a common gray), such that one sees blue and green things that in a sense declare themselves "blue" and "green" while at the same time remaining the concrete and specific blue and green things that they are.

In Godard's films, then, "every sequence of images forms a series in that it tends toward a category in which it reflects itself [*se réfléchit*], the passage from one category to another determining a change in power [*puissance*]" (IT 361; 276). The categories "can be words, things, acts, people" (IT 243; 186); they may be "colors, aesthetic genres, psychological faculties, political powers, logical or metaphysical categories" (IT 361; 276). And through a "generalized serialism" (IT 361; 276) Godard puts these diverse metamorphic categories in relation with one another. Yet Godard's cinema of categories is at the same time a cinema of the body, for in his films, "all the components of the image come together on the body" (IT 252; 193). Each body has its own space, interior spaces frequently taking on their specific characteristics through the constrained movements of the characters (Paul and Camille's apartment in *Le mépris,* the empty villa in *Prénom Carmen,* in which Carmen and Joseph wander, colliding with the walls and with one another as they delineate a space through their bodies). As in the dance scene in *Une femme est une femme,* the characters tend to perform for themselves as if they were in their own theater, their quotidian attitudes constantly being theatricalized into gests that connect those attitudes in series. Yet in Godard, "the attitudes of bodies are the categories of the mind [*l'esprit*] itself, and the gest is the thread that goes from one category to another" (IT 253; 194). The gest is not simply corporeal, but "bio-vital, metaphysical, aesthetic" (IT 253; 194), which means that the body's attitudes and gests extend into the multiple series that constitute the categories of a given film. As a result, a double reading of each Godard film is possible, one in terms of attitudes and gests, and one in terms of categories.

Consider *Prénom Carmen,* for example. Through the complex of references to Merimée's original story, Bizet's opera, and Preminger's film version of the musical *Carmen Jones,* Godard establishes various generic categories (fiction, opera, musical, film), each of which generates series that tend toward the limit of the given category.[18] The parodic or self-conscious handling of stock film scenes (the heist scene, the first love-making scene, the last-words death scene) generates further generic and subgeneric categories. The motif of the film within the film, allusions to video, and the arresting image of the hand against the blue television screen establish "film" itself as a category. The categories of "passion," "doomed love," "femme fatale," implicit in the story line, are made visible and audible in the stylized actions and the shots of the ocean waves (linked to passion through the opening voice-over). Allusions to the apocalypse and the conclusion of Giraudoux's *Electre* (see Powrie 71–72), as well as Carmen's reflections on names and what comes before names, delineate metaphysical categories of life/death and language/pre-language that inform various series of images.

Yet the film may also be approached through the bodies of the characters, through the attitudes that generate the bodies' ambient spaces and form larger patterns linking attitudes in gests. Plots, emotions, themes, and concepts may be seen as secondary products of the generative becoming of the bodies. But through sound and music Godard compels viewers to extend corporeal gests to include non-corporeal elements. The link between sounds and bodies is established early in the film, as Godard, playing a washed-up film director, paces his asylum room, tapping the window, patting the bed rail, striking the typewriter keys, thumping his chest and his skull. Sounds emanate from bodies and their interactions with things and with themselves. The rehearsals of the Beethoven quartets, interspersed throughout the film, provide images of bodies in close contact with sound, the postures and movements of the musicians not only corresponding to the music but also loosely echoing the postures and movements of Carmen, Joseph, and the other characters in the drama. As a result, the gests of the characters and the gests of the musicians form with the music a trans-personal corporeal-musical gest. That gest broadens to include other sonic elements, as the soundtrack alternates in complex patterns between Beethoven's music, the crash of the ocean waves, the cries of seagulls, the occasional voice-overs, the sounds of the dramatic action, and the "absolute silence" of a momentarily dead soundtrack, the sounds sometimes aligned with their corresponding visual images (e.g., ocean sound with ocean image), sometimes not. The patterns that link the attitudes of bodies and the patterns that link music with sounds interact with one another, forming composite gests that connect bodies with sounds while also opening bodies to the *category* of music, with music becoming reflexive as it tends toward the limits of the non-musical ocean waves, seagull cries, and ambient sounds of the drama. In this way, the cinema of the body flows into the cinema of categories, as the body's dynamic becoming joins the becoming of the musical and sonic series.[19]

Chronosigns are of two sorts, those of the order of time, and those of time as series. The chronosigns of the order of time correspond to two different interpretations of time, one in terms of coexisting sheets of the past, the other in terms of simultaneous peaks of the present. Welles and Resnais map sheets of the past, Robbe-Grillet charts peaks of the present. The chronosigns of time as series involve the power of the false, *la puissance du faux,* the potency or force of time as metamorphic becoming. This *puissance* converts sequences of images into series, in which each image subsumes within itself a before and an after. Deleuze distinguishes four different manifestations of the power of the false. In Welles, the characters—men of truth, men of vengeance, forgers and artists— form series that reveal the power of the false. In Rouch, the power of the false is a power of fabulation whereby Rouch and his subjects together become-other as they invent a people and generate truth through their ethnofictions. In Clarke and Cassavetes, the becoming of the body is central, the passage from attitudes to gests forming series that generate space and stories. And in Godard, the cinema of the body merges with a cinema of categories, in which any element—word, thing, act, person, genre, emotion, psychological faculty, aesthetic mode, concept—may form a series that displays the metamorphic power of the false.

In his handling of categories Godard introduces "reflection into the image itself" (IT 242; 186), in the sense both that the image becomes reflexive and that thought becomes visible in the image. There is a sense, however, in which all cinematic images for Deleuze are images of thought, and hence he speaks of the "noosigns," or thought-signs, of the classic cinema and the noosigns of the modern cinema, the one corresponding to an indirect time-image, the other to a direct time-image. All the chronosigns of the modern cinema therefore are also noosigns. In that they call for a new way of seeing, they may as well be called "lectosigns," signs that must be read rather than automatically assimilated within the commonsense coordinates of the sensori-motor schema. What it means to regard chronosigns as noosigns and lectosigns is the subject of the next chapter.

Chapter Six

NOOSIGNS AND LECTOSIGNS: IMAGE AND THOUGHT, SIGHT AND SOUND

Chronosigns are also noosigns and lectosigns, for the time-image is not only an image of time, but also a "thinking image" and a "readable image" (IT 35; 23), an image of thought and an image that must be read. Through the concept of the noosign Deleuze poses a series of questions: What is the relation between cinema and thought? How do images affect the mind, and how does the mind affect images? And for that matter, what is a mind and what is thought? And what does it mean to produce a "thinking image," or to put "reflection into the image itself"? The concept of the lectosign for its part raises a number of questions: In what way must time-images be read as well as seen or heard? What is the cinematic relation between sight and sound, and what happens when in the readable image visual signs and audio signs become autonomous? What are the limits of sight and sound, and what relation might those limits have to one another? These are the questions we will examine in this chapter.

THE CLASSIC IMAGE OF THOUGHT

In 1934, the art historian Elie Faure enthusiastically saluted cinema as the only art capable "of presenting the image of a society that is evolving, at an increasingly sure pace, toward anonymous and collective modes of production" (Faure 621). In a dynamic, mechanical age of mass production, the mechanical art of cinema presents movement and duration directly, showing us through the camera's non-human eye— through unexpected framings, shot angles, show motion, fast action, stop action—features of the world as yet unperceived by human beings. The cinema's moving images directly affect the mind and bring about an "intimate union of the material universe and the mental/spiritual universe [*univers spirituel*]" (621). "In truth," comments Faure, it is cinema's "material automatism itself that causes to surge forth from the interior of these images this new universe that [the cinema] imposes little by little on our intellectual automatism" (618–19).

Faure's faith in cinema rests in his belief that the mechanically generated moving image directly instills a shock in the mind and instigates a new way of thinking, one that unsettles the "intellectual automatism" of our unreflective mental habits. This view Deleuze regards as central to the classic cinema's image of thought,[1] though in Deleuze's formulation of Faure's insight, the unsettling of our "intellectual automatism" gives rise to another form of automatism: "automatic movement causes to rise up within us a spiritual automaton, which in turn reacts on movement" (IT 203; 156). The unusual term "spiritual automaton" Deleuze takes from Spinoza, who in *On the Improvement of the Understanding* argues that the soul (*anima*), like the body, obeys laws of cause and effect, "and is, as it were, an immaterial automaton [*automata spirituale*]" (Spinoza 30). Spinoza, of course, is here responding to Descartes's notion that animals are mere automata, mechanical bodies reacting to fixed physical laws, whereas humans have minds and souls and hence are more than mere machines. Spinoza's point is that the mind cannot be exempt from the law of causality, and that the proper formation and connection of our ideas must follow a necessity equal to that of physical laws. In this sense, the mind is a spiritual automaton, just as the body is a physical automaton.[2] Deleuze adopts the term initially to stress the involuntary nature of thought's response to the moving image, for it is "as if cinema said to us: with me, with the movement-image, you cannot escape the shock that arouses the thinker in you. A subjective and collective automaton for an automatic movement" (IT 204; 156–57). When Deleuze turns to the modern cinema and the time-image, however, he uses the term to suggest as well that the thought aroused by the image is like that of an alien thinker within, an other as remote from our ordinary human world as a wandering mummy or a robotic machine.[3]

To detail the relationship between image and thought in the classic cinema, Deleuze returns to Eisenstein's theoretical writings (see chapter 2). For Eisenstein, we recall, the shot is a germinative "montage *cell,*" and "montage is conflict" (Film Form 37–38). There is collision and conflict within individual shots—collisions of graphic directions, scales, volumes, masses—and in montage there is collision and conflict between shots. Conflict within the shot is potential montage, and "if montage is to be compared with something, then a phalanx of montage pieces, of shots, should be compared to the series of explosions of an internal combustion engine, driving forward its automobile or tractor" (38). Montage "is a *collision,*" each explosive shot colliding with the next, and "from the collision of two given factors *arises* a concept" (37). There is a movement, then, "from the image to thought, from the percept to the concept" (IT 205; 157). The concept engendered by the collision of montage is that of the whole, the organic totality that unites the individual explosive shots. Thus, the image has "a shock effect on thought, and forces thought to think itself as well as to think the whole" (IT 206; 158).

Besides this movement from the image to thought, however, there is also a complementary movement from thought to the image. If Eisenstein argues for an "intellectual cinema," he also recognizes the importance of *pathos* in montage, the "leap" (Nonindifferent Nature 35) from image to image and from quality to quality that increases the emotional and sensual intensity of each image. In the cinematic work of art, there is "a dual process: an impetuous progressive rise along the lines of the highest explicit steps of consciousness and a simultaneous penetration by means of the structure of the form into the layers of profoundest sensual thinking" (Film Form 144–45). What Eisenstein refers to as "sensual thinking" is thought via concrete images and their associative affinities with one another. Such sensual thinking is found in the myths of primitive peoples, but it also forms "the syntax of inner speech," "the flow and sequence of thinking unformulated into the logical construction in which uttered, formulated thoughts are expressed" (130). This inner speech is a kind of "inner monologue," best exemplified, according to Eiseinstein, in "the immortal 'inner monologues' of Leopold Bloom in *Ulysses*" (104). Like the sensual thinking of primitive

peoples, the "inner monologue" of inner speech operates through figures, through sensual images and synecdochic, metonymic, and
metaphoric substitutions of one image for another. Art combines logical thought with the sensual thinking of images and figures, thereby
creating "the true tension-laden unity of form [sensual thinking] and
content [logical thought]" (145).

If the concept of the organic whole of the film is generated by the
individual explosive shots and the pathos of the leap from shot to shot,
then the relationship of parts to whole is that of cause to effect. But in
another sense, the individual parts presuppose the existence of the
whole. The whole, then, is also cause, of which the parts are the individual expressions, or effects. This presupposed whole, however, cannot
be specified except through its parts. Yet it can be felt and thought,
Deleuze writes not as "the *logos* that unifies the parts, but as the drunk-
enness, the pathos that bathes them and spreads out in them" (IT 207;
159). In the "sensual thinking" of the film's "inner monologue," "a
thought of the whole, presupposed, obscure" (IT 207; 159) permeates the
individual images, each of which expresses this affective whole as a specific feeling-image. Further, the syntax of this inner monologue is one of
figures, such as synecdoche, metonymy, and metaphor, whereby an associative link relates one image to the next. In Eisenstein's *Old and New (The
General Line)*, an image of a gush of milk is followed by an image of a fireworks explosion; a leap from one explosive shot to the next generates
pathos and instills a shock in the viewer. Yet to see the fireworks as a *figure* of the gushing milk requires a mental linking of the two images—not
necessarily a conscious linking but a linking through the unconscious
processes of sensual thinking. With the formation of this figural linking
of the two images, the affective power of both images is increased. Thus,
initially we move "from the shock-image to the formal and conscious
concept, but now from the unconscious concept to the matter-image, to
the figure-image, which incarnates the concept and causes a shock in its
turn. The figure gives to the image an affective charge that comes to
redouble the sensory shock" (IT 207; 159).

Two processes, then, may be discerned in the *Old and New*'s
sequence of the gush of milk and the fireworks explosion. The milk shot
and the fireworks shot collide, and that collision instills a shock in the
viewer. That shock impels thought to form a concept of the whole, some
notion of the single entity of which the individual shots are parts—say,

the concept "cosmic celebration of the workers' triumph." The first process thus involves a movement from image to concept, from parts to the whole, from shock-pathos to thought. At the same time, however, the milk shot and fireworks shot are not seen simply as detached and arbitrarily juxtaposed entities. They collide, but they also appear to be individual expressions of some pre-existing whole. That whole is vague and non-rational, as much felt as thought, a kind of dreamlike, intuited affective totality that gives each image its sense of "rightness" (something like the "artistic conception" of the film, that peculiar "feel" of the tone, ambience, rhythm, structure, and so forth of the work that guides Eisenstein in his construction of the work and that gives viewers a sense of the oneness of the film). A sensual thinking in images brings the milk shot and fireworks shot together, such that the one is perceived as a figure of the other. Through the association of the two images with one another, the affective power of each image is increased. Thus in the second process a movement takes place from concept to image, from the whole to the parts, from sensual thought to a redoubled pathos-shock.

Every film establishes a circuit that includes "the sensory shock that raises us from the images to conscious thought, then the thought through figures that sends us back to the images and gives us an affective shock again" (IT 210; 161). Though the circuit may be expressed as a temporal sequence, the two movements, from images to thought and from thought to images, coexist and presuppose one another. For Eisenstein, the successful film should combine the two movements in an organic unity of powerful feeling and critical awareness. But he argues as well that film should inspire action, that critical awareness should lead to a revolutionary consciousness. Deleuze sees here a third relation between image and thought, not that of a movement from one to the other but an identity of the two. Action entails a relation between actors and their surroundings, and the action Eisenstein envisions presupposes a harmonious relation between humans and the world. In an unalienated society, there is an accord between workers and the world they transform through their labor. In such a society, nature becomes a "nonindifferent nature," and this is the nature Eisenstein presents in his films. In *Battleship Potemkin,* for example, Eisenstein establishes various correspondences between nature and humans, the most notable instance being that of the misty Odessa harbor, which expresses the collective mood of sorrow and mourning for Vakulinchuk (see Nonindifferent

Nature 228). Here nature and mass consciousness coincide. Nature takes on new qualities through human action, and as a collective awareness grows, "it is also man who passes to a new quality, in becoming the collective subject of his proper reaction, while Nature becomes the objective human relation" (IT 211; 162). Collective consciousness, human thought in action, or action-thought, is embodied in the images of nature, and in this sense thought and image are identical. And what makes possible this identity of thought and image, humans and nature, is the underlying unity of the sensori-motor schema, here raised from the basic level of the individual's oneness with an ambient environment, to the utopian level of a collectivity's oneness with nature as a whole.

Eisenstein advocates for a particular kind of film, a dialectical cinema of affective collisions and leaps combining to form an organic whole that promotes collective action. Yet despite his manifest differences with other theorists and practitioners, Deleuze argues, the basic outlines of Eisenstein's analysis of thought's relationship to the image are valid for the classic cinema in its entirety. Throughout that cinema, one finds *the relationship with a whole which can only be thought in a superior coming-to-consciousness [prise de conscience]; the relationship with a thought which can only be figured in the subconscious unfolding [déroulement] of images; the sensori-motor relationship between the world and man, between Nature and thought*" (IT 212; 163). The movement from image to thought instigates a "critical thought" [*pensée critique*]; the movement from thought to image manifests a "hypnotic thought"; and the unity of image and thought gives rise to an "action-thought" (IT 212; 163). All three modes of thought coexist in the movement-image and mutually reinforce one another.

THE THOUGHT OF THE OUTSIDE

Central to the classic cinema's image of thought is the unifying presence of the sensori-motor schema, which makes possible a harmonious relationship between thought and image and between humans and the world. Its collapse in the modern cinema signals a break in our relation with the world. When we no longer find credible the sensori-motor schema's interconnecting ties and links that hold the world together, we are faced with the intolerable and the unthinkable. What is intolerable is not some great horror but "quotidian banality" (IT 221; 170), the sense that we are living in a second-rate film, and that we are as clichéd and as hollow as the world that surrounds us. The world's common-sense continuities and regularities, grounded in the sensori-motor schema, seem parodies of themselves. And as the schema's interconnections lose credibility, opsigns and sonsigns appear, pure visual and aural signs disconnected from any organizing schema. We are faced with the unthinkable, that which defies logical thought and yet demands to be thought.

The obvious question posed by the disconnected images is, How can they be reconnected? In the classic cinema, images are linked through their natural harmonies, polarities, and contrasts. The images embody the sensual thinking of an inner monologue, in which images are joined in sequences of synecdochic, metaphoric, and metonymic figures, each image succeeding the next according to its given affinities with the preceding. But with the collapse of the sensori-motor schema, this inner monologue collapses as well. The standard affinities between images no longer hold, and the figures of sensual thinking are no longer viable. The question "is no longer that of the association or the attraction of images. What counts, on the contrary, is the *interstice* between images, between two images: a spacing that causes each image to be wrested from the void and fall back into it" (IT 234; 179). In the classic cinema, the interstice between images is a function of the images, the point at which an image ends, or the point at which an image begins. In the modern cinema, the interstice is primary. The gap between images is not defined in terms of the images; it exists in itself. It is a void between things, a separating force that "spaces" things, that puts space between them. The challenge in the modern cinema is to start with a given image and then "to choose another that will induce an interstice *between* the two. It is not a process of association, but of differentiation, as mathematicians call it, or disparation [a dispersive "rendering disparate"], as physicists call it: a potential being given, one must choose another [image], not any whatever, but in such a manner that a difference of potential is established between the two, which will be productive of a third or of something new" (IT 234; 179–80). One image succeeds another in an additive process, "the method of AND, 'this and then that' " (IT 235; 180), Image C AND Image R AND Image X AND . . . The principle of selection is that of productive difference; one chooses Image R because its conjunction with Image C establishes a dynamic gap between C and R, a gap that generates something new; and then one chooses X according to the same principle.

In the modern cinema, the interstice between images appears directly in the black screen or white screen. The interstice is also evident in discontinuities between visual images and sonic images, as well as in the false continuities (*faux raccords* in French, literally "false joinings") of modern films that violate the norms of standard Hollywood editing. Indeed, all linkages in the modern cinema are ultimately *faux raccords*. The cut between shots is not a rational cut joining images according to a commonsense sequence, but "an irrational cut, which determines the non-commensurable relations between images" (IT 278; 213). The gap of the irrational cut separates two images without belonging to either, in this way resembling an irrational number, which can be used to cut a rational number line in two without itself being represented by a discrete point on that line (hence Deleuze's alternative designations of the irrational cut as "irrational point" and "point-cut").[4] The images conjoined through the irrational cut are not randomly connected, but "there are only re-linkages [*re-enchaînements*, literally "re-enchainings"] subservient to the cut, instead of cuts subservient to the linkage [*enchaînement*]" (IT 278; 213–14). In the classic cinema, of course, one can find occasional irrational cuts—false continuities, disjunctions between sight and sound, dissolves to black or white screens—but such phenomena by and large are momentary aberrations eventually subsumed within commonsense space-time coordinates, whereas in the modern cinema they are manifestations of the interstice as primary source of productive difference.

Modern images are not arbitrarily linked—indeed, much of *Cinema 2* is devoted to an analysis of the connections established between modern images through the various chronosigns: the connections of sheets of the past, of peaks of the present, and of diverse powers of the false. Yet such connections not only defy common sense but have a direct relation to the interstice, or irrational cut, and it is this notion of the interval *between* that provides the key to the modern relationship between images and thought.

The classic image of thought involves a complex movement from image to concept (critical thought) and from concept to image (hypnotic thought), as well as an identity of concept and image (action-thought), but this tripartite schema may also be recast in a bipolar model. Classic images are linked along a horizontal axis according to "laws of association, contiguity, resemblance, contrast or opposition" (IT 361; 276), the natural affinities of images within the unifying sensori-motor schema making possible the figural language of an inner monologue. The relationship between individual images and the whole may be mapped along a vertical axis of integration and differentiation: the whole in one sense is a gathering together of individual images within a unifying concept (integration), but at the same time the whole is present in each image, the whole expressing or unfolding itself in the sequence of different images (differentiation). Along the horizontal axis, images are linked according to rational cuts, the chain of images forming an "extendable world" (*monde prolongeable*) (IT 362; 277), a coherent space-time capable of expansion and continuation in all directions. Along the vertical axis, the images are *integrated* within a unifying, internal self-consciousness and simultaneously *differentiated* within a coherent external world. In the modern image, by contrast, the connections between images are formed through irrational cuts. Images are independent pieces, "disenchained" from the chains of images held together by the sensori-motor schema, which are then "re-enchained" according to their differences from one another. The images cannot be integrated within the concept of an internal self-consciousness, nor can they be treated as differentiations of a whole within a coherent external world. The connections of such images issue from a site beyond any external world, from a pure outside that is always beyond the limits of our coherent commonsense universe. And they instigate a thought that is alien to any rational inner mentality, a thought that is deeper, more inside than any coherent commonsense inside. Hence, if the modern image's horizontal axis is one of irrational cuts that re-enchain previously disenchained images, its vertical axis is one of an outside beyond any external world that is simultaneously an inside deeper than any internal world (see Fig. 3).

In the classic cinema, the whole is an open whole, but in the modern cinema, "the whole is the outside" (IT 233; 179). The outside is manifest in the interstice, the gap or interval between images. The outside is "the constitutive 'and' of things, the constitutive between-two [*entre-deux*] of images" (IT 235; 180). Deleuze may seem to be contradicting himself here, since elsewhere he apparently differentiates the vertical and the horizontal axes of the modern image in terms of an opposition

x174

Figure 3

Horizontal and Vertical Axes of Classic and Modern Cinematic Images of Thought

Classic Cinema

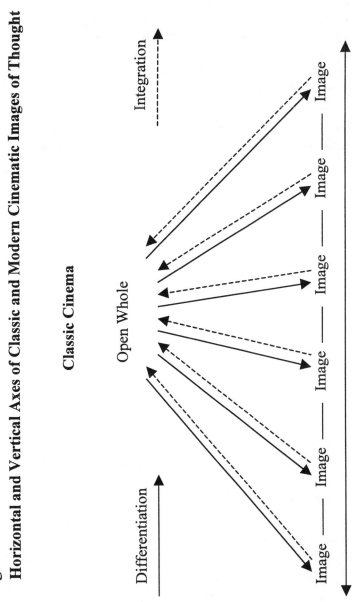

Integration

Open Whole

Differentiation

Horizontal Linkages of an Extendable World

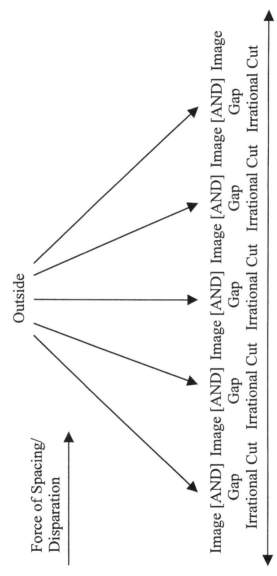

Modern Cinema

of the outside and the interstice, saying that in the modern image "the outside or reverse-side of the image has replaced the whole, at the same time that the interstice or cut has replaced association" (IT 279; 214). Deleuze's point, however, is that the interstice is common to the horizontal and vertical axes of the modern image: the interstice connects images horizontally, and it manifests the outside vertically. The "outside" is the modern counterpart of the classic "whole," a whole paradoxically conceived of as a gap or interval and yet as a generative force, a *constitutive* "between-two of images." The modern whole is "what Blanchot calls the force of 'dispersion of the Outside' or the 'vertigo of spacing': this void that is no longer a motor-part of the image" (IT 235; 180). If in classic cinema each image is an expression of the whole, an unfolding or explication of the whole in an individual part, in modern cinema each interstice is an expression or unfolding of the outside, the outside dispersing itself in multiple interstices, constituting in each interstice non-rational links, spacing the world through the force of its generative intervals. In the modern cinema, "the whole becomes the power [*puissance*] of the outside that passes into the interstice" (IT 236–37; 181).

That passage of the *puissance* or force of the outside into the interstice has a direct effect on thought. In the classic cinema, the collision of images shocks thought, jolting thought into action and forcing it to think the whole. Eventually, thought and image come together in a union of mind and world made possible by the sensori-motor schema. In the modern cinema, images also shock thought, but without thought being able to assimilate that shock within a coherent set of rational coordinates. Logical thought breaks down and experiences its own limits, its "unpower [*impouvoir*]" or "impotence [*impuissance*]" (IT 216; 166). Yet what that unpower reveals is that genuine thinking has not yet begun, that, as Heidegger says, "*most thought-provoking in our thought-provoking time is that we are still not thinking*" (Heidegger 1968, 6). The shock of the modern image "reveals this inability to think [*impuissance à penser*] at the heart of thought" (IT 216; 166). What the modern cinema forces thought to think is the outside, that dispersive, spacing force that passes into the interstice. Thought experiences the outside as "a fissure, a crack" (IT 218; 167), both in the external world and within. Thought, "as power [*puissance*] that has never existed, is born from an outside more distant than any exterior world, and, as power that does not yet exist, confronts an inside, an unthinkable or an unthought deeper than any interior world" (IT 363; 278). The thought instigated by the outside is a "thought outside itself" and an "unthought inside thought" (IT 363; 278). In its encounter with the outside, thought faces "on one hand the presence of an unthinkable within thought, which would be at once its source and its barrier; on the other, the presence to infinity of another thinker within the thinker, who shatters every monologue of a thinking self" (IT 218-19; 168).

THE SPIRITUAL AUTOMATON

"Thought outside itself," the "unthought or unthinkable inside thought," the "alien thinker within the thinker"—all attest to an apersonal, de-realized, "other" thought, the thought of a spiritual automaton. Various figures might represent the spiritual automaton—the robot, the computer brain, the zombie, the alien. Deleuze chooses the mummy, reading Dreyer's films as an extended exploration of this motif, with the heroine of *Gertrud* being perhaps the most complete of his mummy characters. Diverse images of the mummy-like spiritual automaton appear in modern films (and, one might object, such figures are the stock-in-trade of classic sci-fi and horror films), yet what is important, of course, is not the *representation* of the spiritual automaton, but its activation as mode of thought. When Dreyer's characters intone their trancelike sentences, when Rohmer's knights in *Perceval* recite their lines as if in the third person, or when Bresson's actors flatly deliver their monotone phrases, they are not simply acting like mummies. They are enunciating a kind of free indirect discourse, a speech disconnected from any particular speaker or point of view, as if their words issued from some place beyond any external world or some site further inside than any internal world. This free indirect discourse is ultimately just the verbal counterpart of a general "*free indirect vision*" (IT 239; 183) to which the modern cinema aspires. In the absence of the classic cinema's inner monologue that links images in commonsense sequences, vision is disconnected from stable points of view, as if the images were those of a non-human seeing—a floating eye, a prismatic eye, multiple eyes dispersed across space, and so on. The framing, composition, and connection of images attest to different ways of seeing, which are also different ways of thinking. In this sense, the images of the modern cinema are those of the free indirect discourse, the free indirect vision, and the free indirect thinking of a spiritual automaton. The representations of spiritual automata—the various mummified, hypnotized, anesthetized, vacant, transfixed, distracted, or distant characters who wander through modern films—are but indirect signs of the spiritual automaton's speaking, seeing, and thinking that *is* the film itself.

Where is the spiritual automaton? To the extent that modern cinematic images jolt the viewer into "thought beyond thought," the spiritual automaton is in the viewer. But the free indirect seeing and thinking of the spiritual automaton is also in the images, on the screen. The spiritual automaton is thus both inside and outside, inside the viewer and outside in the images. But within the image world as well there is no clear differentiation of inside and outside, between thought and image. The way of seeing and thinking manifest in the images belongs to no localizable or discretely identifiable mind; instead, mind is, as it were, immanent within the images, dispersed, acentered, multiple. Inside and outside communicate with one another in a topological space like that of a Klein bottle, a three-dimensional version of a Moebius strip with an inside and outside that form one continuous domain. Deleuze notes that according to some recent brain research the circuits of the brain form a similarly paradoxical topological space, connections following no single, centralized grid of Euclidean paths, but instead tracing dispersed, multiple, and probabilistic passages, such that the inner and outer surfaces of the brain's folds, its proximate and distant sites, communicate with one another in seemingly impossible ways. If one were to describe the spiritual automaton in corporeal terms, however, one would need to extend this scientific model of a topological brain beyond the closed limits of the skull. If in the modern cinema mind is immanent within the images, and if the images constitute a world, then that world is a topological brain world, in which inside and outside pass into one another, in which thought and image form a single "noosphere" (IT 281; 215).

The image world is the brain world of the spiritual automaton. The brain is the screen.[5] Hence, when Deleuze enumerates the "cerebral components" (IT 281; 215) of the modern image, he simply lists three guises of the interstice—"the point-cut, the re-linkage [*ré-enchaînement*], the white or black screen"—the last of which makes patent the identity of brain and screen. The *point-cut,* or irrational cut, is the interstice as manifestation of the outside. It is "irrational," in that, like an irrational number, it separates two entities without belonging to either. The *re-linkage* is the interstice as "AND," as horizontal connection of images according to non-arbitrary yet unspecified relations of difference. In this sense it is "probabilistic," undetermined and unpredictable at any given juncture, yet related to other interstices through the series of re-linkages the director chooses to create. The series of re-linkages thus resembles a Markov chain, a sequence of chemical reactions in which each reaction is a probabilistic event that affects the next reaction without specifying which one of a limited set of possible reactions it will induce. The *white or black screen,* finally, is the interstice made visible. It is "topological," for in it the outside and the inside merge. "And if the cut grows, if it absorbs all the images, then it becomes the screen, as contact independent of distance, copresence or application of black and of white, of the negative and the positive, of the recto and the verso, of the full and the void, of the past and the future, of the brain and the cosmos, of the inside and the outside" (IT 281; 215). Thus the physical brain of contemporary science, with its non-Euclidean, probabilistic, and topological connections, is a model of the cinematic brain world, whose components of the white or black screen, the re-linkage, and the point-cut are the "topological, probabilistic and irrational" constituents of the "noosphere" (IT 281; 215).

With the breakdown of the sensori-motor schema, the bond between humans and the world collapses. In Eisenstein's schema, thought and image unite in action-thought, since nature is ultimately nonindifferent and humans are capable of harmonious integration with nature. But in the absence of a unifying sensori-motor schema, the world seems alien; its certainties and verities seem hollow parodies of themselves, no longer credible or believable. One of the goals of the modern cinema, says Deleuze, is to make possible a belief in the world—not in some other world, or some future utopian state of this world, but in this world here and now. In other words, modern cinema seeks a new connection between humans and the world. Such a connection requires a different mode of thought, and Deleuze sees such a mode of thought as entailing a form of belief. Belief in turn he relates to the concepts of the problem and choice.

Modern directors connect the world and humans through the chronosigns of sheets of the past, peaks of the present, powers of the false. The chronosigns of each film constitute a kind of problem. A problem Deleuze distinguishes from a theorem, a theorem being a closed set of elements capable of an axiomatic systematization, a problem being an event that intervenes from the outside and thereby constitutes the terms of a subsequent analysis. The example Deleuze gives is that of the passage of a plane through a cone. Various geometrical figures may be defined in terms of the intersection of a plane and a cone—point, straight line, parabola, hyperbola, ellipse—any one of which may be the subject of a theorem. But the general problem of the relationship between the plane and the cone is that of an event, an intervention of a plane coming from outside the cone and creating various figures through its passage. The problem involves choices—which figure to generate via which secant angle of the plane—and Deleuze sees choice as a basic element of any problem (as opposed to a theorem).

Choice, in turn, he regards as central to belief. What Pascal and Kierkegaard show is that belief is a matter of "choosing to choose," of choosing the mode of living of one who is capable of choosing. To choose is to exercise freedom, and to believe is to risk at every moment the freedom of choosing. To choose is to place Pascal's wager, to make Kierkegaard's leap of faith, but also to embrace Nietzsche's *amor fati*—to will the results of each throw of the dice as the outcome one desires.[6] And every problem entails such a choice. Hence, the chronosigns of any given modern film may be seen as the manifestation of a problem, an event intervening from the outside. Each set of chronosigns involves a choice, and the affirmation of that choice is an act of belief. Chronosigns, though, are no ordinary problems. They are not simply interventions from outside, but themselves interventions *of* the outside, instances of non-rational "thought beyond thought" that defy ready assimilation and comprehension. They establish a connection between thought and images, between mind and world, but only one created through the free indirect vision of a spiritual automaton. They make possible belief in this world, but only in this world seen and thought "otherwise."

If we are to sum up Deleuze's treatment of images of thought, we may do so in four ways: in terms of (1) image-thought relations, (2) noosigns, (3) the noosphere, and (4) the relation between noosigns and chronosigns.

(1) The classic cinema establishes three relations between image and thought. In a first movement from image to thought, the shock of

images gives rise to the concept of the unifying whole; in a second movement from thought to image, the inner monologue of sensual thinking serves as the whole that each image presupposes and from which it issues as an expression of the whole; and in a third movement uniting image and thought, world and mind come together through the unifying force of the sensori-motor schema. The modern cinema, by contrast, "develops three new relations to thought: the effacement of a whole or a totalization of images, in favor of an outside that inserts itself between them; the effacement of the interior monologue as the film's whole, in favor of a free indirect discourse and vision; the effacement of the unity of man and world, in favor of a rupture that leaves us only with a belief in this world here and now" (IT 245; 187–88).

(2) Two axes organize the classic image of thought: a horizontal axis of association that links or "enchains" images in rational sequences, and a vertical axis of integration and differentiation, whereby the images are integrated within a whole and each image is in turn a differentiation or unfolding of that whole. There are hence two kinds of classic noosigns. "According to the first kind, images were linked through rational cuts, and under this condition formed an extendable world. . . . The other kind of noosign marked the integration of sequences in a whole (self-consciousness as interior representation), but also differentiation of the whole in the extended sequences (belief in an external world)" (IT 362; 277). The noosigns of the modern cinema also fall into two classes. "The direct time-image, then, has as its noosigns the irrational cut between non-linked images [*images non-enchaînées*] (but always re-linked [*ré-enchaînées*]) [i.e., the horizontal axis relinking one image to the next], and the absolute contact of an outside and an inside, non-totalizable and asymmetrical [i.e., the vertical axis whereby the outside manifests itself in every gap]" (IT 363; 278).

(3) The modern noosigns form a single noosphere, a brain world with three cerebral components: the point-cut, the re-linkage [*ré-enchaînement*], and the white or black screen. The point-cut is "irrational," the re-linkages "probabilistic," and the white or black screen "topological."

(4) The signs of the noosphere are also chronosigns. To the vertical axis of the outside corresponds a given time-image as general problem—the inexplicable and undecidable problem of peaks of the present, or of sheets of the past, or of a particular power of the false. To the horizon-

tal axis of re-linkages corresponds the set of time relations that allow leaps from present to present, or slidings from sheet to folding sheet, or becomings within series that combine before and after in a single event. Hence, when Deleuze contrasts the classic and modern cinematic means of reconciling the continuous and the discontinuous, he says that "when the whole becomes the power of the outside which passes into the interstice, then it is the direct presentation of time or continuity which agrees with [*se concilie avec*] the sequence of irrational points according to non-chronological relations of time" (IT 237; 181). The various irrational points (i.e., irrational cuts, point-cuts, or interstices between images in a horizontal series of re-linked images) take on the continuity of simultaneous presents, coexisting pasts, or metamorphic becomings, and each of these irrational points is the manifestation of a general "point of the outside from beyond the external world" (IT 237; 181), a vertical irrational point of the problem of a particular kind of non-chronological time. "This irrational point is . . . the *inexplicable* of Robbe-Grillet, the *undecidable* of Resnais . . . or again what one might call the *incommensurable* of Godard (between two things)" (IT 237; 182). The passage of the power of the outside into the interstice *is* the event of the inexplicable, undecidable, or incommensurable problem of a given form of non-chronological time. And the re-linkages of interstices *are* the paradoxical continuities that put the scattered points of a shattered chronological time in communication with one another.

SILENT AND AUDIBLE LECTOSIGNS

All chronosigns, besides being noosigns, are also lectosigns. Precisely what Deleuze means by "lectosign" is somewhat elusive. He takes the name, he tells us, from the Greek *lekton,* the Stoic term for the incorporeal of that which is "expressible."[7] Just as the *lekton* of a proposition exists independently of its object, so the lectosign designates the image "when it is grasped intrinsically, independently of its relation with a supposedly external object" (IT 35; 284). To grasp the image intrinsically is first of all to see it as an opsign, that is, as an image disconnected from its external links to the sensori-motor schema. But it is also to understand the image's internal relations, which include sonic as well as visual elements, and to do so, "the entire image must be read no less than seen, readable as much as visible" (IT 35; 22). The image's internal relations of sight and sound are one of the "dimensions or powers [*puis-sances*]" (IT 35; 22) that arise within the opsign/sonsign, and to seize those relations requires an entire "pedagogy" (IT 35; 22) as one learns to see and hear differently. It is important to note that when Deleuze says the image must be read, he is not simply making the banal observation that images must be interpreted, nor is he arguing that the image is a text or coded communication (and hence something subordinate to language).[8] Rather, to read the image is simply to grasp that dimension or power of the time-image produced through its internal relations of sight and sound.

The term "lectosign," then, suggests that the image is separated from its external object, like the *lekton,* and that it must be read in terms of its internal relations of sight and sound. But at one point Deleuze also uses the term in a broader sense to refer to cinematic sight and sound relations in general, noting that "the classic cinema did not lack lectosigns" (IT 365; 279). What might the classic lectosigns be? They would seem to be restricted to the sound era of film, but that is not the case, according to Deleuze, since the silent film is less silent than "quiet," sounds often indicated through visual signs (moving mouths, blasts of steam from a whistle, crashing buildings, etc.) or through writ-ten intertitles. Nonetheless, the advent of sound does change the visual image of the classic cinema. In silent films the visual image retains something of the "naturalness" of the world, that naturalness being characterized by its physical being as sphere of actions and reactions, of material connections between interacting forces. The word appears within images in epistles, notes, billboards, street signs, and so on as well as in intertitles, and always as something that quite literally must be read. The title card may present discourse directly ("I love you"), but its visual rendering of speech as written communication tends to con-vert direct discourse into an implicit indirect speech (He says he loves her). Written words within images (such as a shot of a building on which the words "Plaza Hotel" are painted) have the same effect of forming an indirect verbal communication. Hence, in silent films the visual images are both seen and read, the visible world retaining its nat-uralness and discourse manifesting itself in an indirect fashion.

With the advent of sound, speech is heard as well as read, and sounds become "*a new dimension of the visual image, a new component*" (IT 294; 226). The visual image becomes somewhat denaturalized, in large

part because a new domain is made visible with the advent of sound—
that of *"human interactions"* (IT 294; 227). Deleuze argues that we may
differentiate the preconditions and consequences of speech from certain aspects of acts of speech themselves. In silent films, speech is subordinate to action. The preconditions of a given verbal exchange—the
contextual factors of the physical and social world that situate and
shape the interlocutors, as well as the material and physical consequences of that exchange—are presented directly in the visual image.
The verbal exchange is either rendered indirectly through written signs
or merely suggested through the action that passes from the initial preconditioning situation to a consequent situation. But there is something in acts of speech that may be separated from their preconditions
and consequences, a dimension of "sociability" and "human interaction" that is a distinctive feature of discourse, and this dimension is
what sound films articulate aurally and render visible. Verbal exchanges
have their determinants of class, gender, ethnicity, region, relative for-
mality, and so on, but they also have a simple social function of constituting human interaction, a function resembling that of what linguists
call "phatic" communication, speech meant only to confirm that speech
is going on (e.g., "uh huh," "I see," "yeah, okay," "hear what I'm saying?"
"you know what I mean?").[9] Discourse at this level has its own rhythms
and forms that are relatively undetermined by preconditioning contexts
and consequent situations.

The model of this discursive sociability is the conversation, with its
open-ended rules for taking turns, initiating topics, and ending
exchanges, and its free-form succession of topics, now logically related to
one another, now without any apparent connection. With the introduction of sound in film, such forms of rudimentary sociability as the conversation are directly presented. No longer is speech rendered only as an
indirect function of antecedent conditions and succeeding consequences;
now it has a degree of autonomy. As a result, the visual image's "naturalness," which derives from its cause-effect continuities of structuring conditions and consequences, becomes compromised. An unfixed, relatively
unstructured and hence "unnatural" sonic element of sociability invades
the visual image. Moreover, the free flow of this sociable discourse tends
to take on a life of its own, since it is no longer determined by its structuring context. As a result, the act of speech, "through its autonomous
circulation, propagation and evolution, comes to create the interaction

between individuals or groups, whether distant, dispersed, or indifferent to one another" (IT 295; 227). In this regard, the rumor best models the discourse of sociability. In Lang's *M,* for example, a man reads aloud from a police notice posted in the street; the same text continues as a radio broadcast; then someone in a café reads subsequent sentences of that text to a cluster of citizens, until further rumors and disturbances spread through various crowds and groups throughout the city. A single statement is distributed among multiple speakers, the speech shaping the collective interaction. The discourse of sociability is a circulation of acts of speech passing through individuals, the conversation being "a contracted rumor, the rumor a dilated conversation, the two revealing the autonomy of the communication or circulation" (IT 299; 230). In the great comedies of the classic cinema (Cukor, Capra, and especially Hawks), this autonomous communication reaches one of its highest levels of artistic development as the loose and often anarchic flow of a conversational sociability distributes itself among characters, connecting them in circuits that at times include various social types and classes.

And that flow impinges on the visual image. The visible signs of characters' intentions, motivations, and insinuations must be read in their faces and gestures, since with the advent of sound the characters can lie, deceive, distort, misspeak, hint. The naturalness of the characters' expressive bodies is thereby infected with a potential artificiality and deceptiveness. Verbal exchanges also affect the vectoral space of the image, the glances of the conversational partners shaping camera angles and movements, blocking, montage. The sonic voice "expands in the visual space, or fills it, seeking to reach its addressee across obstacles and detours. It hollows out space" (IT 303; 233). In a more general sense, sound expands the visual image as off-camera voices and ambient noises indicate the continuities of space beyond the frame and into the out-of-field world. And even more important is the way sound fills the "absolute out-of-field" through voice-overs and music. Narrative voices, the voices of reminiscence, of reflection or of commentary, inhabit no clear physical position in relation to the visual image, yet pertain to it as an added dimension. In this way the spoken word enhances the visual movement-image by emphasizing its continuity with the open Whole, of which each shot is an expressive unfolding. The voice-over consciousness speaks from this open whole and imbues the visual image with its presence.

Music has a special effect on the classic movement-image, for according to Deleuze it is capable of directly expressing the open whole. Deleuze insists on one hand that a sonic continuum accompanies the visual image, a continuum that includes dialogue, sound effects, and music in both the relative and absolute out-of-field; and on the other hand that music has the "specific autonomous power" of a "foreign body" (IT 313; 240). Frequently musical performances take place onscreen in classic films and then continue offscreen. As the couple leave the cantina, where they had watched the performance of a guitar soloist, the guitarist's strummings, which had earlier been mingled with the clinking of glasses, the shouts of the crowd, and the couple's conversation, are joined by a studio orchestra, and a seamless passage connects the physical world to the ambient sound world of the film score. Yet if the score belongs to the visual world of the movement-image, it does not simply illustrate it or double its rhythms. In silent films, the score is external to the image, supplied by improvising performers who fashion a kind of running programme-music commentary on the images. With the addition of sound to film, music takes on a greater autonomy. Eisenstein argues that a rhythmic correspondence should unite visual images and their musical accompaniment, but others, like Brecht's collaborator Hanns Eisler, insist that music need not follow the pulse and mood of the visual images.[10] A stirring march may accompany close-ups of weeping faces in a crowd, or a gentle waltz may play over a violent battle scene. In Deleuze's view, music's relation to the visual image encompasses a gamut of possibilities, ranging in function from sonic component of the onscreen scene, through harmonious reinforcement of the film's rhythms, to autonomous "foreign body." What makes possible this continuum of relations is music's participation in the expressive interplay of enfolding integration and unfolding differentiation that relates the open whole and the individual images.

Ultimately, music is distinguished from the visual movement-image in that music, unlike the movement-image, is capable of directly presenting the open whole in an "immediate image," incommensurable with the visual image, "Dionysian, musical: closer to a fathomless Will than a movement" (IT 311; 239). Deleuze's allusion at this point is to *The Birth of Tragedy,* in which Nietzsche cites at length Schopenhauer's analysis of music as "an immediate copy of the will itself" and of the world as "embodied music." For Schopenhauer, music "resembles geometrical figures and numbers, which are the universal forms of all possible objects of experience and applicable to them all *a priori,* and yet are not abstract but perceptible and thoroughly determinate." Hence, music is in a sense "like general concepts, an abstraction from the real," yet it is also perceptible and "gives the inmost kernel which precedes all forms, or the heart of things" (cited in *Birth of Tragedy* 101–102). For Deleuze, the abstract yet perceptible "immediate image" of music is a direct presentation of the open whole, and as such it reacts with the visual images as an autonomous entity, capable of echoing and reinforcing the images, but also of interacting with them "independently of any common structure" (IT 311; 239). "In short," says Deleuze, "to the indirect representation of time as changing whole, the sound cinema adds *a direct presentation, but musical and only musical, non-corresponding.* It is the living concept, which goes beyond [*dépasse*] the visual image, without being able to dispense with it [*sans pouvoir s'en passer*]" (IT 312; 240).

THE MODERN LECTOSIGN

In silent films, then, speech is read in the intertitles, and discourse is always indirect. In classic sound films, discourse is direct and becomes a contributing constituent of the visual image. The visual image of silent films loses its naturalness and thereby becomes something that must be read; the act of speech "becomes visible at the same time that it makes itself heard, but also the visual image becomes readable, as such, as visual image in which the act of speech inserts itself as component" (IT 303; 234). In music, classic sound films find a potentially autonomous element, a direct audio presentation of the whole that accompanies an indirect visual presentation of the whole without corresponding to it. Yet this autonomy is only relative. Music "goes beyond" the visual image, but it cannot "dispense with it," for the score, despite its non-correspondence to the visual images, ultimately attempts to present directly to the ears the same open whole of the sensori-motor schema as presented indirectly on the screen. Only in the modern cinema do sight and sound become autonomous elements. In that cinema, discourse is neither direct nor indirect, but free indirect, and both the visual image and the audio image are images that must be read.

There are various ways in which modern directors create free indirect speech. Dreyer slows the cadences of his actors to a ritual pace;

Rohmer has the characters of *The Marquise of O* and *Perceval* speak in a markedly "written" and uncontemporary style; Bresson elicits distanced, dispossessed performances from his actors; Rouch provokes the subjects of his ethnofictions to engage in a process of fabulation. In all such cases, "there are conditions of strangeness that will disengage, or as Marguerite Duras says, 'frame' the pure act of speech" (IT 331; 253-54). Cinematic free indirect discourse is a pure act of speech, discourse "dis-enchained" from its standard usage and from its linkages with the visual images of the commonsense world. When discourse is made strange, disengaged from its naturalizing contexts, marked and "framed" as discourse, it "folds in on itself, it no longer is a dependent or adjunct of the visual image, it becomes an entirely separate sonic image, it assumes a cinematographic autonomy" (IT 316; 243). At the same time, the visual image attains its own strangeness as discourse turns in on itself and extricates itself from its ordinary visible coordinates. A non-humanized world emerges, one unaffected by conventional linguistic categories. Bresson's disconnected spaces (the Gare de Lyon in *Pickpocket*), Antonioni's vacant, emptied spaces (*L'Avventura, Red Desert*), Pasolini's deserts (*The Gospel According to Matthew, Oedipus the King, Teorema*) are but a few instances of this world dispossessed of its linguistic constituents. "It is as if, speech having removed itself from the image to become founding act [*acte fondateur*], the image, for its part, made the foundations of space rise up, the 'strata,' those mute powers [*puissances*] of the before or after of speech, of the before or after of humans. The visual image becomes *archaeological, stratigraphic, tectonic*" (IT 317; 243).

The modern visual images and sonic images must be "read," in the sense that these images, disengaged and disconnected from their standard contexts, must be reconnected, re-enchained in ways that cannot be anticipated ahead of the appearance of the given images. This notion of reading Deleuze takes from Noël Burch, who in commenting on Ozu's violations of shot/reverse-shot conventions, notes that "the mental reconstitution of a three-dimensional space on the basis of these 'badly joined,' flat images, requires a considerable effort of memory and imagination, i.e., a *reading*" (Observer 174). In his 180-degree cuts especially, Ozu disconcerts the viewer, for there the shot "seems to 'flip over'" (175) like a photographic slide put in the projector the wrong way, flipped around sideways, A facing B left-to-right in one shot (A-B), their positions reversed in the next (B-A). Deleuze says of a similar use of 180 degree cuts in Straub and Huillet's *Moses and Aaron* that it is as if both sides of the film stock were being projected, now run through the machine the right way, now fed through the sprockets with the "inside" surface of the film on the outside. This "turning," or "turning around [*retournement*]" of the image serves as a figure for all the relinkages that anomalous modern images require of the viewer, all the acts of memory and imagination necessary to hold puzzling images in the mind and understand how one image is connected to the next. Hence, the reading of the visual image "is the stratigraphic state, the turning-around [*retournement*] of the image, the corresponding act of perception that ceaselessly converts the empty into the full, the right side into its reverse [*l'endroit en envers,* i.e., recto into verso]. To read is to re-enchain rather than to enchain, to turn, to turn around [*retourner*], instead of following on the right side [*à l'endroit*]" (IT 319; 245).

The "archaeological, stratigraphic, tectonic" nature of the modern visual image Deleuze finds most evident in the films of Jean-Marie Straub and Danièle Huillet.[11] Frequently Straub/Huillet offer long, slow pans of fields, pastures, deserts, and landscapes that have been the sites of massacres, battles, sacrifices, and executions. The buried histories of bloodshed are obliquely alluded to by voices and by shots of written texts or monuments, but the landscapes remain insistently resistant to their histories, like archaeological digs awaiting excavation, or geological faults displaying enigmatic layers in need of explication. Straub/Huillet also consciously emulate Cézanne in their approach to landscapes, attempting to render visible the forces that play through matter, just as Cézanne tries to paint the seismic forces that have generated Mont Saint Victoire. Their effort is not to arouse sensations in the viewers, but to materialize sensation in the landscape, and in this Deleuze sees the fundamental aesthetic of the modern visual image. Once visual images are dis-enchained from the sensori-motor schema, the world's "pictorial or sculptural qualities depend on a geological, tectonic power [*puissance*], like the rocks of Cézanne" (IT 321; 246). In his *Francis Bacon: Logique de la sensation,* Deleuze shows how Bacon similarly makes forces visible in his paintings, "the brutality of fact" bypassing the brain and working directly on the senses through images that defy assimilation in terms of standard visual codes. Like Bacon, such modern directors as Straub/Huillet create images that escape visual clichés and thereby manage to materialize sensation in images shaped by a "geological, tectonic power."[12]

The modern visual image, then, is archaeological, stratigraphic, and tectonic in that it is the site of multilayered forces that materialize sensation and offer the possibility of various re-enchainments with other images, each conjunction of images forcing the viewer to read the image in terms of the re-enchainment actualized in that particular series of images. In the separation of sight and speech, "the visual image reveals its geological strata or foundations, while the act of speech or even of music becomes for its part aerial founder [*fondateur aérien*]" (IT 321; 246). Though autonomous, the visual image and the act of speech interact with one another in a "come-and-go between speech and the image" (IT 322; 247). In Straub/Huillet's *Fortini/Cani*, for example, the poet Franco Fortini reads from his *I Cani del Sinai* [*The Dogs of the Sinai*], his response as an Italian communist Jew to the Israeli-Palestinian Six-Day War.[13] Images of the physical book and of Fortini reading from it emphasize the textual nature of Fortini's act of speech. A further "strangeness" affects his reading in that he is confronting the work ten years after its composition and in excerpts selected by Straub/Huillet, his voice revealing varied reactions to his own words (amusement, surprise, affirmation) as he pronounces them. Amid images of Fortini reading and Fortini's book (as well as two newspaper articles, displayed at length on the screen, the texts of which do not coincide with Fortini's voice-over reading), slow pans of various countryside landscapes intervene. A monument in one shot identifies the village as the site of Nazi brutalities, and Fortini's text alludes to other locales shown on the screen, but the references are often staggered in relation to the images, and always oblique, never taking the form of a commentary on the images.[14] The landscapes serve as monuments to the Italian victims of German violence during World War II, whereas Fortini's text focuses on the violence of the Six-Day War. Fortini's words name the landscapes and allude to their buried histories; they also evoke the unseen Six-Day War and thereby juxtapose the visible site of Italian memory with the unshown bloodshed of the Israeli-Palestinian conflict. Events are enunciated through speech, and the event of the juxtaposition of the two wars is created through the back-and-forth coming-and-going of speech and visual image. "The aerial act of speech creates the event, but always placed crosswise over the tectonic visual layers: they are two trajectories that traverse one another" (IT 322; 247).

In the modern cinema, visual images are re-enchained through the interstices of irrational cuts, and sound, too, is involved in such cuts. In some cases, an act of speech, a sound effect, or a musical passage inserts a disruptive break into a visual continuity. In others, the reverse takes place, a jolting image, for example, appearing suddenly while a lyrical musical phrase continues seamlessly to unfold. And in yet other instances sound and sight mutually reinforce the irrational cut, as in *Fortini/Cani,* with its black-screen punctuation of textual fragments, or in Resnais' *L'amour à mort,* in which music is only heard in the intervals between scenes. But there are films as well in which the primary interstice is that between the visual and the sonic. Marguerite Duras says of *La femme du Gange* that it is two films, a film of images and a film of voices, and Deleuze takes her cinema as an exemplary instance of the modern relation of sight to sound. Deleuze concurs with Duras's judgment that visual images and voices are autonomous in her films, but her suggestion that the two have nothing to do with one another he takes as playful exaggeration. The question for Deleuze is what non-arbitrary relation puts these autonomous elements in contact with one another.

Whereas Straub/Huillet conjoin a stratigraphic vision and overtly political acts of speech, Duras juxtaposes a fluid, oceanographic vision and words of love and desire. The essential liquidity of her visual images engages "a calm fluvial power [*puissance*] which is the equivalent of the eternal, which mixes the strata" (IT 337; 258). The non-coinciding voices of love and desire tend toward an ineffable limit, the words of longing at times passing into song or cries (like the cries of the vice consul in *India Song*). The visible and the audible both tend toward a limit, the visual images toward a point of dissolution into an oceanic flow, the voices toward the thresholds between speech and music or noise. In this regard, Duras simply makes evident what all modern films do. Modern visual images always tend toward a limit, the limit of what ordinary, common-sense sight sees and what a re-enchainment of images makes visible. Likewise, the free indirect discourse of pure acts of speech tends toward the limit of what conventional codes articulate. Fabulation is a becoming, a metamorphic movement beyond a limit. It is a usage of language that puts in variation all components of language, phonic, syntactic, and semantic.[15] The fabulations of Rouch's collaborators, the political statements of Straub/Huillet's speakers/readers, and the songs/cries of

Duras's lovers are all metamorphic, destabilizing usages of language, becomings in language pushing its components toward their limits. In such metamorphic usages, speech "turns around toward a limit that is, as it were, unsayable and yet that which only can be spoken" (IT 339; 260). So likewise in modern visual images, vision "is carried to a limit which is at once something invisible and which nevertheless can only be seen (a kind of clairvoyance, differing from seeing, and passing through *espaces quelconques,* empty or disconnected)" (IT 340; 260).

Vision and speech press toward internally defined limits, but also toward the limit between the two, the point at which seeing differs from speaking and speaking from seeing. That limit separates the two, but in so doing forms the relation between them: "It is the limit of each one that relates it to the other" (IT 340; 260). What Deleuze suggests here is that complementary sonic and linguistic limits haunt the visual image of modern cinema, and that the difference between seeing and speaking is what relates them to one another. The vision is that "of a blind man, of Tiresias," the speech "that of an aphasic or an amnesic" (IT 340; 260), and the two constantly gesture toward one another. "What speech utters, is also what sight only sees through clairvoyance, and what sight sees, is the unsayable that speech utters" (IT 340; 260). Yet at the same time "the visual image will never show what the sound image utters" (IT 364; 279). There is no commensurability but a "complementarity" between vision and voice, an "irrational cut between the two, but which forms the non-totalizable relation, the broken ring of their juncture, the asymmetrical faces of their contact. It is a perpetual re-enchainment" (IT 364; 279).

What makes this "complementary" relation non-arbitrary and specific is that each film centers on a particular problem or set of problems, a generative difference that produces the re-enchainments of visual images, the re-enchainments of acts of speech, and the re-enchaining come-and-go between the two. In *Fortini/Cani,* for example, the problem is that of fascism, racism, and class conflict as they inform Italy's past and shape its views on Israeli-Palestinian relations. The visual linkages of landscapes generate a stratigraphic space of mute memory, the verbal linkages generate the fabulation of an Italian communist Jew betraying his class, ethnic, and even political affiliations as he develops a response to Italy's stance on the Six-Day War. Vision and speech interact and interconnect while simultaneously diverging, the stratigraphic landscapes of buried Nazi bloodshed in disjunction with the discourse about the Six-Day War, but the two pointing toward a single problem, and their conjunction being formed along the line of their specific difference—that of this particular unspeaking vision and this particular unseeing discourse. In *India Song*, the problem is that of the desires of Anne-Marie Stretter, the vice consul, and Michael Richardson. The voices tell of past festivities and the future sufferings of abandonment, disappointment, and suicide, while on the screen appear images of a dance in a present situated in 1937, with interspersed tracking shots along building facades and through dark, empty parks. The voices speak of the visible characters, but not directly of the events taking place on the screen. The visual alternation of interior and exterior shots establishes its own linkage of an enclosed, formal dance world passing into a slowly decaying tropical environment, while the voices for their part interrelate with one another in complex combinations and tend toward ineffable sounds and cries. Vision and voices move toward their proper limits, and their connection is formed through their insistent non-coincidence, the split between seeing and speaking aligning with the split between present actions and incommensurable past/future memories and longings.

If in the classic cinema a sonic continuum connects onscreen events, out-of-field sounds, and an absolute out-of-field realm of reflective voice-overs and music, that continuum takes on a different form in the modern cinema. Speech in *India Song* tends toward an inarticulate cry, and in general the becoming of a metamorphic usage of language involves a sonic disturbance of language that pushes it toward the limits of its conventional articulation. The strangeness of the act of speech in modern films allows a passage of speaking into the musical dimension of chanting or singing, or into the sonic domain of unformed sounds and noises. Many modern directors systematically interrelate musical and non-musical sounds, and others treat the gamut of speech, music, and noise as a single material for sonic manipulation (e.g., Godard's *Prénom Carmen*). What this indicates is that the modern cinema's separation of speech from the visual image is simply one aspect of a larger division of all sound from sight. If, as Duras claims, *La femme du Gange* is a film of images and a film of voices, one may say that every modern film is also two films, a visual film of screen images and an audio film of sounds shaped from the sonic continuum of speech, music, and noises. Not only does the act of speech separate itself from the visual image, but it also resonates with non-linguistic sounds. The modern image is audio-visual, and modern lectosigns exploit the power of a disjunction of sound and sight. Such lectosigns must be read, in that visual images must be re-enchained in series; sonic images, shaped from the continuum of words, music, and sounds, must be re-enchained with one another; and the two strands must be re-enchained in a complementary, non-totalizable, asymmetrical come-and-go that issues from a generative disjunction between the two.

A NOTE ON CINEMA, THEATER, AND TELEVISION

Theater and television are two media with apparent ties to cinema, and in the relation between sight and sound Deleuze finds one means of situating them vis-à-vis one another. With the advent of sound, film might seem a close cousin of the theater, but in Deleuze's view the two have "nothing in common" except "at the level of bad films" (IT 297; 228). Even in the most "stagy" of good classic films, something emerges that the theater rarely captures: "conversation for itself" (IT 300; 231), the ebb and flow of a loosely associative, open-ended discourse of rudimentary sociability. And one of the reasons cinema succeeds in capturing conversation is that it renders the word through the visible in ways that are unavailable to the stage. The voice shapes space in cinema, "itself tracing a path within the visual image" (IT 303; 233). The directional movement of sound is a structural constituent of each shot, and with every change in point of view, framing, angle, and camera movement, the relation of sound to sight shifts. In the theater, by contrast, the spectator's eye and ear remain fixed in a stable space. There is also no out-of-field in the theater, whereas the off-camera space indicated by voices and noises is a basic component of the visual image of the sound cinema. Offstage voices, music and sound effects are not uncommon in the theater, but they never suggest a prolongation of the stage world into a surrounding space. Finally, the sonic continuum of film fuses voices, music, and sounds in a way the theater cannot. Film's manipulation of sound levels and their integration within a single flow (even if that flow is divided into multiple tracks and distributed throughout the projection space, as with surround sound) ensures that, even in the most conventional of films, a seamless sonic/visual space extends from the shot to the out-of-field and into the absolute out-of-field of music and/or voice-over commentary.

Unlike film and the theater, cinema and television are closely and complexly allied. One of the key features of television as a medium is the separability of its audio and visual constituents, and Deleuze asserts that the modern cinema's handling of sound and sight as autonomous elements "would never have arisen without television, it is television that made it possible" (IT 328; 251–52). But this is only one of many ways in which television seems to anticipate the innovations of the modern cinema. The television image is an electronic image, created through a rapid scanning of lines of pixels by a beam of electrons. As the video artist Nam June Paik observes, "the essential concept, in regard to television, is time" (Paik 10), the time of an oscillating electron beam passing over an interwoven mesh of pixels. In this sense, the television image as constant scanning of lines is fundamentally a type of time-image. As electronic image, it lends itself to digitalization, and with the digital image an essential mutability of images emerges. As Edmond Couchot argues, digital images must be regarded as transformable emissions of "immedia," without clear origin or final destination. Images may be computer generated, they may be "morphed" through electronic manipulation, they may be duplicated, simulated, and transferred in an endless circulation of images passing one into another. As a result, television images have no genuine out-of-field, but instead "a right-side and a reverse [recto and verso], reversible and non-superimposable, like a power to turn around on themselves. They are the object of a perpetual reorganization, whereby a new image may arise from any point whatever of the preceding image" (IT 347; 265). In this regard, the digital television image anticipates the modern cinematic lectosign, which must be turned around to be read, seen from the right side and the reverse if it is to be re-enchained in new series. The mutability of the video image also undermines the screen dimensions of up and down, right and left, rendering the screen less a window on the world than the site of transformable data. The video screen becomes "a table of information, an opaque surface on which 'data' are inscribed, information replacing Nature, and the city-brain, the third eye, replacing the eyes of Nature" (IT 347; 265). Thus, the video screen is a brain screen, and in this sense a version of the modern cinema's noosphere.

Yet the television image is not the direct cause of the modern cine-matic image. Without a "powerful will to art" (*une puissante volonté d'art*) (IT 266) no technological innovation leads to genuine artistic creativity. Television, computers, and information technology in general provide external conditions of possibility for creativity in the cinema (and in other arts as well), but internal, properly cinematic concerns are finally what guide directors in their invention of new images. Their innova-tions "depend on an aesthetic before depending on technology. It is the time-image that calls forth an original regime of images and signs, before electronics ruins it, or, by contrast, relaunches it" (IT 349; 267). Duras does not imitate television in *La femme du Gange* but finds prop-erly cinematic means of utilizing the disjunction of sight and sound to fashion new relations between images. Resnais's memory space is con-sonant with the brain world of free-flowing digital information-images, but computers and video screens do not induce his cinematic images. Rather, they provide a general external context within which he devel-ops cinematic means of molding and transforming sheets of the past in the probabilistic and topological folds of a mind world. Each medium has its potential for creative development, and in fact Deleuze sees much of the potential of television as unexploited. Television's main use has been for social control rather than artistic invention, and if any-thing it has been cinema that has shown television what the medium is capable of. The affinities between television and cinema have allowed television to serve as a stimulus to creativity in cinema, but finally it is the cinematic image that has revealed, through the pursuit of its own ends, the nature of the television image.

Conclusion

When Plato recounts the creation of the universe, he says that the creator "resolved to have a moving image of eternity, and when he set in order the heaven [i.e., when he created the sun, moon, and five planets], he made this image eternal but moving according to number, while eternity itself rests in unity, and this image we call time" (Timaeus 37d–e). For Plato, time is a function of movement, the uniform rotation of the planets regulating time and providing a kinetic image of eternity and the truths of mathematics.[1] As for movement itself, Plato and the ancients thought of it as a passage from one ideal pose to another, like a series of statues passing through intermediary states as they succeed one another. As Bergson points out, the Renaissance reconceived motion in terms of a uniform space and a metrical time in which no moment is privileged over another. Yet movement itself eluded Renaissance scientists, Bergson claims, as it did the ancients before them. They spatialized time and separated movement from the moving object, picturing motion as a sequence of discrete points on a line. If time and movement are real, Bergson argues, movement must be grasped as the transformation of a whole, in which any given moving entity, its motion and all surrounding entities form an open, constantly changing totality. That open whole Bergson conceives of as a universe of images, an incessant flow of matter-movement within which certain specialized images appear—living images that interrupt the constant flow of motion. These living images are gaps in the flux of movements, intervals between actions and subsequent reactions.

Bergson's model of an open whole of matter-movement filled with the intervals of living images provides Deleuze with the basic terms of his analysis of the movement-image. On a vertical axis of differentiation, Deleuze treats the frame, shot, and montage as the elements of an expressive enfolding and unfolding of the open whole through individual images. The frame makes a cut in the open whole, montage reassembles a portion of the open whole, and the shot serves as the common element between the cuts and the montage whole. On a horizontal axis of specification, Deleuze situates the various kinds of movement-images, starting with Bergson's perception-image, action-image, and affection-image, then generating the image of Peircean Thirdness, the relation-image, and the intermediary images of the impulse-image and the reflection-image. To each of the movement-images correspond at least two signs of composition and one genetic sign. These are the images and signs treated by the classic cinema, and their disposition is regulated by the sensori-motor schema.

The signs of the perception-image make visible a perception of perception, the signs of perception issuing most often from fixed points of view, but occasionally from a floating, flowing liquid perspective, and at rare moments from a gaseous apprehension-in-things, as if the world had become a meta-cinema of ubiquitously distributed matter eyes. The signs of the affection-image are facial signs, the face's contours reflecting qualities, its intensive traits registering the passage of one quality to another, and the facialized domain of an *espace quelconque* tracing the affective movements of a disconnected or vacant space. The impulse-image arises from an originary world of drives, and its signs are either symptoms, which are qualities or powers related to the originary world, or good and bad fetishes, which are fragments wrested by drives from a real milieu. Action-images are of two kinds, Large Form and Small Form, and the signs of the action-image concern either the sequence Situation-Action-Transformed Situation (S-A-S') or the sequence Action-Situation–New Action (A-S-A'). In the Large Form sequence of S-A-S', actions emanate from an englobing environment, whereas in the Small Form sequence of A-S-A', actions trace a line of the universe that connects one space to another, piece by piece. Reflection-images transform Large and Small Forms into one another, the signs of the reflection-images functioning as so many figures—theatrical/scenographic figures in which an image anticipates a future action (e.g., a simulated event shown in a stage performance foreshadowing a later real event); sculptural/plastic figures in which an image serves as a metaphor for another situation (e.g., Eisenstein's fireworks explosion as a figure for the peasants' joy in *The General Line*); figures of inversion in which Large Form and Small Form images mirror one another; and figures of discourse in which an indirect relation between an action and a situation is given direct expression in discourse. And relation-images, finally, provide visual indications of mental relations, their signs being the *marks* of natural relations, the *demarks* of disrupted natural relations, and the *symbols* that render visible conventional relations formed by law or habit.

The classic cinema manifests a Bergsonian understanding of movement, one that goes beyond the Renaissance model of a spatialized time and a separation of motion and moving object. But for the classic cinema, time remains subservient to movement, as it was for Plato and the ancients. Only with the modern cinema does the relationship between time and movement change. In the modern cinema, aberrant movement is no longer recuperated within a coherent and unified time-space (as when anomalous images and sequences are explained as distorted perceptions, vague memories, dreams, hallucinations, etc.). Instead, aberrant, uncentered movement becomes the rule. Forms of time generate various aberrant movements, and in those movements we see direct images of time. The first indications of a new relationship between time and movement are opsigns and sonsigns, pure visual and sonic images unassimilated within a sensori-motor schema. Certain classic treatments of memory and dreams, such as Mankiewicz's flashbacks and musical comedy's oniric dance worlds, point toward the new time-image, but only in the hyalosigns of the time-crystal does time appear in itself. There, the splitting of time into an actual present and coexisting virtual past is made visible, as opsigns and sonsigns, the shattered shards of time-crystals, are assembled in circuits of images—virtual/actual, limpid/opaque, seed/milieu—that render indiscernible the virtual and the actual.

In chronosigns, the time-image undergoes its fullest development, as sheets of the past, peaks of the present, and various powers of the false generate movements that defy assimilation within commonsense coordinates. In sheets of the past, diverse planes of past time, each a slice from the great cone of the virtual past, are juxtaposed and interconnected through transverse passages that produce incompossible combinations of coexisting past times. In peaks of the present, incompossible presents-of-the-past, presents-of-the-present, and presents-of-the-future are treated as simultaneous present moments, and through abrupt leaps from peak to peak mutually exclusive points of time are put in relation to one another. The movements generated by sheets of the past and peaks of the present make undecidable the distinction between the true and the false, for these paradoxical forms of time bring together past and present events that cannot all be true, but without providing any means of determining which are true and which not. True and false are also undecidable in the chronosigns of time-as-series, those signs in which the vital becoming of time subsumes a retained past and a projected future within a mutative present. In these chronosigns, the power of the false is made manifest in various ways, but always as a force of metamorphosis. In Welles, it is made visible in Nietzschean accounts of vengeful truth seekers, violent betrayers, and artist-fakers. In Rouch, the power of the false is a power of fabulation, whereby Rouch and his African collaborators generate ethnofictions of a future people in formation. In Clarke's and Cassavetes's cinema of the body, corporeal attitudes and gestural patterns constitute trajectories of the power of the false that generate characters, scenes, spaces, and movements. And in Godard's cinema of categories, the power of the false is a force that converts stable classifications into metamorphic series and compels a reading of images as a sequence of incommensurable yet interrelated categories.

The divide between the classic and modern cinema is marked by the collapse of the sensori-motor schema and a reversal of the relation of time to movement. With that reversal, thought's relation to the image also changes, as does the relation of image to sound. The classic cinema's passage from image shock to concept of the whole and from presupposed whole as inner monologue to image-figures depends on a union of mind and world through the sensori-motor schema. With its collapse, the shock of the image induces a thought of the outside, and inner monologue gives way to free indirect discourse as new modes of re-linking images make possible a belief in this world. The classic axes of a vertical integration/differentiation of the open whole and individual parts and a horizontal enchaining of images in regular sequences are replaced by axes of a vertical passage of the outside into the interstice and a horizontal re-enchaining of images through their disjunctive differences from one another. The classic unity of mind and world yields to a topological play of outside and inside whereby brain and world fold into one another. The modern noosphere has as its components the irrational cut, re-linkages, and the white/black screen, and each is a form of the interstice, a vertical-axis divide through which the outside is manifest, a horizontal-axis gap that generates additive series, and an empty hiatus that fills the screen. The interstice is primary as well in the modern lectosign, the split between visual image and audio image serving as the principle of their incommensurable, asymmetrical relationship. In silent film, speech is indirect and literally read; in classic sound film, speech is direct and read in the visual images it shapes; but in the modern cinema, speech separates itself from the visual image, becomes free indirect speech, and forms part of an autonomous sonic continuum. Visual images and sonic images each tend toward their proper limits, and they interrelate through the interstice that marks their mutual limit from one another. Such images must be read, in that they must be re-enchained, visual with visual images, sonic with sonic, and visual with sonic.

Movement-images and time-images are distinct in their manifestation of the relationship between movement and time, but it is not surprising that the two forms of images should on occasion shade into one another. All cinema "brings to light an intelligible matter" which "consists of movements and processes of thought (prelinguistic images) and of points of view taken on these movements and processes (presignifying signs)" (IT 342; 262). This intelligible matter is "a plastic mass, an a-signifying and a-syntactic matter, a non-linguistically formed matter, though it is not amorphous and is semiotically, aesthetically and pragmatically formed" (IT 44; 29). It becomes one kind of "signaletic matter" (IT 43; 29) when regulated by the sensori-motor schema, another when shaped by the paradoxical forces of time. Aberrant movement has been present from the earliest days of film, and with it, the prospect of a new kind of image. "The direct time-image is the phantom that has always haunted the cinema, but it took the modern cinema to give this phantom a body" (IT 59; 41). The invention of this phantom body, the brain world of the spiritual automaton, requires new modes of seeing, hearing, reading and thinking, but those modes are already present within cinema's intelligible matter, virtual modes available for actualization by those filmmakers who are able to create the means of using them.

Deleuze finds in Bergson and Peirce the philosophical foundations of a taxonomy of cinematic images, yet he insists that the concepts he develops come not from a discipline external to cinema but from cinema itself. He rejects the standard structuralist approaches to film, which extend the Saussurean linguistic model to cinema or incorporate film within a general narratology. He also sees as unacceptable the adaptation of psychoanalytic terminology for the theorization of images. Philosophers and film directors are engaged in creative practices; philosophers invent concepts, directors invent images. But when directors talk about films, they no longer are simply directors: "They become something else, they become philosophers or theorists, even Hawks who wanted no theories, even Godard when he pretends to despise them" (IT 366; 280). The concepts of cinema are not produced in films themselves, but those who make movies generate the concepts that belong to film. "Thus there is always an hour, noon-midnight, when one no longer must ask 'what is cinema?,' but instead, 'what is philosophy?' " (IT 366; 280). At that hour directors enunciate a core of basic cinematic concepts, and philosophers work with those concepts to develop related concepts and construct from this collection of concepts a coherent cinematic theory. Deleuze describes his taxonomy of images as a "natural history rather than an historical history" (PP 71; 49), a kind of biological classification of living forms. It is also "a logic of the cinema," he says, and each of his volumes on cinema is "a book of logic" (PP 68; 47). As natural histories, *Cinema 1* and *Cinema 2* seek concepts adequate to the living images they classify. As books of logic, they invent an organizational scheme for the concepts articulated by directors, but articulated by those directors only in a non-philosophical manner. Philosophy, says Deleuze, "is in an essential and positive relation with non-philosophy" (PP 191; 139–140), and the vital elements of philosophy and the arts are "inseparable powers, which pass from art to philosophy and back again" (PP 187; 137). The essential and positive relation between philosophy and the non-philosophy of the arts is evident throughout the noon-midnight hour of *Cinema 1* and *Cinema 2*, an extended hour in which "What is cinema?" and "What is philosophy?" are posed as a single question.

Notes

CHAPTER ONE

1. For illuminating overviews of the development of Deleuze's thought in relation to Bergson's philosophy, see Hardt pp. 1–25, and Ansell Pearson, pp. 20–76.

2. Whether Bergson is a dualist or not is a difficult question, as Lacey points out. Bergson at times seems "to hold a view reminiscent of neutral monism, especially in the version of William James," but "the fact remains that he regarded himself as a dualist, and nowhere, I think, expresses any explicit adherence to neutral monism as such" (92). Bergson's dualism, Lacey says later, "might be described, if rather puzzlingly, as one between perception and memory" (112).

3. Kolakowski notes that Maritain and Hans Ugo von Balthasar likewise find two incompatible systems in Bergson, though they characterize the opposition between the two systems somewhat differently (Kolakowski 103). That incompatible systems should be discovered in Bergson is not surprising, given the fact that interpreters have found widely divergent tendencies in his thought. Mullarkey observes that in general "there have been two ways of taking up Bergson's time-philosophy. The first emphasises its affinities with a naturalistic process philosophy (Whitehead's in particular); the second sees it in the light of the existentialists and phenomenologists who succeeded Bergson in France. Following the first line of interpretation, we find writers like Milic Capek, David Spifle, and Gilles Deleuze; taking the opposite track are Jean Hyppolite, Vladimir Jankélévitch, Maurice Merleau-Ponty and Emmanuel Levinas" (Mullarkey 2).

4. For the sake of economy, I have severely simplified Bergson's complex theory of number. For an extended analysis, see Capek, especially part 2, chapter 16, "An Outline of Bergson's Philosophy of Mathematics" (Capek 176–86).

5. All translations of Bergson are my own. Page references are to the Edition du Centenaire *Oeuvres,* followed by references to the parallel passages in the authorized English translations.

6. Milic Capek, in *Bergson and Modern Physics,* stresses these same passages, remarking that they comprise "the most difficult, most elusive as well as the least known and least understood part of Bergson's thought, which nevertheless was, according to Bergson's own words, an essential part of what he himself called his 'theory of duration' " (Capek 214–15). Capek notes that even Bergson's most ardent admirers (including Vladimir Jankélévitch) were confused and embarrassed by this aspect of Bergson's thought. Far from being an accessory doctrine, argues Capek, "the *very opposite* is true: it is an *essential* part without which the whole of *Matter and Memory* and *Creative Evolution* will remain hopelessly obscure" (222). In Capek's analysis, Bergson's notion of *durée's* contraction/relaxation provides the key for a conception of time-space that is adequate to the developments of modern physics. Capek's reading of Bergson, though formed independently of Deleuze's (and vice versa), is largely consonant with Deleuze's, and Capek's detailed and extensive analyses help clarify many of the points in Deleuze's dense handling of this topic.

7. In *Matter and Memory,* Bergson cites William James on this point, noting that James and other psychologists argue for a basic "extensivity" or "feeling of volume" in every supposedly internal sensation (1959, 350–51; 1911, 288–89).

8. The singleness of *durée* is a complex issue that Deleuze treats at length in "One or Several *Durées?*" chapter 4 of *Bergsonism.* He approaches the issue through the theory of relativity, arguing that Bergson's response to Einstein reveals a coherent interpretation of the theory of relativity, in which different, relative times are so many actualizations of a single, virtual qualitative multiplicity. Capek also addresses the issue of the singleness of *durée* and like Deleuze relates it to Bergson's writings on the theory of relativity. Capek concludes that in the absence of an absolute Here-Now (since all distance involves time, in that the co-presence of events is limited by the finite speed of light) there is no *simultaneity* of time, and thus there are multiple time lines, but there is a *contemporaneity* of time, in that all time lines follow a single arrow of time from the past into the future. In this sense, the multiple time lines of the various events taking place in the universe all unfold in a single contemporaneous movement from the past into the future. (See especially part 3, chapter 8, "Bergson and Einstein. The Physical World as Extensive Becoming," pp. 238–56.) For an excellent summary of the Bergson-Einstein debate and its relation to Deleuze's thought, see Ansell Pearson, pp. 226–27.

9. I follow the practice of the translators of *Cinema 1* and *2* of rendering *tout* and *ensemble* by "whole" and "set," even though in many circumstances both terms could be translated as "whole."

10. Bergson does speak of relations in *Creative Evolution,* arguing that a scientific law is a relation: "But a law, in general, only expresses a relation, and physical laws in particular only translate quantitative relations between concrete things" (1959, 790; 1913, 349). Modern science operates via laws, "that is, via relations. Now, a relation is a link established by the mind between two or several terms. A relation is

nothing outside the intelligence that forms it. The universe thus can be a system of laws only if phenomena pass through the filter of an intelligence" (1959, 796; 1913, 356). Deleuze, like Bergson, sees relations as having "a spiritual or mental existence" (IM 20; 10), and as we have seen, *durée* is "mental" in that it is consciousness (understood, of course, in a peculiarly Bergsonian manner, such that even subatomic particles exhibit consciousness, and hence are mental), but Bergson's treatment of relation as law obviously engages issues different from those Deleuze deals with here.

11. For useful commentaries on the thorny issues related to Bergson's "images," see Lacey, pp. 89-94, 113-18, and Moore, pp. 18-41.

12. My reading of Bergson on this difficult point is similar to Mullarkey's. "If one consequently asks where representation takes place if not in the brain, Bergson's answer will be that, *de jure,* it takes place at the object! . . . Bergson's whole argument is that it is just as likely that perception should occur at the object where we perceive it as it is for it to occur at our eye or our brain. In fact, because the perception is of the object, it is more likely *de jure* to occur at the object than anywhere else" (Mullarkey 47).

13. In his excellent commentary on Deleuze's cinema theory, Rodowick appears to concur with Deleuze that Bergson indeed equates matter and light. He remarks that "this equivalence seems less strange on recalling how Einstein's famous equation rendered matter and energy exchangeable" (Rodowick 27). My own reading is that Bergson equates matter with vibrations, some of which are vibrations of light, and that Deleuze's strategy is to draw out the implications of Bergson's visual figures by here suggesting an equivalence of matter and light; while later, in *Cinema 2,* formulating his own position, which is that the Bergsonian image/ movement/matter flow "bears the characteristics of modulations of all sorts, sensory (visual and sonic), kinetic, intensive, affective, rhythmic, tonal, and even verbal (oral and written)" (IT 43-44; 29).

14. I find Bergson's use of the terms "sensation" and "affection" in *Matter and Memory* somewhat casual; at times, the terms seem synonymous, at others, affection seems the more inclusive term, of which sensation is a subdivision. For our purposes, the distinction is not essential.

15. As one can see, the sense of touch has a special position in Bergson's thought, in that the body's epidermal surface in general serves as a site of both perception and affection. Mullarkey speaks of "the imperialism of touch" (Mullarkey 46) in Bergson, noting that for Bergson "what provides representation with its passive and purely informational *appearance* is of a sensory order: it stems from a pre-reflective identification of our powers of perception *in toto* with one sense alone: that of touch" (45).

16. In the phrase "movement of expression" Deleuze employs the term *expression* in a fashion that is related to, but not identical with, the use of the word we saw earlier in his comments on movement as an expression of the whole. Here, Deleuze is indicating first that the quality expressed is not an imitation or representation of an object or an inner state. In *The Logic of Sense* Deleuze remarks that sense does not

exist outside the proposition that expresses it, but that which is expressed is an attribute of states of things, not a characteristic of the proposition. Expression in this acceptation, then, entails a relation of non-equivalence whereby two things are inseparable yet qualitatively different. The second point he is making is that the expression of a quality marks the emergence of a kind of "subjectivity" or "individuality," taken in an entirely non-Cartesian sense. In *A Thousand Plateaus*, Deleuze speaks of the emergence of a territory as taking place through the isolation of a milieu component that is at once quality and property, *quale* and *proprium*, and that in the quality/property the milieu component ceases to be functional and instead becomes "expressive." The quality expresses the territory, demarcating at once both the territory and the territory's inhabitant. *Expression* in all three senses is part of the logic of expression, in that the virtual open whole expresses itself through explication in multiple actual entities; specific actual entities express the whole by implicating or enfolding the whole in particular manifestations of that whole; and the explicative expression whereby the virtual unfolds in the actual, and the implicative expression whereby the actual enfolds the virtual, involve an inseparable relationship of non-resemblance.

17. In *Difference and Repetition*, Deleuze describes the workings of expression, of explication/unfolding and implication/enfolding, in terms of differentiation, distinguishing between *différenciation* (differentiation in general) and *différentiation* (the French term for differentiation in a mathematical sense). *Différenciation* refers to the divisions of the virtual that are actualized, *différentiation* to divisions within the virtual itself. The entire process whereby difference becomes actualized involves both *différenciation* and *différentiation*, or *différenc/tiation*. (See DR 269–85; 208–21). Here, Deleuze uses the term *différenciation* in what appears to be a broadly inclusive sense that does not draw on his earlier meditations on the word.

CHAPTER TWO

1. Deleuze takes the notion of modulation from Gilbert Simondon, who in *L'individu et sa genèse physico-biologique* contrasts fixed molds, such as one finds in brick making, and modulators, such as the control grid in a simple thermionic (or vacuum) tube known as a triode. Variations in the voltage of the control grid electrode regulate the flow of electrons through the triode, the control grid "shaping" the flow of electrons in a continuously varying manner. I discuss this concept at greater length in chapter 6 of *Deleuze on Music, Painting, and the Arts*.

2. It is important to observe that in Deleuze's brilliant evocation of the shifts of consciousness in Hitchcock's *The Birds*, he is careful to avoid any simplistic identification of a particular point of view with a given person or animal in the film. The film's initial peaceful "humanized nature" is a *camera* consciousness of that humanized nature. When the birds attack, we are given "the perception of a *whole* of birds" (my emphasis), a "Nature entirely 'birdified' [*oeisellisée*]" (IM 34; 20), but not the mere representation of a bird's perception. Rather, what we have is a camera consciousness temporarily imbued with "birdness," which will assume other attributes as it shifts in subsequent scenes.

3. Known at least since Euclid, the Golden Section (or Golden Mean) may be defined as the ratio created when a line segment (AC) is divided into two unequal parts (at point B) in such a way that the smaller part (AB) is to the larger part (BC) as the larger part is to the whole (AB:BC = BC:AC). If AC is one meter long, the larger part (AB) will be approximately 0.618 m in length, the smaller part (BC) 0.382 m; so that 0.382/0.618 = 0.618/1.0. The smaller part (AB) itself may be divided according to the Golden Section, which will generate segments of 0.236 m and 0.146 m (0.146/0.236 = 0.382/0.618 = 0.618/1.0), and this process of division may be continued indefinitely.

4. Deleuze calls the French tendency Cartesian primarily to indicate that the French directors treat movement as an abstract mathematical quantity, which may easily be graphed on Cartesian coordinates. The French tendency also is informed by a Cartesian body-mind dualism, Deleuze shows, and that dualism corresponds to Descartes's distinction between relative and absolute movement, relative movement designating the local motion of individual bodies in relation to one another, absolute movement the motion of the whole as divine force. (See Descartes 168-84.) Bergson calls attention to the paradoxes inherent in Descartes's relative and absolute movement in *Matter and Memory* (1959, 329-30; MM 254-56), and it is perhaps with this in mind that Deleuze alludes briefly to this Cartesian distinction (IM 68; 45).

5. Amengual discusses this scene in detail, contrasting Vigo's treatment of automata with that of German expressionists. In this scene, says Amengual, the expressionist world of doubles is "desacralized in one fell swoop," and its "demons are exorcised" (71).

6. See, for example, Epstein vol. 1, 119-23, and Gance's essay on polyvision, "Le temps de l'image éclatée" [The Time of the Shattered Image], in which he contrasts the "simplistic arithmetic of yesterday's cinema" with polyvision's "algebra accessible to everyone, resolving in fulgurating flashes the most extraordinary poetic equations that the shock of images produce in their simultaneous presentation" (Gance 169). The tenets of Delaunay's simultaneism are most succinctly (if not clearly) expressed in two short texts, "Light" and "Notes on the Construction of the Reality of Pure Painting" (reprinted in Buckberrough, 245-48). See Buckberrough (especially 118-32) for a discussion of the theoretical issues raised by Delaunay's simultaneism.

7. Worringer describes the Gothic line in *Form in Gothic* as one imbued with "passionate movement and vitality, a questing restless tumult," but whose movement is "divorced from organic life" and constitutes a "super-organic mode of expression" (1957, 41). Plants and animal motifs appear in Gothic ornamentation, but they are absorbed within a maze of lines, products of a linear fantasy rather than a close observation of the organic forms of nature. I discuss Worringer's Gothic line at greater length in chapter 6 of *Deleuze on Music, Painting, and the Arts*.

8. Delaunay is deeply impressed with Chevreul's notion of simultaneous contrast, whereby two complementary colors, when juxtaposed, affect one another in various ways. Delaunay is particularly sensitive to the movement generated by simultaneous contrasts of colors, and in this sense may be said to find a "pure mobility" in light. In the short text "Light," Delaunay writes, "Light in Nature creates movement

of colors. The movement is provided by the relationships *of uneven measures,* of color contrasts among themselves and constitutes *Reality.* This reality is endowed with *Depth* (we see as far as the star), and thus becomes *rhythmic Simultaneity*" (quoted in Buckberrough 245). See Deleuze's note, IM 72; 224, for Deleuze's reading of Delaunay and the relationship of simultaneism to French cinema.

9. Deleuze bases his reading of Goethe's color theory on Eliane Escoubas's brilliant essay "L'oeil (du) teinturier." For a more detailed treatment of Deleuze's understanding of Goethe, see chapter 6 of my *Deleuze on Literature.*

10. Deleuze glosses this rather obscure reference to the "abstract spiritual Form of the future" with a parenthetical allusion to Hans Richter's *Rhythmus 21* (1921) and its successors, *Rhythmus 23* (1923) and *Rhythmus 25* (1925). An avant-garde exponent of *der absoluter Film*—a movement that also included Walter Ruttmann, director of the celebrated *Berlin, Symphony of a Great City*—Richter sought in his experimental films to explore abstract relations of time, space, and light and thereby determine what Kurtz calls "the primordial rhythmic function of movement" (cited in Eisner 266). For Richter, abstract formal relations "testified to a profound transcendental meaning" (266). Eisner sees the influence of Absolute Film in such expressionist films as Rahn's *Tragedy of a Street* (1927) and May's *Asphalt* (1928).

CHAPTER THREE

1. Deleuze defines this hodological space as "a field of forces, of oppositions and tensions between these forces, of resolutions of these tensions according to the distribution of goals, obstacles, means, detours" (IT 167; 127–28). Deleuze perhaps draws his sense of Lewin's concept from two sources: Sartre and Simondon. In *The Emotions: Outline of a Theory,* Sartre cites Lewin and remarks, "Thus, one can draw up a 'hodological' map of our *umwelt,* a map which varies as a function of our acts and needs. . . . From this point of view, the world around us—what the Germans call *umwelt*—the world of our desires, our needs, and our acts, appears as if it were furrowed with strict and narrow paths which lead to one or the other determined end, that is, to the appearance of a created object" (Sartre 57). Simondon discusses Lewin's hodological space and the necessity of positing a "pre-hodological space" in *L'individu et sa genèse physico-biologique* (231–238), a discussion Deleuze cites in *Cinema 2* (IT 265; 317).

2. The passage that occasions Deleuze's critique comes from Peirce's correspondence with Lady Welby, published under the title *Semiotic and Significs:* "It appears to me that the essential function of a sign is to render inefficient relations efficient,—not to set them into action, but to establish a habit or general rule whereby they will act on occasion. . . . Knowledge in some way renders them efficient; and a sign is something by knowing which we know something more" (Peirce/Welby 31–32). There are times at which Peirce seems to privilege thought in language as the primary way in which we encounter signs, but he does observe at one point that though "the majority of men commune with themselves in words . . . the physicist, however, thinks of experimenting, of doing something and awaiting the result. The artist, again, thinks about pictures and visual images, and largely in

pictured bits; while the musician thinks about, and in, tones" (cited in Delaney 1993, 141). Whether the use of signs for Peirce necessarily entails linguistic cognition, I would argue, is not as easily determined as Deleuze would allow.

3. I take this reading of Peirce's categories as "modes of being" from Sheriff, who comments further that

> the categories of his architectonic are merely the definition of these three kinds of phenomena, and his general theory of signs is an attempt to describe their interrelationships. In logic they are beginning, end, and process. In biology they are arbitrary sporting, heredity, and the process whereby the accidental characteristics become fixed, that is, chance, law, and the tendency to take habits. In our experience, in psychology we might say, Firstness, Secondness, and Thirdness are feelings, reaction-sensations, and thought. The following are other names for, or rather manifestations of, the same triads: qualities, real existent things, representation/feeling, reaction (change of feeling), habit/monads, dyadic relations, triadic relations/possibility, fact, law/God, Jesus, Holy Spirit (14–15).

4. It is well worth noting that Peirce's voluminous writings have appeared only slowly after his death, and much still remains unpublished. Readers of French have access to Peirce only in a single modest volume of selections translated by Deledalle, who authored one of the few reliable introductions to Peirce in French. Perhaps it is not surprising, then, that Deleuze's engagement with Peirce's arguments is less than thorough. For a helpful commentary on Peirce's theory of perception, see Delaney 118–29.

5. In his influential treatise *Les Passions de l'âme,* Descartes identifies *admiration* as "the first of all the passions" since the emotion of surprise upon encountering something new comes upon us "before we know whether the object is agreeable to us or not" (*Oeuvres,* v. 3: 998–99). (This quality of newness is important to Deleuze since it suggests a connection between *admiration* and Peirce's Firstness, the category of the new.) Descartes defines *admiration* as "a sudden surprise of the soul, which causes it to pay attention to objects which seem to be rare and extraordinary" (*Oeuvres* v. 3: 1006). Descartes argues that there are only six *passions primitives: admiration,* love, hate, desire, joy, and sadness. Desire he characterizes as "an agitation of the soul caused by spirits that dispose it to want in the future things which it represents to itself as agreeable" (1977, v. 3: 1019). The painter Charles Le Brun, in his 1668 address to the Academy of Painting and Sculpture, "Conférence sur l'expression générale et particulière," proposes a theory of the passions and their facial depiction that echoes Descartes's treatise at several points, including those passages in which Le Brun describes *admiration* and desire. See Montagu, *The Expression of the Passions* 1994, for the text of Le Brun's "Conférence" (112–24; translation, pp. 125–40) and parallels between Descartes's and Le Brun's texts (156–62).

6. Deleuze treats Stoic incorporeals at length in *The Logic of Sense.* For a discussion of Deleuze's appropriation of themes from Stoic philosophy, see my *Deleuze and Guattari* chapter 3.

7. Buñuel's *Los Olvidados* could easily be considered an example of naturalism, in the standard sense of the term, and one might make a similar case for *Susanna, El,*

Diary of a Chambermaid, and *Veridiana* (especially the final banquet scenes). Most commentators emphasize the surreal and experimental elements in Buñuel's films (perhaps at their most extreme in *The Phantom of Liberty*), but Deleuze's unorthodox approach to naturalism has the advantage of suggesting an inherent affinity between the naturalistic and the surreal (which in Buñuel is most evident in *The Exterminating Angel*). (In *Cinema 2* [134–35; 102–103], Deleuze does offer a reading of Buñuel's late work as a departure from the movement-image, citing *Belle de jour, The Discreet Charm of the Bourgeoisie, That Obscure Object of Desire,* and *The Phantom of Liberty* as manifestations of the time-image.) Losey is not commonly regarded as an exponent of naturalism, though *King and Country* and *The Servant* might easily be assimilated to that category. Palmer and Riley, however, do attribute to Losey characteristics that are consonant with Deleuze's analysis of Losey as a naturalistic director. Of *Accident* and *The Go-Between,* they say that "both of these films are also unusually rich in evoking the palpable presence of their physical world as a force in its own right." They also argue that "Losey's finest films are characterized by a layering of unresolved tensions not just between social classes, but between calm surfaces and passionate depths, between intellect and emotion, between places and the characters who live in them, between communities and those who intrude on them" (Palmer and Riley, 13).

8. Deleuze cites Burch's analyses of such shots, which Burch labels *plans-rouleaux* (scroll shots). In commenting on two such shots in *Sisters of Gion,* Burch says,

> in both these 'scroll-shots,' the pro-filmic organization of architectural space is such that the passing lens produces successive tableaux which appear as both discrete and inter-penetrating. This is a major effect of the *e-makimono* [the traditional Japanese painted hand scroll]. In these shots Mizoguchi achieves a corresponding fusion of the two fundamental and opposite aspects of lateral camera-movement as such: successive stages versus steady flow. (To the Distant Observer 229)

For a balanced consideration of Burch's notion of the "scroll shot," as well as a subtle analysis of Mizoguchi's pre-war films, see Kirihara, especially pp. 126–28.

9. The "montage of attractions" has received considerable attention in Eisenstein studies. For a thoughtful examination of this difficult concept, as well as an illuminating treatment of Eisenstein's montage practices in general, see Aumont, especially pp. 41–51.

10. Fontanier most often speaks of seven types of figures, though his taxonomy may be reduced to four categories. He divides figures into two basic kinds: tropes and non-tropes. Tropes are of two types, "tropes properly speaking" and "tropes improperly speaking." Non-tropes include "figures of words properly speaking" (within which category Fontanier includes figures of Diction, figures of Construction, figures of Elocution, and figures of Style) and "figures of thought absolutely independent of words" (Fontanier 221). Deleuze's use of Fontanier is most strained in his reference to Fontanier's third category of "figures of words properly speaking," in that under this rubric Fontanier includes some forty-five separate figures, of which Inversion is only one, and Fontanier's "Inversion" seems to bear at best only a nominal similarity to Deleuze's cinematic "figure of inversion."

11. There is actually some difficulty in establishing the precise cinematic parallel to Fontanier's "figures of thought." In his remarks on Fontanier, Deleuze alludes to figures of thought "already present in Chaplin's talkies" (IM 250; 183). Deleuze's allusion is presumably to his discussion of Chaplin's "radical, original usage" of sound that introduced into cinema the "Figure of discourse" (IM 236; 172). Yet Deleuze also says that the nature of figures of thought can be disclosed only "later, in another chapter"—presumably, the chapter on the relation-image. It would seem that the fourth of the reflection-images (the discursive figure) and the three relation-images (which we will examine shortly) are all "figures of thought." We might note that in the *Cinema 1* glossary, Deleuze offers an alternative labeling of the relation-image, referring to it as the "mental image (relation)" (IM 292; 218). In *Cinema 2*, Deleuze speaks of the "discursive image" in Chaplin (and its counterpart in the Marx Brothers' films, the "argument-image") as a "mental image" (IT 88; 65). It appears that Deleuze does not find a clear-cut distinction between the last kind of reflection-image (the discursive figure) and the relation-image, but that in the discursive figure he sees an area of transition from reflection to relation that gradually increases the presence of the "mental" in the movement-image. (On the "mental" and its general presence in the movement-image, see IM 268; 198.)

12. Deleuze, we should note, also makes the somewhat cryptic observation that the discursive figure "is a situation or action of discourse, independently of the question: is the discourse itself realized in a language?" (IT 49;33). It would seem from this remark that the discursive figure need not manifest itself in linguistic signs. The sense of Deleuze's observation hinges on the double meaning of "discourse" as "speech" and "argument." Deleuze says of *The Great Dictator* and *Monsieur Verdoux* that what counts is not the opposition of good and bad situations but "the underlying *discourses*, which are expressed as such at the end of these films" (IM 235; 172). The discourses are "underlying [*sous-jacents*, subjacent]," i.e., unstated. Presumably, they are also capable of overt presentation in a form that is not explicitly or directly linguistic. Although Deleuze offers no example of a non-linguistic discursive figure, he does read the ending of *The Great Dictator* in a way that complicates the relationship between language and what he is calling discourse. Clearly, Deleuze finds *The Great Dictator*'s concluding speech (which he refers to as its *discours final* [IM 236; 172]) sentimental and philosophically problematical, but "whatever its intrinsic value" (IM 236; 172) the Jewish barber's discourse "is identified with all human language [*langage*], represents everything that man can say, in relation to the false tongue [*langue*] of nonsense and terror, of noise and fury, that Chaplin invents with genius and puts into the mouth of the tyrant" (IM 236; 172). The underlying discourse of the film—the argument that two divergent situations (democratic community and totalitarian state) foster good or bad actions—is directly presented in the final speech, but as much through the form of its delivery as through its actual content. The film's argument is only partially articulated in the literal words; its most profound elements are demonstrated in the image of the Jewish barber using language in a way that counters the violence of the dictator's speech. Chaplin's concluding discursive figure may not be non-linguistic, but it includes within it elements

that communicate a discourse (an argument) without explicitly articulating that discourse. In this sense, perhaps, the figure is discursive "independently of the question: is the discourse itself realized in language" (IT 49; 33).

13. Deleuze notes that Peirce does not directly treat the distinction between natural and abstract relations, but Deleuze sees in Peirce's differentiation between the dynamic interpretant and the final interpretant a somewhat similar opposition. Such a parallel, however, seems doubtful, and here especially the limited Peircean corpus to which Deleuze has access is evident. Dynamic and final interpretant are but two terms of a complex set of triads, starting with the components of the sign (representamen-object-interpretant) and continuing with the subcategories of the immediate interpretant (which further subdivides into hypothetic, categorical, and relative interpretants), the dynamic interpretant (emotional, energetic or logical) and the final interpretant (gratific, practical, or scientific/pragmaticistic). Indeed, one might argue that Peirce's entire semiotic enterprise is devoted to unraveling the complexities of what are commonly referred to as natural, habitual, or abstract relations.

CHAPTER FOUR

1. Deleuze identifies a similar emergence of the opsign and sonsign in France with the New Wave around 1958 and in Germany around 1968. The earliest instances of the opsign, however, Deleuze finds in the pre-War films of Yasujiro Ozu, whose relatively low camera placements, 360-degree shooting space, austere camera movements, and extended shots of inanimate objects and landscapes undermine spatio-temporal continuities and help fashion an *espace quelconque*, "whether through disconnection or through vacuity" (IT 26; 15). Deleuze concentrates on what Burch calls Ozu's "pillow shots," the landscapes and still lifes that function to "*suspend the diegetic flow*" (Burch, *To the Distant Observer* 160). Deleuze differentiates between Ozu's landscapes and still lifes, arguing that the still lifes are genuine time-images (see esp. IT 27–28; 17–18). In a sequence of a woman smiling, a prolonged shot of a vase, the woman weeping, for example, a change has occurred in the woman, but in the unmoving vase, we see the *duration* of the object, "that which remains throughout the succession of changing states" (IT 28; 17). That duration is the *form* of time, the unchanging form of all that changes, and hence an image of time. Deleuze notes, however, that Ozu's still-life images of "time in person" (IT 27; 17) do not seem to have had an immediate influence on directors either in Japan or in the West.

2. Deleuze does not explicitly identify the Serbs as a seed-crystal, but a similar parallel of seed-milieu and local action–sociohistorical context informs his remarks on Tarkovsky's *The Mirror*. (Deleuze argues for a roughly similar version of this parallel in his comments on Herzog's *Heart of Glass,* the seed-milieu pair manifest in the film's two components, the search for the secret recipe for ruby glass [seed] and Hias's apocalyptic prophecies amid vast Romantic landscapes [milieu].) Perhaps Deleuze's clearest example of the seed-milieu relationship comes from *Citizen Kane*. When the paperweight globe falls from Kane's hand and shatters as he intones "Rosebud," a visual seed of artificial snowflakes merges with the snowclouds of Colorado and an aural seed of the enigmatic word begins to spread to include the

memories, stories, and histories presented throughout the rest of the film. For a brilliant elaboration of this example, see Rodowick, p. 93.

3. Deleuze finds signs that Camilla, too, might eventually escape the theater in the troupe leader's closing remark (as Truffaut records it in the appendix to Bazin's *Jean Renoir*): "You will find your happiness only on a stage each evening—that is, in forgetting yourself. Through the characters you incarnate, perhaps you will discover the true Camilla" (Bazin, *Renoir* 261). Renoir produced three versions of *The Golden Coach*, in English, French, and Italian, no one of which satisfied him, though he considered the English the original (Durgnat 286). The English version of the troupe leader's remark differs significantly from Truffaut's transcription and seems to emphasize the closed nature of the theater world: "Your only way to find happiness is on any stage, any platform, any public place during those two little hours when you become another person, your true self."

4. Amengual develops this notion in "Fin d'itinéraire: du 'côté de chez Lumière' au 'côté de Méliès' ":

> Festival architectures, aggregate of independent islets, all constructed as realistically as possible, defying their precariousness and their provisional finality, exacerbating their expressivity in order to signify better that which they represent: Palace of Discovery, Pavilion of Siam, Temple of Industry, Salon of Electricity, Spanish Pavilion . . . Antiquity according to *Satyricon,* the unconscious of Guido in *8½* and that of Juliet in *Juliet of the Spirits,* the Venice of *Casanova,* the metropolis of *Fellini-Roma,* the faraway Rimini of *Amarcord,* the feminist 'seminar' of *The City of Women,* Fellini builds them out of solid stuff, divides them into alveoli juxtaposed as so many *mansions,* distributes them in 'pavilions,' orders them into galleries, assigns them to collections: women, visions, sensual delights, vices, dreams, monsters, torments, existential attitudes. (90–91)

CHAPTER FIVE

1. Deleuze does not indicate how the future is to be integrated into the "totality of time" of the virtual past. My conjecture is that, as time passes, the whole of the past is contracted into the present and thrust forward into a future, and in this sense the future may be seen as a projection, or forward thrust, of the past.

2. Deleuze argues that "it is the possibility of treating the world, life, or simply a life, an episode, as a single and same event, that founds the implication of presents" (IT 132; 100).

3. Deleuze alludes here to Augustine's meditation on time in book 11 of the *Confessions.* In section 20 of book 11, Augustine reasons that only the present truly exists, and that the past is simply a memory of a once-present-moment and the future an anticipation of a present-moment-to-be. Hence, rather than speak of past, present, and future, we should say that "there are three times: the present of the past, the present of the present, and the present of the future" (tempora sunt tria: praesens de praeteritis, praesens de praesentibus, praesens de futuris) (Augustine II, 314). Despite Deleuze's playful reference to the "augustinism" of those who treat the event as a simultaneous enfolding of multiple presents, he is not arguing that

Augustine promotes this view of time himself. For commentaries on Augustine's theory of time, see Kirwin 162–86 and Teske.

4. See especially Morrissette's "Post-Modern Generative Fiction: Novel and Film" (1975) and his books *The Novels of Robbe-Grillet* (1975) and *Intertextual Assemblage in Robbe-Grillet: From Topology to the Golden Triangle* (1979).

5. See Gardies pp. 118–20. While commenting on the music and the excision of the rape scene, Robbe-Grillet observes that in filming the script "Resnais respected each detail in a scrupulous fashion," and yet "nevertheless he transformed everything. . . . Despite everything, the film is his" (118).

6. Deleuze compares Resnais's handling of sheets of the past to the "baker's transformation" that Prigogine and Stengers discuss in *Order out of Chaos* (268–77). If a square sheet of pastry dough is stretched to form a rectangle twice the height and the same width as the original square, then folded onto itself, and finally rolled out to form another square, initially contiguous points on the sheet may end up widely separated from one another, and conversely, distant points may become contiguous. Repeated stretchings, foldings, and rollings of the dough will create diverse configurations of points. This topological model of a malleable surface may be used generally as a means of conceptualizing statistical probabilities in an indeterminately related set of elements. Deleuze's point, I believe, is that Resnais's sheets of the past are like sheets of pastry dough, each a stretched, folded, rolled-out metamorphosis of another.

7. See especially Bazin's *What Is Cinema?* pp. 33–35. "*Citizen Kane* can never be too highly praised. Thanks to the depth of field, whole scenes are covered in one take, the camera remaining motionless. Dramatic effects for which we had formerly relied on montage were created out of the movements of the actors within a fixed framework" (33).

8. Deleuze finds a similar development in seventeenth-century painting. As Wölfflin shows, the Renaissance space of parallel and isolated planes gives way in baroque painting to a transverse, in-depth space of interrelated and interacting planes.

9. The phrase "invitation to recollect" Deleuze takes from Claudel, who in *L'Oeil écoute* says of Rembrandt that "the art of the great Dutchman is no longer a copious affirmation of the domain of the contemporary [*l'actualité*], a festival given to our senses, the perpetuation of a moment of joy and color. It is no longer the present that we regard, it is an invitation to recollect" (195–96).

10. The apparent exception would be *Je t'aime, je t'aime*, in which past events are oriented around the fixed point of Ridder's time-machine repetition of a love scene with his wife. Deleuze insists, however, that even here the present "floats," for the repeated instant is itself ambiguous, a moment when the couple's love is at once increasing and fading, and hence participating in two different sheets of the past (IT 153; 117).

11. In this explanation I have maintained Deleuze's pairing of the inexplicable with peaks of the present and the undecidable with sheets of the past, though I see no impediment to characterizing both chronosigns as inexplicable and undecid-

able, save that Deleuze's exposition of peaks of the present involves the figure of implication/explication, whereas his description of sheets of the past does not.

12. The English translation of *Cinema 2* misidentifies *F for Fake* as *It's All True. F for Fake,* Welles's last film, appeared in 1973. *It's All True,* released in 1993, is an assemblage of long-lost footage shot by Welles in 1942, including a sequence for a project titled "My Friend Bonito," pieces of a documentary on the carnival in Rio, and several scenes from a docudrama about the heroic voyage of four Brazilian fishermen, "Four Men on a Raft."

13. For descriptions of Rouch's films through 1979, see Eaton pp. 1–34. Stoller discusses six of Rouch's films in detail, including *Jaguar* (pp. 131–44) and *Les maîtres fous* (pp. 145–60). For a brief introduction to Rouch's cinema, see Issari and Paul pp. 67–82. For insightful commentary on Rouch, see Eaton pp. 40–53 and Fieschi (available in English translation in Eaton pp. 67–77).

14. *Les maîtres fous,* we might note, directly inspired Jean Genet's *Les noirs* and Peter Brook's production of *Marat/Sade* (Eaton 6–7).

15. Rouch describes a striking instance of provocation he instigated while filming *Chronique d'un été.* Rouch had assembled a group of French and African students, and during their casual conversation together he decided to ask one of the French girls about the tattoo the Nazis had put on her wrist, "because the Africans did not comprehend our concern about anti-Semitism. When I posed the question, the isolation and assumptions of cultures emerged dramatically. . . . Suddenly the Europeans began to cry and the Africans were totally perplexed. They had thought the tattoo was an adornment of some kind. All of us were deeply affected. The cameraman, one of the best documentary people around, was so disturbed that the end of the sequence is out of focus. . . . Now, is this a 'truthful' moment or a 'staged' moment? Does it matter?" (Georgakas, Gupta, and Janda 1978, 18).

16. Brecht's German term is *Gestus,* an uncommon Latinism used to refer to particular elements of a stage performer's actions. Brecht's English translator has used the equally uncommon English word *gest* to render the German term. In French translation, Brecht's *Gestus* is left untranslated, and Deleuze follows suit, using *gestus* to refer to Brecht's concept and his own version of it.

17. Comolli identifies a formal element in Cassavetes that reinforces the movement of bodies which interests Deleuze. In *Faces,* says Comolli,

the filming with two cameras, in suppressing the notion of 'continuities' [*raccords*], immediately establishes the impression of a spatio-temporal continuity, of a space-time in continuous expansion, such that the sensation of fluidity is added to that of speed: the variations in size of the shots, the changes in angles do not break the movements of the characters but underline them, add to their mobility and to their diversity, conserve and increase their acquired forces [*élans*], so that through the combination and the multiplication of these two mobilities (within the frame, and between frames), a general movement of the film is produced, a movement that gives the impression of itself creating, through its own force, the particular movements of which it is composed. Everything takes place as if the rhythm of the film were the generator of itself, once the initial impetus is given, the starting speed established. In this way, as far as the development of the fiction is concerned, a purely formal logic (that of the linkages of movements) replaces the psychological. (38)

Deleuze comments that "as a general rule, Cassavetes retains only the space that belongs to bodies, he composes space with disconnected pieces that a gest alone ties together. It is the formal linkage of attitudes that replaces the association of images" (IT 251; 193). One might argue that the self-generating linkage of movements observed by Camolli is the formal counterpart of the gest, the "formal linkage of attitudes," and that the mutually reinforcing movements of camera and performers generate the space of the film.

18. For helpful analyses of the multiple allusions in *Prénom Carmen*, see Conley and Powrie. Also insightful are the essays of Bergala and Lardeau. For a fascinating look at François Musy's work on the film's soundtrack, see Musy.

19. Deleuze indicates a final complication in the relationship between bodies and music in *Prénom Carmen:* whereas the attitude of the body "is like a time-image, that which puts the before and the after in the body, the series of time," the musical gest "is already another time-image, the order or ordering of time, the simultaneity of its points, the coexistence of its sheets" (IT 254; 195). The music/sound patterns, it would seem, depend much less on the *puissance* of time's forward thrust for their coherence than do corporeal patterns. The film's musical gest is treated in such a way that the pattern is manifest at various junctures as a simultaneous, coexisting presence, so that this particular category—music—in this particular usage becomes an instance of the order of time rather than time as series. If the power of the false forms horizontal series, music here forms a vertical series "in depth." Deleuze observes a similar handling of the category of the pictorial in Godard's *Passion,* in which bodies are subsumed within the gests of tableaux based on famous paintings. Hence, he says, it is possible that "the limit or category in which a series is reflected itself forms another series of a higher power [*puissance*], at that point superimposed on the first: thus the pictorial category in *Passion* or the musical category in *Prénom Carmen*. There is in this sense a vertical construction of series, which tends to rejoin coexistence or simultaneity, and to reunite the two kinds of chronosigns" (IT 361; 276).

CHAPTER SIX

1. The "image of thought" is a theme Deleuze deals with at several points in his work. See especially PS 115–23; 159–67, DR 169–217; 129–67, and QP 38–59; 35–60.

2. Bidney especially stresses the importance of the spiritual automaton in Spinoza's thought. "The originality of Spinoza consists in the fact that he for the first time applied the doctrine of laws of becoming to the mind as well as to the body. . . . The mind he considered as a 'spiritual automaton' subject to necessary laws of its own, even as the body was subject to the universal laws of motion" (Bidney 14). For an excellent treatment of the *automate spirituel* in Deleuze, see Bensmaïa, "Les transformateurs-deleuze"

3. Deleuze notes that Jean Epstein, like Faure, praises cinema for its "automatic subjectivity" (Epstein v. 2: 63). It is worth adding that in his preface to *The Intelligence*

of a Machine (1946), Epstein remarks that "the images created by this other optical system, this sort of robot-brain, which is the cinematographic instrument," tend "to modify, more or less, thought in its entirety" (Epstein v. 1: 255).

4. Deleuze cites Spaier's discussion of the mathematical concept of the "irrational cut" upon introducing the term. As Spaier points out, classical arithmetical theory posits a fundamental opposition between quantity and number, the one being characterized by material continuity, the other by mental discontinuity. Méray and Dedekind overcome this classical dualism by defining number by the concept of the "cut" [*coupure*]. A given number is simply defined as a cut in a continuous line, whereby two classes are created "such that all the terms of one are smaller than those of the other" (Spaier 39). In the case of an irrational number such as the square root of two, a cut in the continuous line may be made, but the irrational number will not belong to either of the classes it separates, since it cannot be assigned a precise value. (Two, being a prime number, has no square root, though it may be assigned an approximate value, e.g., $1.4145 \times 1.4145 = 2.0008$.) Hence, the only difference between a rational and an irrational cut is that "the rational number must always be contained either in the inferior class, or in the superior class of the cut, whereas no irrational number can form a part of the one or of the other of the classes that it separates" (Spaier 159).

5. "The brain is unity. The brain is the screen. I don't believe that linguistics and psychoanalysis offer a great deal to the cinema. On the contrary, the biology of the brain—molecular biology—does" (BR 366).

6. Deleuze discusses Nietzsche's *amor fati* and differentiates it from Pascal's wager in *Nietzsche and Philosophy* (NP 41–43; 36–38).

7. The Stoics divide the world into two categories: actual bodies, which have real existence, and "incorporeals," which do not exist so much as they "insist" or "subsist." Incorporeals are of four kinds: the void, place, time, and the *lekton*. The *lekton* is that which is added to a sonic body to give it meaning. When a Greek and a barbarian hear a Greek sentence, they both apprehend the same sonic body, but for the Greek something has been added to the body—the *lekton,* or the "expressible"—and the sound has been rendered meaningful. The meaning is expressed by the sonic body, yet the meaning does not fully belong to it, but in a sense hovers over it like an incorporeal fog or aura. For a more detailed discussion of the *lekton,* see chapter 3 of my *Deleuze and Guattari*

8. Deleuze does briefly suggest an affinity between lectosigns and language when discussing Bergson and the virtual past. Bergson's "time-image" necessarily extends itself into a "language-image and a thought-image" (IT 131; 99). When we remember, we leap into the preexisting virtual past. In a parallel fashion, we leap into the preexisting linguistic realm of meaning (*sens*) when we use language, and into the preexisting realm of ideas when we think. "Thus chronosigns never cease to extend themselves into lectosigns, into noosigns" (IT 131; 100). *Sens,* of course, Deleuze identifies with the Stoic *lekton,* but this does not mean that the linguistic domain of *sens* is central to the lectosign. Language is simply one possible element of the lectosign, either as something heard (the dialogue of characters) or seen (e.g., written words on the screen).

9. Deleuze takes the notion of "sociability" from Georg Simmel, who argues that just as there is in humans a basic impulse to create and an impulse to play,

in the same sense one may speak of an impulse to sociability in man. To be sure, it is for the sake of special needs and interests that men unite in economic associations or blood fraternities, in cult societies or robber bands. But, above and beyond their special content, all the associations are accompanied by a feeling for, by a satisfaction in, the very fact that one is associated with others and that the solitariness of the individual is resolved into togetherness, a union with others. (Simmel 121)

10. See Eisenstein *Film Form,* pp. 152–53, 177–178, *Nonindifferent Nature,* pp. 332–34, and especially *The Film Sense* pp. 175–216, with the accompanying diagram of shots and score from *Alexander Nevsky.* Eisler offers several examples of discontinuities between music and dramatic events in *Composing for the Films,* pp. 20–30.

11. For helpful introductions to Straub and Huillet, see Sandford, pp. 27–36, Franklin, pp. 75–88, and Turim. For an extended treatment of Straub and Huillet's German films, see Byg.

12. For a discussion of Deleuze's analyses of Bacon and Cézanne, see chapters 5 and 6 of my *Deleuze on Music, Painting, and the Arts.*

13. For the text of the French subtitles to *Fortini/Cani,* with an accompanying description of the film's forty-nine shots, see Huillet.

14. In an excellent analysis of *Fortini/Cani,* Turim comments that Straub and Huillet

have developed a strategy in which the verbal text performs a significant and autonomous discursive task. The visual series comments on that verbal argument, rather than the inverse. The visual in *Fortini/Cani* assists the discourse as a metacritical reframing of the original essay, and one is tempted to replace the image/voice-over paradigm with voice/image-over, as images surround the voice, supplying new spaces and meaning through which it can be heard. (343–44)

15. This metamorphic, destabilizing usage of language Deleuze calls a "minor" usage, and he develops this notion at length in *Kafka: pour une littérature mineure.* For an exposition of the concepts of minor literature and the minor usage of language, see chapters 4 and 5 of my *Deleuze on Literature.*

CONCLUSION

1. Cornford remarks of this passage that for Plato, time "cannot exist apart from the heavenly clock whose movements are the measure of Time. . . . Plato's view of Time as inseparable from periodic motion is no novelty, but a tradition running throughout the whole of Greek thought, which always associated Time with circular movement" (Cornford year 97, 103). Number is an essential constituent of the movement of time in that the regular motion of the planets conforms to mathematical proportions, and through observation of the uniform rotation of the planets humans learn mathematics. "The purpose of the Demiurge is that mankind shall learn to count and develop mathematics by the exercise of reckoning periods of time, days, months, and years" (115). It is to this conjunction of time, movement and number that Deleuze refers when he says that the time that is dependent on movement may be defined "in the manner of the ancient philosophers, as the number of movement" (IT 51–52; 35).

Works Cited

Amengual, Barthélemy. "Fin d'itinéraire: du 'côté de chez Lumière' au 'côté de Méliès.' " *Études cinématographiques* 127–130 (1981): 81–111.

———. "Monde et vision du monde dans l'oeuvre de Vigo." *Études cinématographiques* 51–52 (1966): 49–87.

Ansell Pearson, Keith. *Germinal Life: The Difference and Repetition of Deleuze.* London: Routledge, 1997.

Augustine. *Confessions.* Ed. Pierre de Labriolle. 7th edition. Paris: Société d'Édition "Les Belles Lettres," 1969.

Aumont, Jacques. *Montage Eisenstein.* Trans. Lee Hildreth, Constance Penley, and Andrew Ross. Bloomington: Indiana University Press, 1987.

Bazin, André. *Le Cinéma français de la Libération à la Nouvelle Vague (1945–1958).* Ed. Jean Narboni. Paris: Cahier du cinéma, Éditions de l'étoile, 1983.

———. *Jean Renoir.* Ed. François Truffant. Paris: Gérard Lebovici, 1989.

———. *What Is Cinema?* Trans. Hugh Gray. Berkeley: University of California Press, 1967.

Bensmaïa, Réda, "Les transformateurs-deleuze ou le cinéma comme automate spirituel." *Quaderni di Cinema/Studio* 7–8 (July December 1992): 103–116.

Bergala, Alain. "Les ailes d'Icare." *Cahiers du cinéma* 355 (January 1984): 5–8.

Bergson, Henri. *Creative Evolution.* Trans. Arthur Mitchell. New York: Henry Holt, 1913.

———. *Matter and Memory.* Trans. Nancy Margaret Paul and W. Scott Palmer. London: George Allen and Unwin, 1911.

———. *Mind-Energy.* Trans. H. Wildon Carr. New York: Henry Holt, 1920.

———. *Œuvres.* Edition du Centenaire. Ed. André Robinet. Paris: Presses Universitaires de France. 1959.

———. *Time and Free Will.* Trans. F. L. Pogson. New York: Macmillan, 1910.

Bidney, David. *The Psychology and Ethics of Spinoza: A Study in the History and Logic of Ideas.* 1940. Reprint, New York: Russell and Russell, 1962.

Bogue, Ronald. *Deleuze and Guattari.* London: Routledge, 1989.

———. *Deleuze on Literature*. New York: Routledge, 2003.

———. *Deleuze on Music, Painting, and the Arts*. New York: Routledge, 2003.

Bonitzer, Pascal. *Le champ aveugle: essais sur le cinéma*. Paris: Gallimard, 1982.

Brecht, Bertolt. *Brecht on Theatre: The Development of an Aesthetic*. Ed. and trans. John Willett. New York: Hill and Wang, 1964.

Buckberrough, Sherry A. *Robert Delaunay: The Discovery of Simultaneity*. Ann Arbor, MI: UMI Research Press, 1982.

Burch, Noël. *Theory of Film Practice*. Trans. Helene R. Lane. New York: Praeger, 1973.

———. *To the Distant Observer: Form and Meaning in the Japanese Cinema*. Rev. and ed. Annette Michelson. Berkeley: University of California Press, 1979.

Byg, Barton. *Landscapes of Resistance: The German Films of Danièle Huillet and Jean-Marie Straub*. Berkeley: University of California Press, 1995.

Capek, Milic. *Bergson and Modern Physics. A Reinterpretation and Re-evaluation*. Boston Studies in the Philosophy of Science, vol. 7. Dordrecht, Holland: D. Reidel, 1971.

Claudel, Paul. *L'Oeil écoute*, in *Oeuvres en prose*. Ed. Jacques Petit and Charles Galpérine. Paris: Gallimard, 1965.

Comolli, Jean-Louis. "Deux visages de 'Faces'." *Cahiers du cinéma* 205 (October 1968): 38.

Conley, Verena Andermatt. "A Fraying of Voices: Jean-Luc Godard's *Prénom Carmen*." *L'Esprit Créateur* 30 (Summer 1990): 68–80.

Cornford, Francis Macdonald. *Plato's Cosmology: The Timaeus of Plato*. New York: Humanities Press, 1937.

Courchot, Edmond. "Image puissance image." *Revue d'esthétique* 7 (new series) (1984): 123–33.

Delaney, C. F. *Science, Knowledge, and Mind. A Study in the Philosophy of C. S. Peirce*. Notre Dame Ind.: University of Notre Dame Press, 1993.

Deleuze, Gilles. *Francis Bacon. Logique de la sensation*. Paris: Editions de la différance, 1981.

Deleuze, Gilles and Felix Guattari *Kafka: pour une littérature mineure*. Paris: Minuit, 1975.

Demonsablon, Philippe. "Le Plus court chemin." *Cahiers du cinéma* 48 (June 1955): 52–53.

Descartes, René. *Oeuvres philosophiques*. Vol. 3. Ed. Ferdinand Alquié. Paris: Garnier, 1973.

Durgnat, Raymond. *Jean Renoir*. Berkeley: University of California Press, 1974.

Eaton, Mick, ed. *Anthropology—Reality—Cinema: The Films of Jean Rouch*. London: British Film Institute, 1979.

Eisenstein, Sergei. *Film Form: Essays in Film Theory*. Ed. and trans. Jay Leyda. New York: Meridian, 1957.

———. *The Film Sense*. Trans. Jay Leyda. New York: Harcourt, Brace, 1942.

———. *Nonindifferent Nature*. Trans. Herbert Marshall. Cambridge: Cambridge University Press, 1987.

Eisler, Hanns. *Composing for the Films*. New York: Oxford University Press, 1947.

Eisner, Lotte. *The Haunted Screen*. Trans. Roger Greaves. Berkeley: University of California Press, 1969.

Epstein, Jean. *Ecrits sur le cinéma*. 2 vols. Paris: Seghers, 1974.

Escoubas, Eliane. "L'oeil (du) teinturier," *Critique* 418 (March 1982): 231–42.

Fahle, Oliver, and Lorenz Engell, eds. *Der Film bei Deleuze/Le cinema selon Deleuze*. Weimar: Verlag der Bauhaus-Universität/Paris: Presses de la Sorbonne nouvelle, 1997.

Faure, Elie. *Oeuvres Complètes d'Elie Faure*. 3 vols. Paris: Jean-Jacques Pauvert, 1964.

Fieschi, Jean-André. "Dérives de la fiction: notes sur le cinéma de Jean Rouch." In *Cinéma: Théorie, Lectures*. Ed. Dominique Noguez. Paris: Klincksieck, 1973, pp. 255–64.

Flaxman, Gregory, ed. *The Brain Is the Screen: Deleuze and the Philosophy of Cinema*. Minneapolis: University of Minnesota Press, 2000.

Fontanier, Pierre. *Les Figures du discours*. 1818–1830. Reprint, Paris: Flammarion, 1977.

Franklin, James. *New German Cinema: From Oberhausen to Hamburg*. Boston: Twayne, 1983.

Gallie, W. B. *Peirce and Pragmatism,* Rev. ed. New York: Dover, 1966.

Gance, Abel. "Le temps de l'image éclatée." In Sophie Daria, *Abel Gance: Hier et Demain.* Paris: La Palatine, 1959, pp. 167–75.

Gardies, André. *Alain Robbe-Grillet.* Paris: Seghers, 1972.

Georgakas, Dan, Udayan Gupta, and Judy Janda. "The Politics of Visual Anthropology: An Interview with Jean Rouch." *Cinéaste* 8 (summer 1978): 16–24.

Groethuysen, Bernhard. "De quelques aspects du temps. Notes pour une phénoménologie du Récit." *Recherches philosophiques* 5 (1935–36): 139–95.

Hardt, Michael. *Gilles Deleuze: An Apprenticeship in Philosophy.* Minneapolis: University of Minnesota Press, 1993.

Heidegger, Martin. *What Is Called Thinking?* Trans. J. Glenn Gray. New York: Harper and Row, 1968.

Huillet, Danièle. "Texte des sous-titres français de *Fortini/Cani.*" *Cahiers du cinema* 275 (April 1977): 15–39.

Issari, M. Ali, and Doris A. Paul. *What Is Cinéma Vérité?* Metuchen, N.J.: Scarecrow Press, 1979.

Kant, Immanuel. *Critique of Judgement.* Trans. J. H. Bernard. New York: Hafner, 1951.

Kennedy, Barbara M. *Deleuze and Cinema: The Aesthetics of Sensation.* Edinburgh: Edinburgh University Press, 2000.

Kirihara, Donald. *Patterns of Time: Mizoguchi and the 1930s.* Madison: University of Wisconsin Press, 1992.

Kirwin, Christopher. *Augustine.* London: Routledge, 1989.

Kolakowski, Leszek. *Bergson.* Oxford: Oxford University Press, 1985.

Lacey, A. R. *Bergson.* London and New York: Routledge, 1989.

Lara, Philippe de. "Le bal des vauriens." *Cinématographe* 38 (May 1978): 36–37.

Lardeau, Yann. "Fugit amor." *Cahiers du cinéma* 355 (January 1984): 9–11.

Maldiney, Henri. *Regard Parole Espace.* Lausanne: Editions l'Age d'Homme, 1973.

Marks, Elaine U. *The Skin of the Film: Intercultural Cinema, Embodiment, and the Senses.* Durham, N.C.: Duke University Press, 2000.

Michelson, Annette. "L'homme à la caméra: de la magie à l'épistémologie." In *Cinéma: Théorie, Lectures,* ed. Dominique Noguez. Paris: Klincksieck, 1973, pp. 295–310.

Mitry, Jean. *The Aesthetics and Psychology of the Cinema.* Trans. Christopher King. Bloomington: Indiana University Press, 1997.

Montagu, Jennifer. *The Expression of the Passions. The Origin and Influence of Charles Le Brun's Conférence sur l'expression générale et particulière.* New Haven, Conn.: Yale University Press, 1994.

Moore, F. C. T. *Bergson: Thinking Backwards.* Cambridge: Cambridge University Press, 1996.

Morrissette, Bruce. *Intertextual Assemblage in Robbe-Grillet: From Topology to the Golden Triangle.* Fredericton, New Brunswick: York, 1979.

———. *The Novels of Robbe-Grillet.* Rev. and expanded ed. Ithaca, N.Y.: Cornell University Press, 1975.

———. "Post-Modern Generative Fiction: Novel and Film." *Critical Inquiry* 2 (winter 1975): 253–262.

Mullarkey, John. *Bergson and Philosophy.* Notre Dame, Ind.: University of Notre Dame Press, 2000.

Musy, François. "Les mouettes du Pont d'Austerlitz: Entretien avec François Musy." *Cahiers du cinéma* 355 (January 1984): 12–17.

Narboni, Jean, "Visages d'Hitchcock." In *Alfred Hitchcock,* ed. Jean Narboni et al. Paris: Editions de l'étoilé-cahier du cinéma, 1980, pp. 31–37.

Nietzsche, Friedrich. *The Birth of Tragedy and the Case of Wagner.* Trans. Walter Kaufmann. 1872, 1888. Reprint, New York: Random House, 1967.

Paik, Nam June. "Entretien avec Nam June Paik," with Jean-Paul Fargier, Jean-Paul Cassagnac, and Sylvia van der Stegen. *Cahiers du cinéma* 299 (April 1979): 10–15.

Palmer, James, and Michael Riley. *The Films of Joseph Losey*. Cambridge: Cambridge University Press, 1993.

Pasolini, Pier Paolo. *Heretical Empiricism*. Ed. Louise K. Barnett, trans. Ben Lawton and Louise K. Barnett. Bloomington: Indiana University Press, 1988.

Peirce, Charles S., and Victoria Lady Welby. *Semiotic and Significs. The Correspondence between Charles S. Peirce and Victoria Lady Welby,* ed. Charles S. Hardwick with James Cook. Bloomington: Indiana University Press, 1977.

Philippe, Claude-Jean. "Les Westerns d'Anthony Mann." *Études cinématographiques* 2 (winter 1961): 289–300.

Plato. *Timaeus*. Trans. Benjamin Jowett. In *Collected Dialogues,* ed. Edith Hamilton and Huntington Cairns. Princeton, N.J.: Princeton University Press, 1961.

Powrie, Phil. "Godard's *Prénom: Carmen* (1984), Masochism, and the Male Gaze." *Forum for Modern Language Studies* 331 (January 1995): 64–73.

Prédal, René. "Alain Resnais." *Études cinématographiques* 64–68 (1968): 3–184.

Prigogine, Ilya, and Isabelle Stengers. *Order out of Chaos*. New York: Bantam, 1984.

Regnaut, François. "Système formel d'Hitchcock (fascicule de résultats)." In *Alfred Hitchcock,* ed. Jean Narboni et al. Paris: Editions de l'étoilé-cahier du cinéma, 1980, pp. 21–30.

Robbe-Grillet, Alain. *Last Year at Marienbad*. Trans. Richard Howard. New York: Grove, 1962.

———. *Pour un nouveau roman*. Paris: Minuit, 1963.

Rodowick, D. N. *Gilles Deleuze's Time Machine*. Durham, N.C.: Duke University Press, 1997.

Rohmer, Eric, and Claude Chabrol. *Hitchcock: The First Forty-Four Films*. Trans. Stanley Hochman. 1957. Reprint, New York: Frederick Ungar, 1979.

Rouch, Jean. "The Camera and the Man." In *Principles of Visual Anthropology,* ed. Paul Hockings. The Hague: Mouton, 1975, pp. 83–102.

Sandford, John. *The New German Cinema*. Totowa, N.J.: Barnes and Noble, 1980.

Sartre, Jean-Paul. *The Emotions: Outline of a Theory*. Trans. Bernard Frechtman. New York: Philosophical Library, 1948.

Serrano, Jacques, ed. *Après Deleuze: philosophie et esthétique du cinema*. Marseilles: Place publique, 1997.

Sheriff, John K. *Charles Peirce's Guess at the Riddle: Grounds for Human Significance*. Bloomington: Indiana University Press, 1994.

Simmel, Georg. *Simmel on Culture: Selected Writings*. Ed. David Frisby and Mike Featherston. London: Sage, 1997.

Simondon, Gilbert. *L'individu et sa genèse physico-biologique*. Paris: Presses Universitaires de France, 1964.

Spaier, Albert. *La pensée et la quantité*. Paris: Alcan, 1927.

Spinoza, Benedict de. *Improvement of the Understanding, Ethics and Correspondence*. Trans. R. H. M. Elwes. Washington, D.C.: M. Walter Dunne, 1901.

Stoller, Paul. *The Cinematic Griot: The Ethnography of Jean Rouch*. Chicago: University of Chicago Press, 1992.

Teske, Roland J. *Paradoxes of Time in Saint Augustine*. Milwaukee, Wis.: Marquette University Press, 1996.

Toubiana, Serge. "Le cinéma est deleuzien." *Cahiers du cinéma* 497 (December 1995): 20–21.

Truffaut, François. *Hitchcock*. New York: Simon and Schuster, 1967.

Turim, Maureen. "Jean-Marie Straub and Daniéle Huillet: Oblique Angles on Film as Ideological Intervention." In *New German Filmmakers: From Oberhausen through the 1970s*. Ed. Klaus Phillips. New York: Frederick Ungar, 1984, pp. 335–58.

Vertov, Dziga. *Kino-Eye: The Writings of Dziga Vertov*. Ed. Annette Michelson, trans. Kevin O'Brien. Berkeley: University of California Press, 1984.

Wölfflin, Heinrich. *Principles of Art History*. Trans. M. D. Hottinger. New York: Holt, 1932.

Worringer, Wilhelm. *Form in Gothic*. Trans. Sir Herbert Read. London: Alec Tiranti, 1957.

Yakir, Dan. "*Ciné-transe:* The Vision of Jean Rouch. An Interview." *Film Quarterly* 31 (spring 1978): 2–11.

Index